Pete and Nancy

THE GARDENER'S YEAR

THE GARDENER'S YEAR

John Ferguson and
Burkhard Mücke

Special photography by Jacqui Hurst

BARRON'S

NEW YORK · TORONTO

The Gardener's Year
© Frances Lincoln Limited 1991
Text © John Ferguson and Burkhard Mücke 1991
Illustrations © Frances Lincoln Limited 1991

First U.S. edition published 1991 by
Barron's Educational Series

International Standard Book Number: 0−8120−6184−5
Library of Congress Catalog Card No.: 90−23339

Library of Congress Cataloging-in-Publication Data
Ferguson, John, 1940−
    The gardener's year / John Ferguson and Burkhard Mücke. — 1st
U.S. ed.
        p.   cm.
    Includes index.
    ISBN 0−8120−6184−5
    1. Gardening — United States.   I. Mücke, Burkhard, 1945−
II. Title.
SB453.F43   1991
635′.0973—dc20   90−23339
                                                                CIP

All inquiries should be addressed to:
Barron's Educational Series, Inc.
250 Wireless Boulevard
Hauppauge, New York 11788

Printed and bound in Italy by New Interlitho S.p.A.
Set in Ehrhardt by Bookworm Typesetting, Manchester
Originated in Hong Kong

CONTENTS

INTRODUCTION

"To every thing there is a season,
And a time to every purpose under the heaven;
A time to be born,
And a time to die;
A time to plant,
And a time to pluck up that which is planted."
(Ecclesiastes 3)

Many gardeners, and certainly not only novices, are often a bit uncertain about when to tackle some of the tasks which confront them in their garden. Just when is the best time to plant a rhododendron, to prune back a rampant clematis, to divide that overgrown clump of hardy asters, or to dig a new garden pond? *The Gardener's Year* answers such questions. It is first and foremost a practical guide to the most important tasks of the gardening year. For each of these jobs there is often a best time, perhaps not the only possible time, but generally a season of the year that is most likely to guarantee success and minimize failure.

A garden is a rich and fascinating living structure. Even in the smallest city garden, you can discover much more than you might at first expect. Another goal of *The Gardener's Year* is to sharpen your awareness of the seasonal events which take place in your garden and in your immediate environment.

Plants, like all other living beings, are subject to the manifold influences of weather, climate, and situation. Thus, environment to a large extent determines whether any plant will prosper at a particular location, when it will begin growth, flower, and bear fruit, when it will become dormant for the winter, and when it will reach the end of its lifespan, become senescent and finally die. Consequently, a division of the gardening year into the four calendar seasons of spring, summer, fall, and winter is not precise enough for many of the important gardening tasks which confront you each year. At the same time, it is futile to recommend that a shrub be pruned in April, for example, for April in Maine or Wisconsin is very different from April in Georgia or Southern California.

Every garden has its own individual climate, specific to its location. The beginning of spring at any location, for example, will not be determined by the calendar date for the astronomical first day of spring, but will be dependent on a number of conditions, some fixed and some variable. The location of the garden in degrees of latitude and longitude, the elevation above sea level, the distance from the ocean or other large bodies of water, the slope of the terrain, and exposure to the sun and the prevailing winds are examples of fixed conditions which play an important role in the climate of your garden. Whether the garden is in the city or in the open countryside is also quite important; the warmth and shelter a city provides can have a great effect on the advance and duration of the seasons. Add to these factors the relatively inconstant patterns of the weather from year to year, or the totally unpredictable phenomenon of a late or an early spring, and you soon come to the realization that each garden and its local climate are unique.

The cycle of the seasons
Up to the beginning of the present century our ancestors were well aware of the cycle of the seasons and the recurrent labors which were appropriate to a particular time of the year. Before the twentieth century, the large majority of people still lived and worked on the land or were only a step removed from the patterns and rhythms of the countryside. Most of us today have lost that instinctive awareness of a continuous, cyclical development and pattern of change in the natural environment.

That the exact dates for just when any plant will break into growth, when it will blossom and bear fruit vary from year to year and from place to place was recognized long ago. The very oldest records come to us from Japan, where such observations have a long tradition. In fact, astonishing as it may seem, the annual appearance of the cherry blossoms has been registered since the year 812 and the dates are recorded in the archives of the imperial court The first real attempt to study these phenomena with scientific precision was made in the middle of the eighteenth century, when the famous Swedish botanist Carl Linnaeus began recording his systematic observations. It was he who founded and first coined the name "phenology" for the branch of biology which combines the methods of ecology and meteorology.

Phenology is the study of life-cycle phases of plants and animals as they occur throughout the year and of the timing of biological events and in relation to seasonal climatic changes. In his *Philosophia Botanica* (1751), Linnaeus outlined methods for compiling annual plant calendars of leaf opening, flowering, fruiting, and leaf fall, together with climatological observations so as to show how areas differ one from another. The methods and aims of phenological observations have remained essentially unchanged since the days of Linnaeus. He himself instituted a network of phenological stations in Sweden, but the main center of activity for the past hundred years has been in Germany and other countries of central Europe. The heyday for phenological observations was during the period from about 1880 until 1940. At present there is a loose network of phenological observation stations spanning continental Europe from Italy and Greece to Norway, Sweden, and Finland, with the center of interest in West Germany although, as yet, there is no equivalent such network or organization in the U.S.A.

The Marsham family record

One of the most fascinating collections of phenological data is the Marsham Family Phenological Record, the remarkable product of the private observations of six generations of an English family, beginning first in 1736 at their Norfolk estate, Stratton Strawless Hall, about 6 miles/10km north of Norwich and then, after 1858, at Rippon Hall near Stratton. The oldest part of the Marsham document was discovered by chance in 1924, hidden under the floorboards of an old mill. Robert Marsham and his descendants kept extensive records from 1736 up till 1925. Year for year, the leafing of thirteen trees such as hawthorn, birch, beech, oak, and horse chestnut, and the flowering of snowdrops, wood anemone, and hawthorn were recorded, as well as the movements of several migratory birds and even the first croaking of frogs. The average date for the first appearance of the snowdrop there was January 16; the earliest date was December 15 1838; and the latest was February 19 1895.

THE PHENOLOGICAL CALENDAR

These phenological observations, together with others carried out at many locations around the world, have made it possible to construct a natural biological calendar in which the seasons are not defined by arbitrary dates but by the leafing out, blossoming, or fruiting of certain common indicator plants. Thus the beginning of pre-spring is when the first snowdrops open their blossoms and this date will vary from place to place, from garden to garden, by as much as six to eight weeks. Although latitude and, to some extent, the buffering effects of the oceans are the most important factors determining the transition of the seasons, local factors can cause considerable variation, even at the same latitude. Altitude, for example, is important. The average temperatures drop about 3.56°F/2°C for every 330ft/100m you climb, which means a shorter growing period at higher altitudes; so, for example, for each 300ft/90m of extra altitude, the total growth season in the eastern USA is shortened by five days.

HOW TO USE THIS BOOK

Following the rhythm of nature reflected in the phenological calendar, we divide the year into nine seasons each marked by an easily observed natural signal. Each chapter opens with a portrait of the garden in the particular season and discusses plants that enhance the garden at that time. Then a practical section explains the gardening tasks that are best done in that season. The recommended program of work is given in the following order in every season: trees and shrubs, roses, climbing plants, herbaceous perennials, annuals and biennials, bulbs and tubers, the water garden, lawn and meadow, and container plants. Step-by-step illustrations show you how to do particular tasks. The final chapter outlines general gardening techniques.

Plant lists

Each chapter includes lists of plants in bloom in that season – or, late in the year, plants that have decorative fruits, berries, leaves, or stems. They are grouped by their color or by scent or by their usefulness in attracting bees and butterflies to the garden. They are listed within each group in order of type –

Season	Begin/end	Signal plant	Signal
Pre-spring	Begin	Snowdrop (*Galanthus nivalis*)	flowers
		Hazel (*Corylus avellana*)	catkins release pollen
	End	Goat willow (*Salix caprea*)	flowers
		Cornelian cherry (*Cornus mas*)	flowers
Early spring	Begin	Wood anemone (*Anemone nemorosa*)	flowers
	End	Horse chestnut (*Aesculus hippocastanum*)	leaf buds open
		European whitebark birch (*Betula pendula*)	leaf buds open
Spring	Begin	Early apple varieties (*Malus*)	flowers
		Horse chestnut (*Aesculus hippocastanum*)	flowers
		Lilac (*Syringa vulgaris*)	flowers
	End	Hawthorn (*Crataegus monogyna*)	flowers
		Laburnum (*Laburnum anagyroides*)	flowers
		Mountain ash (*Sorbus aucuparia*)	flowers
Early summer	Begin	European elder (*Sambucus nigra*)	flowers
		Snowberry (*Symphoricarpos albus*)	flowers
		Black locust (*Robinia pseudoacacia*)	flowers
	End	Large-leaved linden (*Tilia platyphyllos*)	flowers
		Common privet (*Ligustrum vulgare*)	flowers
Midsummer	Begin	Small-leaved lime (*Tilia cordata*)	flowers
Late summer	Begin	Snowberry (*Symphoricarpos albus*)	ripe berries
		Mountain ash (*Sorbus aucuparia*)	ripe berries
Early fall	Begin	Meadow saffron (*Colchicum autumnale*)	flowers
		European elder (*Sambucus nigra*)	ripe berries
	End	Cornelian cherry (*Cornus mas*)	ripe fruits
Fall	Begin	Horse chestnut (*Aesculus hippocastanum*)	nuts ripen & leaves color
		European beech (*Fagus sylvatica*)	nuts ripen & leaves color
		English oak (*Quercus robur*)	nuts ripen & leaves color
	End	Ash (*Fraxinus*)	leaf fall
		Larch (*Larix decidua*)	leaf fall
		Large-leaved linden (*Tilia platyphyllos*)	leaf fall
Winter	No indicator plants: winter is a period of dormancy for most native plants		

Note: Agricultural meteorologists recognize three stages in fall, but since there are no gardening jobs which cannot be done just as well in late fall as in mid-fall, we have combined these two stages into one season – fall.

that is, trees and shrubs, roses, climbers, perennials, annuals and biennials, bulbs, and water plants. A few are rare or unusual but all are well worth growing if you come across them.

USDA Plant hardiness zones
Where plants are discussed in the introductory text to the seasons, their hardiness – that is, the likelihood of their surviving through winter – is given in terms of the U.S. Department of Agriculture hardiness zones, which are areas defined by average annual minimum temperatures.

Zone 1	Below −50°F/Below −45.6°C
Zone 2	−50° to −40°F/−45.6° to −40°C
Zone 3	−40° to −30°F/−40° to −34.5°C
Zone 4	−30° to −20°F/−34.5° to −28.9°C
Zone 5	−20° to −10°F/−28.9° to −23.3°C
Zone 6	−10° to −0°F/−23.3° to −17.8°C
Zone 7	−0° to −10°F/−17.8° to −12.3°C
Zone 8	−10° to −20°F/−12.3° to −6.6°C
Zone 9	−20° to −30°F/−6.6° to −1.1°C
Zone 10	−30° to −40°F/−1.1° to −4.4°C

CHAPTER 1

PRE-SPRING

"Already now the snowdrop dares appear,
The first pale blossom of th'unripened year;
As Flora's breath, by some transforming power,
Had changed an icicle into a flower..."

Mrs. Barbauld

How fitting it is that the blossoming of the common snowdrop (*Galanthus nivalis*) signals the beginning of pre-spring, for there is no other flower which so reassures us that winter has finally lost its grip on the landscape. Spring itself is yet some weeks away, and cold spells of unfriendly weather are likely to set in, keeping us out of the garden just when we are impatient to get started. But the sturdy little snowdrops are brave enough to stand up to the last of winter's skirmishes and for gardeners there is a multitude of tasks that can be finished during this season.

Common snowdrops grow naturally in deciduous woodlands, along cool, moist streams. If you want to observe the beginning of pre-spring closely, you can plant several clumps of snowdrops in suitable places throughout your garden. Their cultivation is easy, but only if they like your garden soil and location. A cool spot with dappled shade and moist, rich soil containing plenty of humus which never dries out too much in summer are all that they really desire.

Snowdrops are usually offered for sale as dry bulbs for fall planting, but it is much safer to buy them as growing, even flowering, plants and to set them out now in the garden. If the spot is to their liking, they will continue to grow and to spread for generations. Snowdrops look their best in natural informal plantings, under spreading deciduous trees and shrubs, together with daphne, winter aconites, and hepaticas, for example. Any bees that venture out of their hives for their first flights of the year will welcome such a planting for early nectar and pollen. The catkins of hazel (*Corylus avellana*) usually begin to shed their pollen at about the same time as the snowdrops bloom. The flowering of the goat willow (*Salix caprea*) signals the end of pre-spring.

THE PRE-SPRING GARDEN

Sunlit tree trunks and a filigree of twigs and bare branches against a clear blue sky, shining miniatures such as hepaticas, winter aconite, anemones, and hellebores hugging the ground and nestling among tree roots for protection against cold stormy blasts, and late snow, elusive scents – these are the elements of the garden in pre-spring. The cheerful mood of the open woodland can be created in even the smallest town garden. A single well-placed shrub can be sufficient. A broad

witch hazel underplanted with pink-flowering *Erica carnea* or a white abeliophyllum standing on a carpet woven of ivy, hepaticas, snowdrops, and winter aconites would be sufficient to make an impact in a smaller setting.

Shrubs for structure and interest

Without a doubt the hardy deciduous shrubs, more than any other group of plants, determine the structure, mood, and main focus of interest in the pre-spring garden and no other genus of deciduous shrubs has more to offer at this time of year than *Hamamelis*, the witch hazel. Rich in color and pefume, its spiderlike flowers defy frost, snow, and icy winds, to open during every interlude of milder weather. The petals are like narrow strips of tissue paper, bunched together along the leafless branches. The best known species, the Chinese *Hamamelis mollis*, has bright canary yellow blossoms with dark maroon eyes that shine and glow for weeks on end. Slow-growing, it eventually forms a broad, attractive shrub, 8ft/2.5m high. The most valuable witch hazels for your garden are *H.* 'Pallida', which has pale lemon yellow flowers with long petals, and *H. mollis* 'Brevipetala,' with its short, stubby clusters of a warm ocher yellow hue. Both have the sweet, spicy fragrance of the Chinese witch hazel, so reminiscent of cowslips.

Numerous excellent hybrids between the Chinese and Japanese witch hazels, classified as *Hamamelis* × *intermedia*, have extended the range of color to coppery-orange and even deep red. 'Jelena', for example, is a striking hybrid with dense clusters of large copper orange blossoms, each with a maroon heart; 'Diane' is rich red and 'Goldcrest' golden yellow. Hybrid witch hazels are vigorous shrubs, superb in color and form, but often lacking the richness of scent of the Chinese parent.

All witch hazels thrive on a deep, rich woodland soil. They are tolerant of lime in moderation, but grow more freely on slightly acidic soil. They should be planted in an open position or woodland edge.

A sunny forest glade might be your inspiration for a sheltered corner of the garden with either a warming wall or a dark hedge as background. There is no better spot than this for *Abeliophyllum distichum* which, in spite of its eye-catching

Lenten roses – hybrids of *Helleborus orientalis* are easy to grow in shade, and flower in a range of colors, the handsome evergreen foliage is splendid in all seasons.

appearance and delicious almond scent, is still relatively uncommon in our gardens. It grows naturally in hilly regions where winters are cold and summers decidedly hot. Consequently, although hardy to zone 5, abeliophyllum prefers a warm, sunny spot in which to grow.

Covered with sprays of ivory white, starry flowers similar in form and size to those of forsythia, abeliophyllum is one of the most valuable shrubs for the pre-spring garden. Its small size – 5-6ft/1.5-1.8m in height and spread – and slow rate of growth make it just as useful in the smallest of gardens as in larger woodland settings. Shining above a carpet of one of the rose- or red-colored varieties of *Erica carnea*, abeliophyllum would be one of the highlights of this season. Later in the year, the leafy shrub remains neat, if not particularly noteworthy in appearance and resembles somewhat its close relative, the common privet. Abeliophyllum thrives in any ordinary soil but flowers more freely when growing in a heavy, neutral loam.

In most locations, pre-spring is actually the main flowering season for those shrubs which are often called winter-flowering. Among them is winter sweet, *Chimonanthus praecox*, whose flower buds are hardy to zone 7 and which has one of the sweetest scents imaginable. It grows slowly, but in time can reach 11ft/3.5m. It is also lazy about flowering for the first few years after planting; however, once established, it blooms dependably every year, impervious to the worst weather. The curious, stiff flowers are translucent straw yellow in color, thick and waxy in texture, and about ¾in/20mm in diameter. They seem to be produced most freely when growing in full sun in poor soil.

A close relative of the witch hazel and also a native of the Orient, *Corylopsis pauciflora* is a delightful garden shrub. The individual flowers are small and pale yellow, borne in clusters and partially enclosed in waxy yellow bracts. Bright crimson anthers on pink filaments protrude from the flowers and give enough extra color to prevent them from seeming insipid. Their scent is sweet, reminiscent of cowslips. Another yellow-flowering shrub is *Stachyurus praecox*, whose rigid, hanging spikes of waxy flowers look as if suddenly frozen while swaying in a stiff breeze. It is hardy to zone 7 and tolerates a wide range of soils.

Sarcococca, the Christmas box, is a little-known genus of small evergreen shrubs, ideal for planting in groups beneath large trees and shrubs. *S. confusa* and *S. humilis* are especially pleasant shrubs of neat and unassuming habit, never calling much attention to themselves until some mild day in pre-spring when a soft breeze carries their warm sweet scent, almost like heather honey, in your direction. Their tiny flowers are indeed little more than tufts of stamens and stigmas. Sarcococcas are happy in any soil and thrive in shade.

Underplanting

At the lowest level, you can underplant everything with the earliest spring-flowering bulbs. Be guided by your good taste alone and plant masses of these little gems wherever they fit into your color schemes. *Anemone blanda* is available in a variety of good forms, mostly shades of blue and white. *Chionodoxa*, known as glory of the snow, is best in its blue forms. The flowers of *C. luciliae* are bright blue with white centers and *C. sardensis* has blossoms of deepest gentian blue. *Eranthis*, the winter aconite, can give weeks of golden yellow flowers if you plant the two species *E. hyemalis* and *E. cilicica* together with their common hybrid, *E × tubergenii*. Snowdrops, *hepatica* and the tiny *Scilla bifolia* can be tucked in under every deciduous shrub and hedge, so long as the soil is suitable.

A bright and cheerful miniature for a shady spot under deciduous shrubs: the attractive arrowhead leaves of *Arum italicum* 'Pictum' are marbled in silver and green; they appear in fall and remain throughout winter until spring. Here they make an effective foil for the golden yellow *Eranthis* flowers.

PLANTS FOR PRE-SPRING

Blue and mauve
Primula juliae
P. × pruhoniciana varieties
Anemone blanda 'Blue Star'
Chionodoxa luciliae
Crocus etruscus 'Zwanenburg'
C. sieberi 'Violet Queen'
C. tommasinianus 'Whitewell
    Purple'
Hepatica nobilis
Iris bakeriana
I. histrioides + I.h. 'Major'
I. reticulata + I.r. 'Cantab,'
    'Royal Blue'
Scilla bifolia
S. mischtschenkoana

Yellow and orange
Chimonanthus praecox
Cornus mas
Corylopsis pauciflora
Hamamelis × intermedia 'Jelena'
H. mollis 'Brevipetala,'
    'Goldcrest,' 'Pallida'
Jasminum nudiflorum
Stachyurus praecox
Crocus ancyrensis
C. angustifolius
Eranthis cilicica
E. hyemalis
E. × tubergenii
Iris danfordiae
Narcissus cyclamineus + N.c.
    'February Gold,' 'Tête-à-
    Tête'

Red and pink
Daphne mezereum
Erica carnea 'Myretoun Ruby,'
    'Vivellii'
Hamamelis × intermedia
    'Diane'
Prunus mume 'Kagoshimako'
P. 'Accolade'
P. × subhirtella 'Fukubana'
Rhododendron 'Praecox'
Viburnum × bodnantense 'Dawn'

Corydalis bulbosa
C. solida
Helleborus atrorubens
Primula denticulata
P. × pruhoniciana varieties
Anemone blanda 'Charmer,'
    'Rosea,' 'Pink Star'
Crocus imperati
C. tommasinianus 'Taplow Ruby'
Cyclamen coum

White and cream
Abeliophyllum distichum
Erica carnea 'Snow Queen'
Lonicera × purpusii
Pieris japonica 'White Cascade'
Prunus incisa 'Praecox'
P. × yedoensis
Sarcococca confusa
S. humilis
Viburnum farreri
Corydalis bulbosa
Helleborus niger
H. orientalis
Primula denticulata
P. × pruhoniciana varieties
Anemone blanda 'White
    Splendour,' 'Bridesmaid'
Crocus biflorus weldenii 'Fairy'
C. versicolor
Galanthus nivalis
G. 'S. Arnott'
G. plicatus
Leucojum vernum

Scented plants
Abeliophyllum distichum
Chimonanthus praecox
Corylopsis pauciflora
Daphne mezereum
Hamamelis mollis 'Brevipetala,'
    'Goldcrest,' 'Pallida'
Lonicera × purpusii
Prunus mume 'Kagoshimako'
P. × yedoensis
Sarcococca humilis
Stachyurus praecox

Viburnum × bodnantense 'Dawn'
V. farreri
Iris bakeriana
I. histrioides
I. reticulata
Petasites fragrans

**Plants for bees and
butterflies**
Acer rubrum
Anemone blanda cultivars
Cornus mas

Corylus avellana
Crocus species
Daphne mezereum
Eranthis species
Leucojum vernum
Salix caprea (male)
S. daphnoides pomeranica
S. × smithiana
Sarcococca species

Crocus tommasinianus, a very hardy wild species from Yugoslavia, is one of the best crocuses for naturalizing in sunny or semishady parts of the garden where it should be allowed to seed itself without being disturbed.

PRE-SPRING TASKS

TREES AND SHRUBS

Planting

As soon as the soil is dry enough to be workable and has started to warm up again after the winter, planting of trees and shrubs can be resumed. Never, however, plant in muddy or partly frozen ground. Where winters are extremely cold or arrive early, pre-spring planting of all woody plants is much safer than planting in the fall and is best for all the less hardy species. Don't forget to water the newly planted trees faithfully if the season is dry. (See page 152 for details about planting bare root trees.)

Many trees and shrubs, in particular the broadleaved evergreens, are vulnerable to frosts and drying winds while they are still small, although they are hardy when fully grown, established plants. Rhododendrons, magnolias, pieris, kalmia, and even some species of holly and cotoneaster are just a few such plants. (These shrubs are usually sold with a root ball or as container-grown specimens.) Thus, pre-spring is generally considered to be the ideal season for planting broadleaved evergreens of all kinds. The gradually warming soil encourages the growth of strong new roots needed to replace the water lost by constant transpiration from the evergreen leaves. Even so, temporary protection against drying winds or late frosts is often necessary. Anything that reduces the force of the wind, such as burlap sacking, straw mats, or a row of pine branches stuck in the ground will provide sufficient protection. If the weather turns dry, as well as watering the roots, the leaves should be sprayed overhead with water periodically. (For information on planting container-grown or balled-root shrubs, see page 153.)

Fertilizing

With deep-rooted woody plants, particularly those standing in grass or mixed borders, fertilizer must be applied early enough so that the spring rains can wash it beyond the greedy roots of grass or herbaceous perennials before these are active enough to intercept the dissolved nutrients.

Uptake of minerals by the roots of trees and shrubs begins well before new growth of leaves and shoots and nutrient requirements are highest at this time. Consequently, about two-thirds of the annual fertilizer amount should be applied now. Normally, young trees planted in well-prepared soil do not require any additional fertilizing for at least three years.

As trees and shrubs grow and their roots penetrate into the surrounding soil outside the prepared planting hole, their growth may slow. In such cases, a commercial tree fertilizer can be applied now. For rhododendrons, camellias, and other acid-loving shrubs, special fertilizers, rich in nitrogen, are recommended. (For methods of feeding trees and shrubs, see page 160.)

Protection

Newly planted trees and shrubs, especially the evergreens, may still need protection against drying spring winds and sun until they have established a good root system. As a rule though, it is now time to remove winter protection from shrubs before warmth under the protective layers can induce premature growth – susceptible to late frosts – and before any pests or diseases can start to multiply unchecked. Choose an overcast, windfree day to remove protection, in order to avoid the sudden shock of bright sun. In locations where dangerous night frosts are still likely, keep mats and screens handy, so that you can put them back in place quickly.

Where protection against wind or sun is still deemed necessary, then sackcloth screens should be erected to provide protection without allowing the buildup of warm air around the plant. Sometimes all that is necessary is to surround the plants with cut pine branches stuck into the ground. Against minor frosts even a slight cover of pine branches or a sheet of newspaper can suffice to save new growth. But remember that drying out is a more serious danger than cold. The combination of dry soil, full sun, and gusty spring winds can do horrifying damage to foliage in a very short time.

Removal of props and ties

Tree stakes are needed only until sufficient new roots have grown out into the surrounding soil to establish a secure anchorage. If the tree has been properly planted, stakes should not be needed after the second winter, although in very exposed locations, an additional year could be advisable. Pre-spring is the best time to remove a stake and tie since the tree will be starting to make active root growth and new leaf growth will not have begun. When removing a stake, saw it off at ground level, rather than try to rock it loose, which might damage vitally needed young root growth.

With actively growing trees that are to remain staked for another year, examine ties to be sure that they are secure and have not become too tight. The best brand name ties allow for a certain amount of expansion, but any tie may cut into the cambium layer unless slackened periodically.

Frostlifting

Newly planted trees and shrubs that have not yet had time to become well anchored are often lifted by the action of alternating freezing and thawing weather or are loosened by strong winter winds. Unless this is remedied, the fine root system of the young plants will be damaged, so check recent plantings now, and where necessary, tread firm the loose soil around the plants.

Layering

Pre-spring is the best time to propagate by layering (see page 157).

ROSES

Planting

Roses can be successfully planted during this season whenever the weather and soil conditions permit. For most locations late fall is a better time for planting, but where winters are cold and without a dependable snow cover, pre-spring is safer. Also if roses are to be planted in a heavy, water-retentive clay soil, where root growth may be slow during the fall and winter months, then pre-spring is best. The only real drawback to spring planting is that top and root growth begin almost simultaneously, and, if early spring weather is unseasonably warm, the top may temporarily outstrip the roots, so the bushes will require careful watering.

Protection and tidying

As the soil thaws and starts to warm up, the winter protection can be removed. If possible, choose a quiet frostfree day with an overcast sky in order to minimize shock to the plant which could be caused by wind or sudden bright sunlight.

Pre-spring is also the ideal time for a thorough cleanup in the rose garden. Remove any leaves that remain on the rose plants, then rake up and remove all old leaves and other debris from the ground around the bushes. Pest eggs and disease spores may be carried over from one year to the next on the fallen leaves, so if you suspect them to be infected remove them from the garden; otherwise they may be composted.

Planting roses

1 Right Prepare the rose by cutting damaged roots back to healthy tissue, and shortening any excessively long roots to about 8in/200mm. Cut back all shoots to three or four strong buds and cut out any weak or damaged stems. Soak the roots in water for at least an hour before planting.

3 Right Fill the planting hole with soil improved with a small handful of bone meal and, preferably, good ripe garden compost. As you fill, shake the bush gently from time to time to ensure that spaces around the roots are completely filled with fine soil. Firm the soil lightly with your hands as you proceed.

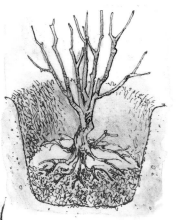

2 Right In well-prepared soil, dig the planting hole wide enough to accommodate the spread-out roots and deep enough for the graft union – the point at which the green stems join the brown rootstock – to be covered with about 2in/50mm of soil after the hole has been filled in.

4 Left When the hole is over half full, flood it with water. After the water has drained away, shovel in the remaining soil. This procedure ensures that all the roots are in intimate contact with the soil and no air pockets remain, and the loose soil on top acts as a mulch, preventing drying out and caking of the surface.

Annual pruning of roses
Below In the first year, cut back hybrid teas, floribundas, and climbers hard, so that only 2–4 buds remain on each shoot. This severe pruning establishes a strong root system and plenty of new shoots will appear by early summer.

Right In later years, remove weak stems and branches that rub against each other or that cross through the center and any diseased, damaged, or dead wood. This gives an open, vase-shaped plant, allowing air and sunlight to all parts, reducing the chance of disease.

Left For bigger, showier blooms, shorten all remaining canes to 3 to 5 strong buds. However, this further pruning is not needed for roses left to grow as shrubs; even hybrid teas and floribundas can be left thus.

Pruning

All roses that need pruning during dormancy can safely be pruned now as soon as the forsythia bushes in the neighborhood burst into blossom. At this time the topmost buds on the strongest rose canes should be just starting to swell. The aim is to prune as early as possible in order to produce an early crop of flowers without risking loss from late frosts. Pruning too late wastes the energy that the plant has invested in the young shoots that are cut off and delays flowering.

Pruning roses can be a complex topic, but in general, you can treat roses like the deciduous flowering shrubs they are. A handy simplification classifies roses into two main groups.

The first group comprises the wild species and their hybrids, the old garden roses, and modern shrub roses. Many roses in this group will benefit from regular annual pruning but it is not such a stringent requirement as for roses in the second group. All you need to know about a rose in this group is whether it flowers on the current season's growth or on the growth of the previous season. For any rose that flowers on this year's new growth, now is the right time to prune. Most only need some thinning and shaping each year, but very little cutting back. Cut out any shoots that spoil the shape of the shrub and remove any old canes that have produced little new growth.

The second group includes the hybrid teas, the floribundas, and the climbers, all of which flower on the current season's growth and respond well to regular annual pruning. In earlier times, these roses were cut back almost to ground level to produce mammoth flowers for exhibition. Nowadays the goal is more often plenty of attractive flowers on healthy, long-lived bushes, and less severe pruning is usual. Regardless of group, pruning of all roses serves a common purpose: to promote a symmetrical bush and to encourage vigorous new growth.

Fertilizing

Established roses should be given a topdressing of a complete balanced fertilizer or a commercial rose fertilizer as soon as growth begins or shortly after pruning. Any good balanced fertilizer is suitable so long as it contains a high proportion of potassium, particularly if the soil tends to be light and sandy. Commercial rose foods are formulated to fill the roses' specific needs and should be relatively low in nitrogen and high in potassium, with a good balance of the major trace elements, particularly iron and magnesium.

Before applying dry fertilizer, be sure the soil is moist to avoid burning the roots. Water the roses the day before. On the following day, loosen the soil surface to a depth of 1in/1–2cm and scatter the measured amount of fertilizer beneath the bush, and as far as the edge of its root zone, while avoiding direct contact with the stems. Water in the fertilizer thoroughly. On good soils, one topdressing should sustain the rose throughout the summer. Where the soil is poor or light and sandy, apply a second dressing in early summer.

CLIMBING PLANTS

Pruning clematis

Pre-spring is the ideal season for pruning any climbing plants that bloom late in summer or fall on new wood formed this year. Typical are many popular species and varieties of clematis. Hard pruning now will prevent them from becoming tangled masses of growth, bare and unsightly at the base, and producing their flowers only at the top, far out of sight. The complicated instructions for pruning clematis that are so often found can be much simplified by dividing the clematis into three categories, based on the age of the shoots on which flowers appear.

The first group is the easiest to prune: it comprises all clematis species and hybrids that flower in summer and fall, for example, the species *C. orientalis* and *C. tangutica* and hybrids such as 'Ernest Markham,' 'Hagley Hybrid,' 'Perle d'Azur,' 'Comtesse de Bouchaud,' 'Gypsy Queen,' 'Lady Betty Balfour,' and 'Ville de Lyon.' These should be cut back virtually to ground level each year. All of last year's growth should be pruned to the lowest pair of strong buds. Many of these clematis freeze back almost to ground level anyway, so that pre-spring pruning entails removal of dead wood.

Pruning of the second group of clematis hybrids can be somewhat more complicated. These hybrids flower from spring to midsummer on short side shoots produced from buds along last year's old growth. At the same time new growth is formed that can flower a second time during late summer and early fall. To this repeat-flowering group belong, for example, 'Henry,' 'Lady Northcliffe,' 'Lasurstern,' 'Marie Boisselot,' 'Nelly Moser,' 'The President,' and 'William Kennett.' Two methods of pruning are possible. They may either be treated as belonging to the first group and pruned back hard each year, in which case they will flower only once in late summer. Or they may be left unpruned or only lightly pruned (see page 86), removing only dead, damaged, or diseased shoots, until they finally become unsightly, straggly, and bare at the base. Then they must be rejuvenated by cutting back hard to within 2-3ft/600-900mm of the ground in pre-spring.

Early-flowering clematis constitute a third major group and are pruned later, immediately after the blossoms have faded.

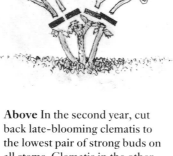

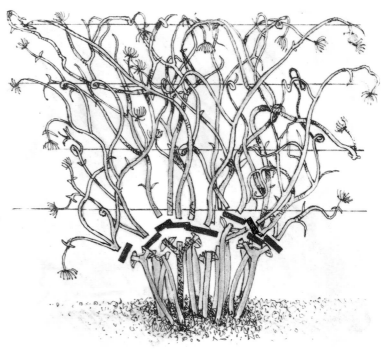

Pruning clematis
Above In the first year, prune all species and hybrids back to the lowest strong buds. In all three groups of clematis this initial pruning is essential for establishing a good framework and maximum branching from low down on the plant.

Above In the second year, cut back late-blooming clematis to the lowest pair of strong buds on all stems. Clematis in the other two groups should have all their main growths shortened by about one-half, back to a strong pair of buds.

Above In subsequent years, again hard prune all the stems of late-blooming clematis. Repeat-flowering clematis can be pruned this way or more selectively in midsummer.

Pruning wisteria

With its breathtaking cataracts of fragrant lilac-blue blossoms, wisteria is truly the queen of all hardy climbers. But instead of the desired floral deluge, the disappointing reality may be a rampant, tangled mass of jungly stems, smothered in dense foliage with hardly a bloom.

More often than not, it is pruning alone that makes the difference. It is not difficult, but it must be done faithfully each year, in two steps, one in midsummer and again during pre-spring. Pruning in two stages serves to concentrate the energies of the shoots toward the formation of flower buds and to confine the plant's naturally robust growth to the available wall space.

A freshly planted wisteria should have its main shoot cut back 2½-3ft/750-900mm from ground level and any side shoots cut away from the base. For the first two or three years after planting, a young wisteria may make only a limited amount of growth, until a strong root system has been built up.

Pruning wisteria

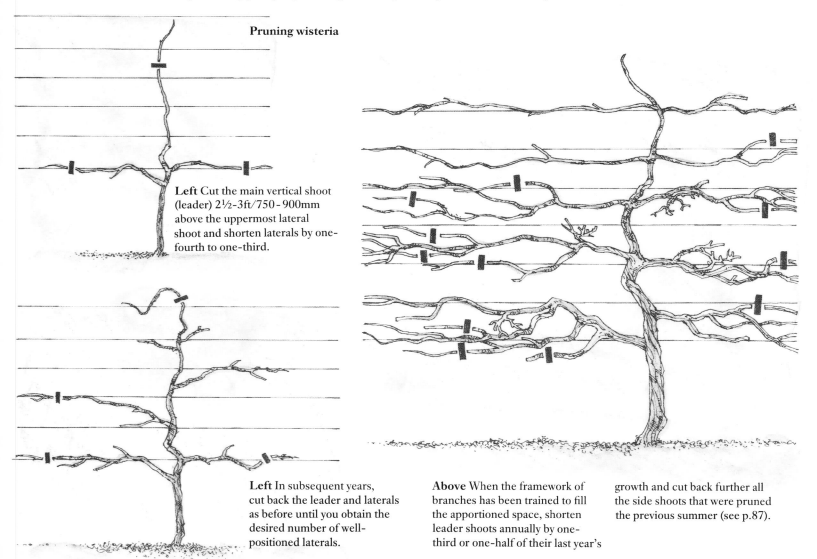

Left Cut the main vertical shoot (leader) 2½-3ft/750-900mm above the uppermost lateral shoot and shorten laterals by one-fourth to one-third.

Left In subsequent years, cut back the leader and laterals as before until you obtain the desired number of well-positioned laterals.

Above When the framework of branches has been trained to fill the apportioned space, shorten leader shoots annually by one-third or one-half of their last year's growth and cut back further all the side shoots that were pruned the previous summer (see p.87).

HERBACEOUS PERENNIALS

Planting
Generally speaking, the best time to plant herbaceous perennials is shortly after they have finished flowering, especially if perennials are being divided and replanted within the garden. Most modern nurseries, however, grow young plants in small pots or containers, which allows planting throughout most of the year. Even so, the optimal planting times for most herbaceous perennials are still fall or pre-spring to early spring.

As with trees and shrubs, pre-spring planting of herbaceous perennials is always preferable wherever the garden soil tends to be heavy, cold, or wet, and where winters arrive early and linger long, especially if the young plants are not reliably hardy.

In particular, now is the best time to plant those herbaceous perennials that blossom in summer and fall, for example, Japanese anemones, *Aster amellus*, and *A. dumosus*. Certain other plants like anthemis, lupins, nepeta, penstemons, scabious, verbascums, all ferns, and, of course, all sun-loving Mediterranean plants and perennials with silvery-gray or woolly foliage tend to respond much better to planting now, when conditions are becoming increasingly amenable to growth. Again, special attention must be given to watering during the first few weeks after planting, until the plants have developed enough roots to fend for themselves. (For planting techniques, see page 159.)

This is the very best time to plant ornamental grasses of all sorts. It is not yet too dry, and the warming spring weather gives them the best chance to establish themselves quickly and to grow away strongly; planted in the fall, they seldom get off to such a good start. Planting procedures are the same as for other herbaceous perennials. As with all spring plantings of container plants, it is advantageous to soak the root ball well before planting.

Frostlifting
One of the dangers of fall planting is that the young plants may be lifted by frost during the winter before they have been able to produce enough roots to anchor themselves firmly, so check all herbaceous perennials, particularly those newly planted, as soon as the soil has thawed. If any have been lifted or loosened, they should be firmed in again or even replanted if it seems necessary.

Tidying
The time has come to tidy up the herbaceous and mixed borders, to remove the traces of the past winter and to prepare the stage for the entrance of spring. Winter protection should be removed in two or three stages, instead of all at once, since harsh winds and cold may still follow spells of mild weather. An overcast, humid day is best for the job of uncovering plants. Dead vegetation that has provided winter protection should now be cut back to the ground to make room for new growth. Gather up dead leaves and other debris at the same time.

Cutting back ornamental grasses
Many ornamental grasses, especially the taller species, are attractive throughout the winter, as the foliage dries and pales or takes on warm-colored hues which shine in the low-lying winter sun. Even more important for the well-being of the grasses, the dead stalks and foliage provide valuable protection for the crowns of the plants during the winter. But now, all grasses that are not evergreen should be cut back to within 2in/50mm of the ground so that the growth of new shoots will not be hindered. This can be easy with grasses like molinia, which can be tidied up practically with the bare hands, or it can be treacherous and backbreaking as in the case of some of the more robust miscanthus species, whose cut stalks can be as sharp as daggers. Sturdy pruning clippers or hedge clippers are the best tools for achieving a good, clean cut. You can also use electric hedge clippers to obtain an effortless cut, close to the ground.

Smaller evergreen species, such as carex and luzula, should not be cut back at all; only dry, dead leaves removed. Similarly, evergreen festuca species should be freed of all brown leaves around the base. Using the hand as a comb – or even a broad-toothed metal comb – the dead blades can then be teased out from the crown.

Hoeing and fertilizing
After the borders have been freed of debris and as soon as new growth is visible, the soil around the plants should be hoed or lightly dug. Work from the paths or from boards laid out in the beds so as not to compact the soil. If bulbs have been planted in the border, then the soil should be worked over shallowly and with great care.

Weed seeds will be germinating already. Removing them while they are small is much easier than later when the herbaceous perennials have produced top growth. Any perennial weeds, such as ground elder, thistle, or couch grass, must be dug out as soon as they appear.

Apply a dressing of organic fertilizer around the plants and lightly work it in. Herbaceous perennials respond well to an annual feeding with well-composted farmyard manure, garden compost (free of weed seeds), or a commercial balanced organic fertilizer, based on peat or composted tree bark. Where compost or manure is not readily obtainable, feeding with a brand name organic fertilizer each spring brings excellent results. Plants that tolerate lime can also be fed with bone meal, which is a good source of phosphorus.

All of these organic fertilizers are slow-acting and release their nutrients only when the soil conditions are conducive to growth. This makes them superior to mineral fertilizers and they are therefore generally safer to use with perennials.

ANNUALS

Sowing indoors

If a suitable area for cultivating seedlings is available, then you can make the first sowings of half-hardy annuals indoors. The place must be warm enough to promote rapid germination, with a temperature somewhere between 59 and 68°F/15 and 20°C and with sufficient light, either from the sun or from artificial plant lights, to encourage strong stocky seedlings once the seeds have germinated.

A greenhouse or cold frame makes success easier, but fair results can also be achieved on the windowsill, provided that light is good enough. Don't overestimate the intensity of light shining through your windows; it may not be sufficient for growth. The intensity falls off very rapidly with the distance from the glass as well, so the area with useful illumination is often limited. If the light is insufficient for seedlings or your space is cramped then it is better to wait for a few weeks. If you have to make do without a greenhouse, then special plant lights give the best results.

1 Right Fill a seed flat or pot with potting mix, level off and firm with a board or the base of another pot, to about ⅓in/ 10mm below the rim. Always use well-drained, impeccably clean seed flats and pots – disinfect and rinse them if they have been used before – and fresh brand name seed mix.

2 Right Although you can scatter seed over the surface in a flat, it is easier to transplant seedlings sown in rows. Make sure that the potting mix is uniformly moist but not wet and make shallow rows by pressing a ruler or similar straightedge into the soil.

3 Left Shape the seed packet into a small funnel and scatter the seeds as evenly and as thinly as possible along the rows. Gently tapping the packet may help to release the seeds slowly.

4 Left Cover most seeds with a layer, equal to their own depth, of seed mix, sand, or vermiculite. Use a sieve to achieve a fine, even coverage. Very fine seeds should not be covered at all or they will fail to germinate.

5 Right Water in the seeds, using a fine sprayer, a sprinkler bulb, or a watering can with a fine rose. Alternatively you can stand the containers in water until the surface is moist, then allowing the containers to drain, although this method is unsuitable for loamless seed mixes which tend to float.

6 Right Place the container in a propagator to prevent water loss and maintain an even temperature. Alternatively, cover flats with a sheet of glass, seal pots in plastic bags. Cover containers with newspaper against intense sunlight until the first seedlings appear, and then remove the covering.

BULBS AND TUBERS

Tuberous begonias

If you get them started off now, tuberous begonias can brighten up borders or a shady spot on the balcony or patio from early summer until late fall. The dormant tubers are generally available during the late winter; buy them early, the bigger the better, and start them indoors, 6-8 weeks before you plan to set them out.

Place the tubers in shallow boxes of damp peatmoss, setting them so that the tops are barely covered. The round side of the tuber is the bottom and the concave side is the top. The growth rate varies from tuber to tuber, so as each send up about half an inch (one centimeter) of growth, it should be transplanted to a 6-8in/150-200mm pot of fresh potting mix. Keep the mix moist but not soggy – if the leaves turn yellow, you are overwatering. After the young plants get under way, fertilize weekly with a dilute high-nitrogen plant food and grow on in a sunny spot until moving them outdoors in early summer.

Dahlia cuttings

By means of a simple trick, a single dahlia tuber can be made to produce several plants, each of which will flower as profusely as the planted tuber and may even come into flower earlier. This propagation method is especially useful for building up stocks of new – and expensive – varieties. Pre-spring and spring are good times to propagate dahlias using this method, but the exact time is largely governed by the available warmth in the greenhouse: at least 60°F/16°C is necessary for good results.

Planting begonias
Below and left A begonia tuber is round at the bottom and concave at the top where growth buds may be emerging. Plant the tubers 3in/80mm apart, water regularly and keep at 64° to 75°F/18° to 24°C in good light but out of direct sun.

Taking dahlia cuttings
1 Right Plant the dahlia tubers in pots or boxes containing any good potting mix. Cover them with mix, leaving the crowns exposed. Keep the potting mix moist, but take care that the crowns, from which new growth will emerge, do not become wet.

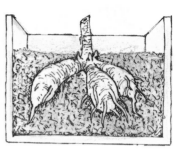

3 Right Remove the lowest leaves and trim the shoots just below the leaf joint.

5 Right Place the pots in a warm sheltered place or cover them with a plastic bag over a frame. After two or three weeks, pot the rooted cuttings individually.

2 Left When the shoots are about 3in/8mm long, cut them with a sharp knife, just above the first basal joint, allowing further growth for later cuttings.

4 Left Insert the cuttings 1in/25mm deep in pots containing a peat and sand mix.

WATER GARDEN

Cleaning and tidying

In the water garden there are a few simple but important tasks that can save a great deal of hard work – and frustration – later on. As soon as the surface ice melts and new life begins to stir in the lowland areas, you can start with the annual cleanup. Any decaying plant matter from water garden plants or the leaves of nearby trees will destroy the quality of the water and promote growth of ugly algae later on as the water warms up and so it should be fished out of the water as soon as you see it. But do not disturb any eggs or frogs or other amphibians. Cut back all dead and withered reeds, grasses, and other herbaceous plants that are still standing, to make way for new growth.

Weed the low and bank areas while you are tidying, but do not tread on the wet ground more than necessary. Stay on the stepping stones or lay out planks temporarily to allow access to the wetter areas. Take special pains to remove any perennial weeds and seedlings of trees such as willow, poplar, or maple, which may become impossible to remove later without upsetting the planting.

If you have fish in your pond, they should not be fed until the water temperature rises above 50°F/10°C. Any water or air pumps that were not in use over the winter should be checked and serviced now.

LAWN AND MEADOW

Maintenance

It is always best to keep off the grass as much as possible at this time of year, certainly so long as the ground is still frozen or very wet. You should note, however, where standing puddles or wet patches indicate compaction and bad drainage and take remedial action. In most cases, fortunately, faulty drainage can be remedied simply by spiking the turf with an aerating tool, followed by a topdressing of gravel or sharp sand. Do not drive a fork into the ground instead of an aerator as it is likely to make the condition worse by compacting the soil even more where the prongs enter.

If the aerator cannot reach the impermeable layer, then you may have to dig one or more French drains deep enough to break through the obstructing layer.

Rejuvenation and repair, aerification, removal of moss and thatch, and topdressing are normally done in the fall, but any of these operations that you could not finish before winter can just as well be completed now (see page 161). A flexible springtine lawn rake is essential for leveling worm casts, removing winter debris, and breaking up small amounts of thatch. It also lifts up the grass blades and weed stems, which allows more efficient cutting at first mowing. If the lawn has been lifted by frost or the tunneling of moles, then it must be rolled before mowing can begin.

CONTAINER PLANTS

Pelargonium care

Overwintered dormant pelargoniums (geraniums) will be ready to break into new growth and need attention now if they are to develop into sturdy, compact plants for summer display on the balcony or patio. If you pruned them back by one-third of their height before moving them into their winter quarters, then they may be cut back once more by an equal amount. Otherwise they should now be pruned back hard. Always cut back to an outward facing bud, so that new shoots will not grow inward toward the center and cross each other.

If the pelargoniums were overwintered in their old containers, then it is best to remove them, to shake off much of the old potting mix from the roots, and to repot in fresh mix – moderately heavy, with good drainage but not more than about one-fourth peat or other organic matter. Pelargoniums seem to flower better when slightly pot bound, so keep their roots restricted. When repotting, ram the mix down very firmly. You may replant in the old containers or pot up in individual pots for replanting later.

As soon as the stems start to plump up, new shoots will break. From now on, your pelargoniums need 59-68°F/15-20°C warmth, moderate watering, and plenty of light.

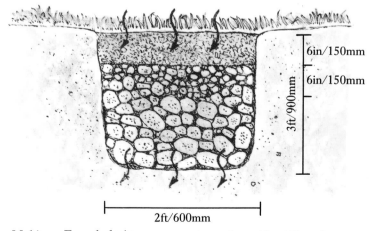

Making a French drain

To construct a French drain, dig a hole at least 2ft/600mm square and 3ft/900mm deep. Fill it to within 1ft/300mm of the surface with rubble or large stones; cover this with a 6in/150mm layer of gravel, or coarse sand and above that a 6in/150mm layer of good topsoil.

CHAPTER 2

EARLY SPRING

"Loveliest of trees, the cherry now
Is hung with bloom along the bough,
And stands about the woodland ride
Wearing white for Eastertide."

A. E. Housman

Early spring begins with the flowering of the dainty wood anemone (*Anemone nemorosa*). Sometimes called fairies' windflower, it grows naturally in deciduous woodlands and often appears, together with primroses, along hedgerows or banks. The small white, or pinkish white, pendulous bells are well adapted to the changeable weather of early spring: only on sunny days do the blossoms open fully, so neither late snows nor cold drizzle can reach the sensitive flower parts to spoil the pollen.

Midway through the season, the dandelion's ostentatious show appears in meadows and unmowed lawns. At the same time the blackthorn or sloe (*Prunus spinosa*) opens its white blossoms, a dazzling haze set against black leafless twigs, the wild sweet cherry or mazzard (*Prunus avium*) blooms pure white, flowering just as the leaves start to expand, and the Norway maple (*Acer platanoides*) is truly spectacular when the leafless branches are covered with bunches of acid yellow flower clusters. However, the most charming sight is the leafing out of the birch, an infallible sign that winter has indeed lost its hold on the land. At the very end of early spring, sour cherries and pear trees bring the first flush of white blossoms to orchards and gardens.

Only a few of these signal plants for early spring are suitable for a place in the garden, but all the others are so common that one or more is certain to be near enough to allow easy observation and comparison with the progress of the season within the garden.

The white wild form of the wood anemone is attractive and suitable for naturalizing under hedges in wilder parts of the garden. It may be too vigorous for small gardens, though, for its creeping rhizomes soon form large patches. Plant them in fall in a partly shaded border, choosing the position carefully, as the area should be planted with ferns or other shade-loving plants to fill gaps when the foliage dies down.

Early spring is the season for exploring the sunny woodland edge, for strolling over the wild meadow, or for lingering on the flowery bank, strewn with starry white windflowers, sweet violets, and golden daffodils.

Fritillaria imperialis 'Lutea Maxima,' the yellow crown imperial, is one of the most stately and dramatic flowers of the early spring garden. It grows easily in any neutral or alkaline soil as long as it remains relatively dry in summer.

THE EARLY SPRING GARDEN

The garden in early spring might well be inspired by Nature's own design: trees and shrubs flowering in clouds of white blossom with an occasional pink or delicate rose-colored shrub blended in, to give a tempered warmth to what might otherwise be too frosty a picture. Such ethereal whites and pinks need a secure foundation, although early spring is definitely not the season for hot reds or strident orange tones; once again Nature serves as model. On the ground, a flowery carpet of yellows, creams, and blues could echo the warm sunny bank or the verdant meadow crowded with daffodils.

Most early-flowering, hardy bulbs, which are valuable for their brilliant, if ephemeral appearance in the garden, are relatively small plants. This makes them ideal for borders underneath deciduous shrubs and, especially, for planting in flower meadows, since they blossom while the grass is still short. In imitation of the forest's edge, anemones, scillas, chionodoxa, grape hyacinths (*Muscari*), crocuses, and of course daffodils may be planted together with violets, primulas, hellebores, and pulmonaria, which are all at their prime now, to give the desired color effects. There is a wide selection of delectable spring bulbs; particularly, narcissus, crocus, and the rather sinister snake's head fritillary (*Fritillaria meleagris*), that flourish in grass and may well naturalize to give a flowery meadow worthy of a poet's praise. Whatever you plant, it is important that a period of six weeks or so be allowed between flowering and the first mowing. This should be sufficient time for the bulbs to store enough energy for the next season and for the foliage to begin to die down naturally.

Blossoming trees and shrubs

One of the most attractive shrubs flowering in early spring is also one of the easiest to grow: *Amelanchier lamarckii*, the snowy mespilus, cannot compete perhaps with the exquisite magnolias or opulent ornamental cherries, but it does possess an airy grace of its own that enables it to blend in well with many other shrubs. It is especially valuable because it has two seasons of beauty: in early spring the branches are laden with snowy white blossoms, which appear together with the young, silvery pink or copper-colored leaves, and the fall foliage colors are magnificent. In the intervening months, it is a pleasant, unobtrusive shrub, well adapted for informal settings, such as the fringe of a deciduous woodland or in a background hedge, but it is also effective as a freestanding specimen. During the summer the small, fleshy black fruits ripen and are eagerly eaten by many birds. Amelanchiers grow mostly as bushy shrubs or small trees which may eventually attain a height of 23ft/7m. Hardy to zone 4, they grow on virtually any soil so long as it is neither too dry nor too wet.

The real jewels of this season are the early magnolias, which flower before their leaf buds break. Their splendid blossoms are the largest of any to be seen at this time of year and, because they open in such lavish abundance while the branches are still quite leafless, the effect is doubly enhanced.

Magnolia stellata is often the first to open its delicately fragrant, starry white flowers. It forms a neat, rounded bush, with a reliably attractive, bowl-shaped silhouette. This species is without a doubt the best for smaller gardens as it flowers while still young, takes many years to reach its final height and spread of 10ft/3m, is hardy to zone 5, and tolerant of a wide range of soils, so long as they are not waterlogged. Indeed, its only fault is that the large, but rather delicate blossoms come so early that they are susceptible to frost; however, they are produced in such abundance that a succession of new blossoms generally replaces the first crop, should they be damaged. A wonderful blue-and-white china effect can be obtained by underplanting *M. stellata* with a sea of blue flowering bulbs, such as one of the blue varieties of *Anemone blanda* or *A. nemorosa*, or with grape hyacinths (for example, *Muscari armeniacum* 'Cantab').

A few days later, the lovely willow-leaved *Magnolia salicifolia* 'Pendula' opens its white flowers, with their rich fruity perfume. They are rarely damaged by frost and the tree itself is one of the hardiest of the genus. *M. salicifolia* grows as a slender elegant tree, eventually reaching 26ft/8m. Even young specimens flower freely and older trees are smothered in blossoms. The flowers are 3-4in/7-10cm in diameter and are the smallest of all the magnolias; the leaves are narrow, willowlike and give off an aromatic scent, reminiscent of lemon, when bruised. It prefers moist soil rich in humus and will refuse to grow on an alkaline one.

The same soil conditions are required for *Magnolia denudata*, known as the Yulan magnolia, which blooms at about the same time. Its gleaming pure white flowers open as upright goblets, but soon spread to a broad bowl form; they release their pleasant scent, suggestive of violets, particularly intensively at night. The blossoms are large, up to 6in/15cm in diameter.

A group of charming hybrid magnolias, known as *Magnolia × loebneri*, extends the range of color from white to delicate pink. There are several named varieties, all of which are spectacular small trees, flowering with profusion even as young plants. What is more, *M. × loebneri* is tolerant of a wide range of soils and will grow on poor, alkaline soils. *M.* 'Leonard Messel' is the best known of this group; it forms a magnificent plant, with fragrant flowers of a deep lilac-pink.

Towards the end of this season the most ornamental of the pear trees flowers, the weeping willow-leaved pear (*Pyrus salicifolia* 'Pendula'). With its beautiful silvery gray foliage, this elegant tree is a welcome alternative to the full-sized weeping willow for the small garden. Its graceful foliage and weeping form are perfect as a contrast to the rather rigid leaves of the ornamental cherries. The creamy white flowers open simultaneously with the downy silver leaves; together they present a delightful picture. The willow-leaved pear is hardy to zone 5 and tolerant of extremes in climate and soil; it eventually reaches a height of about 23ft/7m.

Ornamental cherries

The ornamental cherries are graceful, small trees, worthy of space in even the smallest garden. They are hardy and unproblematical, succeeding on any reasonable, well-drained soil and asking only for full sun in order to retain a symmetrical shape. One of the earliest to flower during this season is *Prunus* 'Moerheimii,' which bears single flowers of the palest pink, appearing before the leaf buds break. It forms a small picturesque weeping tree with a wide, dome-shaped crown, eventually reaching a height of 19ft/6m and width of 13ft/4m. In contrast, *Prunus* 'Umineko' is a small, upright cherry tree covered with delicate single blossoms of purest white just as the leaves start to show. During the summer, the foliage is a lush, dark green, which changes beautifully to shades of bright yellow, amber, and brown in fall.

'Mount Fuji' is considered to be, together with its sister 'Tai Haku,' the loveliest of the white-flowering Japanese cherries. 'Mount Fuji' is a small but vigorous, spreading tree which often adopts a weeping shape – the branch tips can be weighted down to the ground when heavy with blossoms. The fragrant flowers themselves are very large, both single and semidouble in large hanging clusters, with shining bright green leaves carried above as a perfect foil to the pure white blossoms. The handsome foliage changes to attractive shades of amber and russet in fall. 'Mount Fuji' eventually attains 20ft/6m in height and 33ft/10m in diameter.

For the smallest garden, where there is only space for one small tree flowering in early spring, there is a perfect ornamental cherry: *Prunus* 'Hally Jolivette' is a small graceful tree which will never exceed 13ft/4m in height. Its form is dense and slender, becoming more rounded with age. In flower, the elegant willowy stems are covered with small, semidouble, faintly pink blossoms which continue over two to three weeks.

Woodland flowers

Among the loveliest of all the spring flowers are the dog's tooth violets, or trout lilies, *Erythronium*. Plants of the open deciduous woodland, they grow best in partly shaded spots with a cool, moist but free-draining soil, rich in humus. They are easy to grow and will gradually make imposing colonies if they find your garden to their liking.

One of the most adaptable species for the garden is *Erythronium tuolumnense* which bears up to five bright buttercup yellow, turk's-cap flowers per stem, held over glossy plain green leaves. It is relatively tolerant of poor soil conditions and will flower freely even on sandy soils.

Similarly tolerant are two quite vigorous hybrids: 'Pagoda' has lovely flowers of a vivid shining sulphur yellow; 'Kondon' has somewhat paler yellow blossoms. Both have marbled leaves, like the equally lovely *Erythronium* 'White Beauty', which is one of the best forms to choose for the garden. It has large white flowers with a ring of yellow and russet about the center and leaves mottled with bold brown marks. 'White Beauty' carries its turk's-cap flowers on stems 10–12in/25-30cm high. It is prolific in the garden and tolerates more dryness than most of the other erythroniums. A thriving colony of 'White Beauty' surrounded by masses of *Anemone apennina* with their fernlike foliage is an unforgettable sight. Indeed, all the erythroniums associate particularly well with other woodland dwellers such as polygonatum, trilliums, hellebores, and hepaticas.

The blue forms of *Anemone nemorosa* are especially charming in the early spring garden: 'Allenii' has exquisite pale silvery

The Californian dog's tooth violet, *Erythronium revolutum*, likes moist, loose soil. Its delicate pink petals look well growing here with rose-flowering *Ribes sanguineum* and deep blue grape hyacinths (*Muscari*).

lavender-blue blossoms 1½in/4cm in diameter, the largest of the species; those of 'Robinsoniana' are a paler lavender; and the large, long-lasting blossoms of 'Royal Blue' are intense blue with a suggestion of warm rose on the backs of the petals. The dark green foliage of the last variety shows a light touch of red as well. All of these anemones grow 4-5in/100–120mm tall and naturalize well under deciduous shrubs and trees.

A. apennina has the same delicate ferny foliage as the other spring anemones and has bright blue starry flowers which open flat whenever the springtime sun reaches them. It spreads freely by means of its slender black rhizomes and can make drifts of blue underneath magnolias and ornamental cherries. It is never invasive, however, and discreetly withdraws underground during the summer. It is happiest in humus-rich soil in semishade under deciduous shrubs where it can be left undisturbed to increase over the years to give the desired massed effect.

PLANTS FOR EARLY SPRING

Blue and mauve
Aubrieta cultivars 'Blue
    Emperor,' 'Doctor Mules,'
    'Schloss Elkberg'
Brunnera macrophylla
Mertensia pulmonariodes
Omphalodes verna
Pulmonaria saccharata
    'Frühlingshimmel'
Vinca minor 'La Grave'
Viola labradorica purpurea
V. odorate 'Queen Charlotte',
    'Triumph'
V. × wittrockiana cultivars
Myosotis cultivars
Anemone apennina
A. blanda 'Blue Star'
A. nemorosa 'Robinsoniana',
    'Allenii,' 'Royal Blue'
Chionodoxa luciliae gigantea
Hyacinthus orientalis cultivars
Muscari cultivars
Scilla siberica 'Spring Beauty'

Yellow and orange
Corylopsis spicata
C. sinensis sinensis
Cytisus × praecox 'Allgold',
    'Gold Speer'
Forsythia × intermedia 'Beatrix
    Farrand,' 'Karl Sax,'
    'Lynwood'
Hamamelis japonica
    'Zuccariniana'
Mahonia aquifolium 'Apollo'
Rhododendron species, cultivars
Salix hastata 'Wehrhahnii'
Adonis vernalis
Alyssum saxatile 'Citrinum'
A. s. 'Compactum'
Doronicum orientale
Epimedium perralderianum
E. pinnatum colchicum
E. × versicolor 'Sulphureum'
Hylomecon japonicum
Cheiranthus cheiri cultivars
Erysimum × allionii

Viola × wittrockiana cultivars
Erythronium 'Pagoda'
E. tuolumnense
Fritillaria imperialis 'Lutea,'
    'Lutea Maxima'
Iris bucharica
Narcissus bulbocodium
N. 'Peeping Tom' and other
    early cultivars
Tulipa Fosteriana 'Sweetheart,'
    'Orange Emperor'
T. Kaufmanniana 'Berlioz,'
    'Corona,' 'Fritz Kreisler'

Red and pink
Cercis canadensis
C. siliquastrum
Chaenomeles × superba 'Crimson
    and Gold,' 'Fire Dance,'
    'Hollandia'
Magnolia × soulangeana 'Lennei'
M. × loebneri 'Leonard Messel'
Pieris 'Forest Flame'
Prunus 'Pink Perfection'
P. subhirtella 'Fukubana'
P. × yedoensis 'Moerheimii'
Rhododendron species + cultivars
Ribes sanguineum
    'Pullborough Scarlet'
Arabis caucasica 'Monte Rosa'
Bergenia 'Abenglut', 'Ballawley,'
    'Bressingham Bountiful'
Epimedium × rubrum
Pulmoonaria saccharata
    'Pink Dawn'
P. vallarsae 'Margery Fish'
Viola × wittrockiana
    cultivars
Anemone blanda 'Pink Star'
Erythronium dens-canis
    'Carneum,' 'Roseum'
Fritillaria imperialis 'Maxima'
F. meleagris 'Charon,'
    'Poseidon,' 'Artemis'
Hyacinthus orientalis cultivars
Tulipa Fosteriana
    'Madame Lefeber'

T. Kaufmanniana
    'Daylight,' 'Alfred Cortot'

White and cream
Amelanchier laevis
A. lamarckii
Chaenomeles speciosa 'Nivalis'
Magnolia denudata
M. × loebneri 'Merrill'
M. salicifolia
M. × soulangeana
    'Alexandrina,' 'Brozzonii,'
    'Speciosa'
M. stellata
Prunus 'Hally Jolivette'
Pyrus salicifolia 'Pendula'
Rhododendron species + cultivars
Viburnum 'Anne
    Russell'
V. × burkwoodii
V. × carlcephalum
Arabis caucasica
    'Schneehaube'
A. procurrens
Bergenia 'Schneekönigin,'
    'Silberlicht'
Iberis sempervirens
    'Findel,' 'Snowflake'
Primula denticulata 'Alba'
Pulsatilla vulgaris
    'Weisse Schwan'
Sanguinaria canadensis
Tiarella cordifolia
Trillium grandiflora
Vinca minor 'Gertrude Jekyll'
Viola × wittrockiana cultivars
Anemone blanda 'White
    Spendour,' 'Fairy'
A. nemorosa
Erythronium citrinum
Fritillaria meleagris 'Aphrodite'
Hyacinthus orientalis cultivars
Iris bucharica
Narcissus early cultivars
Tulipa Fosteriana
    'White Empress'
T. Kaufmanniana 'The First'

Scented plants
Corylopsis spicata
C. sinensis sinensis
Magnolia denudata
M. × loebneri 'Merrill'
M. salicifolia
M. × soulangeana
M. stellata
Prunus × yedoensis
Rhododendron species + cultivars
Viburnum 'Anne Russell'
V. × burkwoodii
V. × carlcephalum
Primula auricula
Viola odorata
Cheiranthus cheiri cultivars
Erysimum × allionii cultivars
Viola × wittrockiana hybrids
Crocus varieties
Hyacinthus
Iris bucharica
Muscari varieties

Plants for bees and butterflies
Acer platanoides
A. rubrum
Amelanchier lamarckii
Salix hastata 'Wehrhahnii'
Prunus varieties with
    single flowers
Daphne laureola
Erica carnea cultivars
Ribes sanguineum cultivars
Alyssum saxatile
Arabis caucasica
A. procurrens
Aubrieta cultivars
Doronicum orientale
Iberis sempervirens
Primula species
Cheiranthus cheiri varieties
Myosotis varieties
Anemone species
Muscari varieties

EARLY SPRING TASKS

TREES AND SHRUBS

Pruning

It is now time to prune or finish pruning shrubs that flower in late summer or fall on new wood produced this year. The same applies to shrubs planted for the winter effect of their brightly colored stems.

Late-flowering shrubs to be pruned now include:

Buddleja davidii
Caryopteris × *clandonensis*
Ceanothus (deciduous)
Ceratostigma
Elsholtzia stauntonii
Hydrangea paniculata

Lespedeza thunbergii
Perovskia
Spiraea japonica 'Albiflora,' 'Anthony Waterer,' 'Bullata,' 'Froebelii,' 'Little Princess'
Vitex agnus-castus

Shrubs with colored stems to be pruned now include:

Cornus alba 'Sibirica'
C. stolonifera 'Flaviramea'
Rubus biflorus
R. cockburnianus

Salix alba 'Britzensis,' *S. a vitellina*
S. daphnoides
S. irrorata

Pruning of both groups should be completed as quickly as possible before new growth begins. The same method is used for both, although with shrubs grown for the winter color of their young stems the point from which the young shoots arise can either be close to the ground or even near to shoulder level so that the display of color is at the optimal height to fit in with the planting design. Ornamental brambles (*Rubus*) should be cut back to the ground. The secret with all of these shrubs is to keep them eternally young; vigorous new shoots are always longer and more brightly colored or bloom more freely than older, unpruned growths.

Planting conifers

Many conifers can be planted now, before new growth begins. Indeed, early spring is, in most gardens, the preferred time to plant any of the less hardy species, such as the cedars, the false cypresses (*Chamaecyparis*), Japanese cedar (*Cryptomeria*), Chinese fir (*Cunninghamia*), Japanese umbrella pine (*Sciadopitys*), or the hemlocks.

Planting at this season, however, can be somewhat risky for larger specimens, particularly those which are to maintain a rigid conical form, and careful watering may well be necessary. The buds at the ends of the shoots will be breaking during the next few weeks and are very sensitive to dehydration. All conifers require a maximum of moisture when their new growth is expanding and especially young, freshly planted trees need a constant, uninterrupted supply of moisture at the roots. Should the swelling buds be damaged by an unseasonal drought, then the new growth may be uneven and the

Pruning late-flowering shrubs

 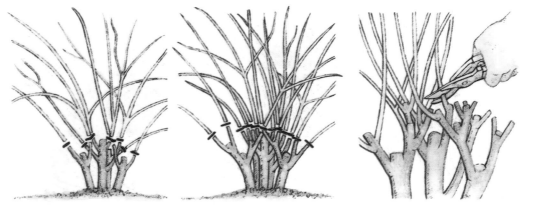

Hard pruning will produce a well-shaped shrub that flowers vigorously in late summer or fall. On shrubs grown for winter effect, the same treatment promotes longer, more brightly colored stems.

Cut back the flowering stems as low down as possible – certainly to within one or two pairs of buds from where they arise on the main basal stems.

In subsequent years, new basal stems grow and new shoots arise from the pruned stems. Cut all stems and shoots back to a similar height.

Using sharp pruners, cut new shoots cleanly, almost at their point of origin. If the framework becomes congested, remove some basal stems entirely.

symmetrical form of the tree impaired. Smaller conifers, as well as any of the larger species which normally have a more irregular growth habit, are much less problematical and can be planted now without hesitation. In any case, remember that a conifer is always losing some moisture, even if the weather is still cool and growth is at a standstill. A newly planted conifer requires all the same considerations, precautions, and care recommended for broad-leaved evergreens (see Pre-spring, page 14).

HEDGES

Most hedges planted now or since last fall should be cut back hard in early spring. But there are exceptions and the clipping regimen will be largely dictated by the species of hedging plant chosen (see page 154 for pruning techniques).

Planting

Early spring is also the preferred time for planting evergreen hedges. Without a doubt, broad-leaved evergreens, such as holly, box, privet, euonymus or cherry laurel, or conifers, such as yew, juniper, or red cedar, all do best when planted in early spring, when the conditions are favorable for quick growth of new roots which are necessary to replace the water lost continuously by the transpiration of the evergreen leaves. Should they be planted when root growth is slow, the leaves may become dried out during cold dry weather. (See pages 115 and 131 for details on planting hedges.)

ROSES

Pruning and fertilizing

If you have not completed the pre-spring pruning of your roses (see page 16), you should do so as quickly as possible, before new growth has proceeded too far. Similarly, if you have not already fed your roses, then you should do so now.

CLIMBING PLANTS

Planting

Early spring is a good time to plant clematis, honeysuckle, wisteria, and most other climbing plants that have been grown in containers.

Climbing plants can work wonders for you, but only if you provide them with what they need most: adequate space for their roots in good, rich soil with sufficient water when they need it. Unfortunately, the soil at the base of most walls is all too often the worst in the garden: hot, full of trash and building debris, consisting mainly of lime, builder's sand, or compacted clay. So, before you plant a climber, you are likely to have to do a good deal of strenuous digging in order to

create just the sort of conditions that guarantee years of satisfactory growth and continued flowering. It is best to dig the entire area to be planted to a depth of at least 20in/500mm – even deeper if you can – and just as wide. Remove any rubble that crops up. If the soil is terribly poor, then the only solution is to replace it entirely with good fresh garden soil. Otherwise, work in plenty of ripe compost, rich topsoil, peat or composted tree bark. After refilling with improved soil, it is a good idea to wait for the soil to settle before planting. When you are ready to plant, dig out the planting hole about 1ft/300mm away from the wall. Many climbers, clematis and wisteria for example, can be planted slightly deeper than they stood before, with their root balls covered by 1-2in/20-40mm of soil. Set the plant in its hole, leaning toward the wall. Clematis may be planted lying almost on its side, with the lower part of the main shoot shallowly covered with soil.

Water is of utmost importance; if the root ball is dry, immerse it in a bucket of water before planting, long enough for it to become saturated. Never plant in dry soil; if it appears dry when digging the planting hole, fill the hole once or twice with water and allow this to drain through before planting.

It is good practice to lead the young plant to the wall, or its support, using a temporary stake, which should be put in place before filling in the hole and firming the soil. After planting, water again thoroughly. A mulch of pulverized tree bark, straw, compost or dried peat is an ideal means of conserving soil moisture and maintaining a cool root run during hot weather. Make sure that the newly set plants do not suffer from lack of water at any time during their first year.

Many climbers, clematis in particular, are typical dwellers of the sunny woodland edge: they prefer to grow with their roots in cool, moist shade and send their shoots upward into the full sun. In your own garden plant them so that their roots are shaded by other low-growing plants.

Clematis care

Routine care of established clematis, and indeed of most other climbing plants as well, consists primarily of reducing competition from weeds and vigorous neighbor plants, of maintaining a thick layer of mulch around the bases of the plants, of watering during dry weather; and of fertilizing, especially if they are growing in a narrow border along a wall where there is only restricted root run and soil nutrients quickly become exhausted. A good balanced fertilizer should be scattered around the root area of the climber and lightly worked into the top layer of soil. After thoroughly watering in the fertilizer, you should top up the mulch layer. Mulching with well-rotted compost not only keeps the soil cool and moist in summer, it also provides a little beneficial nourishment for the plants.

Older clematis which have not been pruned regularly each year often become unsightly and quite bare of leaves and flowers in the lower parts. This is often the case with *Clematis montana* and other vigorous species which do not as a rule require yearly pruning. These can be rejuvenated now by the renewal pruning method for the second group of hybrids described in pre-spring (page 17). It is also not too late to rejuvenate clematis hybrids from that group.

Sowing annual climbers

Annual climbing plants are invaluable for quickly covering fences, screens, trellises, and even entire walls of building with a soothing cloak of living green. In the course of a single summer, they can cover and camouflage almost any structure, ranging in size from under 3ft up to more than 20ft/1.6m, depending on the species chosen and the suitability of the planting site.

Now is the time to start sowing seeds of annual climbers indoors. Most of them require temperatures around 68°F/20°C to germinate. Large seeds which are easy to handle should be sown, singly or three to a pot, in small individual containers. Otherwise, sowing may be performed as described for annuals on page 20. As soon as the young seedlings appear they will need as much light as you can give them until, when there is no longer any danger of frost, they are finally planted out.

HERBACEOUS PERENNIALS

Staking

Any herbaceous perennials that will need support during the coming year should be staked early, certainly before they reach half their expected height. Staking early is important; once the plants have grown too large, it is virtually impossible to support them so that their natural habit is preserved and once kinks develop in weak stems they can never be straightened. There are various types of support; for taller plants, sturdy bamboo canes or wooden stakes are commonly used; for shorter plants, a few pieces of twigs or sticks stuck into the ground around the plant are sufficient. Simple as the operation sounds, staking is often done poorly – or much too late – with inadequate, unsightly results. Always select supports suitable for the job; strong enough to serve their purpose but not so tall as to poke up above the plants themselves. Neatness and as far as possible unobtrusiveness are also important. Use no more supports than necessary and position them to best advantage, so that as the plants grow the supports will be hidden by foliage.

Division

Many herbaceous perennials form broad, overgrown clumps after several years in one spot; quite often the center of such a clump becomes bare and the plant ceases to thrive and flower as profusely as in its youth. Then the time has come to uproot the entire plant, to divide it and replant the strongest of the outermost shoots. Except for a few very short-lived species, most herbaceous perennials need to be uprooted and divided every four or five years. Otherwise, their overly crowded roots have to compete for moisture and nutrients from the soil, which eventually becomes exhausted. Without rejuvenation, the plants become too weak and diseased to survive.

Generally speaking, the best time to divide is just after the plant has finished flowering. That is when vegetative growth is strongest and a new shoot system is developing. With perennials that flower in fall, however, this usually means waiting until early spring since

Supporting perennials

Right Twiggy pea sticks make good unobtrusive supports for weak-stemmed perennials. Insert them into the ground around the growing plant and bend them inward. By the time the plant is fully grown they will be virtually obscured.

Right If stakes are used, cross the twine between stake and stem in a figure eight loop to prevent the stem rubbing against the stake. Begin tying early and continue in several stages as the stems lengthen and eventually flower.

Right You can support wide-spreading clumps by inserting 3 or 4 stakes around it; slope them outward to allow for growth. Tie string between the stakes, adding additional string as the plant grows.

winter would be unsuitable. This is the time to divide such late-flowering herbaceous perennial as hardy asters, rudbeckias, perennial sunflowers, golden rod, phlox, helenium, and monarda. In addition, many of the less hardy perennials are also best divided now, after the rigors of winter are past, as are all ferns and ornamental grasses.

It is good practice to divide early, when the crown buds are still small enough to survive division unscathed. Try to end up with individual plants that have two or three stems or growth buds. It is a common mistake to make the divisions too large; small vigorous divisions are always preferable. Replanted in enriched soil, they will blossom abundantly the following fall (see *Division* page 159).

If you have not completed these tasks in pre-spring, there is still time in spring, too, to plant all those late-flowering herbaceous perennials which delight us with their richly colored flowers in late summer and fall.

Planting ferns and ornamental grasses

Hardy ferns and ornamental grasses are particularly valuable in the modern garden because of their graceful forms and textures. Early spring is an excellent time to plant hardy ferns and is not too late for ornamental grasses if you have not planted in pre-spring. They will be delivered as container-grown plants and require no special treatment.

Ferns as a rule prefer a loose, damp but well-drained soil, with a high humus content. Slightly to strongly acidic soil is a requirement for most ferns, but some, among them *Asplenium trichomanes*, the dainty little maidenhair spleenwort, need some lime in the soil. Ferns tend to grow slowly for the first year or so. During this time they should never suffer for lack of water. A permanent mulch of leaf mold, compost, or dried peatmoss suits them well.

Mulching

Once the soil has warmed up, mulch around your herbaceous perennials before they have grown large enough to hamper spreading the mulch material. Because mulch is a form of insulation, do not apply the mulch before the soil has warmed up; otherwise, the soil may remain cool too long and retard growth. You may want to scatter an appropriate fertilizer before applying the mulch.

ANNUALS

Sowing outdoors

There is a practical, though not botanical, distinction between hardy and half-hardy annuals: hardy annuals are those that grow well when sown outdoors as soon in early spring as the ground can be brought into condition. They will not be harmed by light frost and make satisfactory growth at fairly low temperatures. Now is a good time to begin sowing hardy annuals outdoors. They will reward you with an early and abundant crop of flowers.

Sowing indoors

Continue indoor sowing of half-hardy and tender annuals. Species that need only a short time for germination and precultivation, such as *Lobelia*, *Phlox*, and *Salpiglossis* may also be sown now.

Pricking on

As soon as seedlings from indoor sowings in pots and flats start to produce their first set of true leaves, the time has come to prick them into new containers. Never wait too long before transplanting

1 Right Prepare the new containers for the seedlings by using a stick or dibble (round-ended stick) to make a hole large enough to receive the roots of the young plant.

2 Left Holding the seedling carefully by a leaf (cotyledon) – never by the stem – pry it loose from the seeding mix and gently place it in the prepared hole.

3 Right Use the stick to push the mix gently against the roots. Water with a fine spray and keep the seedlings shaded for the first few days.

young plants into new soil: even if they are still very small, the seedlings barely feel any shock and will continue to grow with unchecked vigor if moved on early. The purpose of pricking on is to give the seedlings more growing room and occasionally a more nourishing soil. At the same time, the slight damage inflicted on the seedlings' roots during pricking on induces them to branch and fill the substrate densely with more numerous, but shorter roots, which ensures better growth of plants, when they are planted out in individual pots or outdoors.

BULBS

Dividing snowdrops

Now is the best time to divide and replant any snowdrops (*Galanthus*) which have become overcrowded and show signs of deterioration. This is one of the few exceptions to the general rule that bulbs should not be moved while growing. Snowdrops are always best transplanted while in full growth, preferably just after they have flowered: divided into single bulbs, they should be replanted immediately, before they have time to dry out. Although they may look rather bedraggled for a time, they will soon recover. Indeed, the secret of establishing new plants quickly is to buy and plant them while the leaves are still green. Some nurseries supply them in this condition; they may be more expensive than dried bulbs, but they are well worth the extra cost.

Fertilizing

Spring-flowering bulbs benefit from fertilizing now when the bulbs are breaking into active growth and perhaps once again later, just after the blossoms have faded.

As soon as the leaves appear above the surface, you can scatter

Potting up begonias

Transplant each tuber as soon as it has started strong growth – the first leaves should be about 2in/50mm long. Carefully lift the plant and insert singly into 6in/150mm pots filled with rich soil or a commercial potting mix, just as deep as they stood before. Give each plant moderate warmth, generous light, and plenty of fresh air, but no direct scorching sun.

quick-acting balanced plant food. If possible, use a complete fertilizer which is rich in potassium or a special commercial fertilizer for bulbs. After fertilizing, water in well. Isolated clumps can be fed individually by applying a dissolved plant food with the watering can. This method is especially suitable for daffodils, tulips, lilies, and any particularly fastidious species.

With proper fertilizing and care, most bulbs can remain in one spot and flower satisfactorily for many years. Not until they become too dense or the plants show signs of weakness is it necessary to remove the bulbs and to replant.

Tuberous begonias

Growth rate varies from tuber to tuber, but most begonias started earlier should be so far along by now that they may be potted individually. As soon as the roots have filled the pots, watering can be increased somewhat and the plants can be fertilized weekly with a dilute plant food. Not until all danger of frost is past can they be moved outdoors.

WATER GARDEN

Planning a pool

Early spring is an ideal time to begin construction of a new garden pool, in order to be finished in ample time to allow planting in spring, the best season for setting out all sorts of aquatic plants. First it is most important to select a suitable site. Once installed, a pond is virtually impossible to move and should be considered and built from the beginning to be a permanent feature. All aquatic plants enjoy full sun and will only prosper and flower well if they receive a minimum of 8 hours of direct sunlight each day in the summer. So the ideal spot for the pool is in full sun, sheltered from strong winds but well away from any shading trees whose leaves will also land and decompose in the pool, releasing poisonous gases and fouling the water.

There are also aesthetic aspects to consider when choosing the site for your pool. A body of water is found naturally only at the lowest spot in the landscape. Consequently, for your pool to look right, it must be situated at a low – preferably the lowest – part of the garden. Only a strictly formal pool can be raised higher than the surrounding area and still look attractive.

The shape of a pool is largely a matter of personal choice, but generally a formal garden demands a geometrical pool design. A pool with a more natural irregular shape is best suited to an informal garden; it is advisable, however, to choose a simple shape with easy, broad curves which can easily be realized. A large pool is always ecologically more stable and therefore easier to manage than a small one; so, plan to build the largest pool possible within the limits imposed by your garden setting.

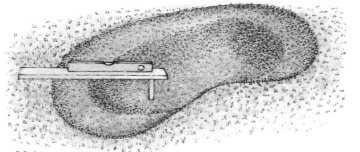

The depth of the pool is also important. A pool less than 2ft/60cm deep may freeze solid for most of its depth during the coldest winters and may heat up so much in hot weather that the aquatic plants and animals may suffer. Various aquatic plants require different depths at which to grow; this should also be taken into account while planning your pool. It is sensible to contemplate first the plants you wish to include at all costs in your water garden and then create just those conditions they require rather than to select plants after the completion of the pool. Most water lilies, submerged free-swimming aquatics, and other common deep water plants are well satisfied with a water depth of at least 2ft/600mm but only seldom require more than 3ft/900mm so you can safely plan for the deepest zone of your pool to be somewhere between these measurements. Water-edge aquatic plants, which are to inhabit the shallows around the pool, are able to grow in various depths of shallow water; however, most of the commonly available species prefer to have not more than 4in/100mm of water over their crown. So if you allow for the height of the planting containers in which they will grow, a shelf, or other shallow water zone about 10in/250mm deep is adequate. Certainly every informal pool should have at least two zones with different depths of water.

Making a pool

1 Above Dig a contoured hole with slopes and ledges for water-edge plants. Check the surrounding area, at least 1ft/300mm wide, is level all round by rotating a level on a plank anchored by a vertical support. Remove sharp objects and line the hole with 1in/30mm layer of fine moist sand to give extra puncture protection.

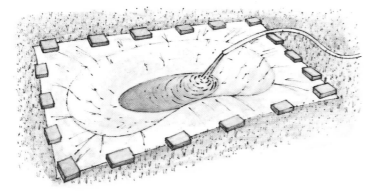

2 Above Stretch the liner over the hole, with plenty of overlap and anchor it with stones. As the liner stretches under the weight of the water trickling in, slide it from under some stones and pull it up under others until it fits the contours of the hole. When the pond is full, trim the surplus liner.

Construction

The cheapest and easiest method, particularly if you plan to do the work yourself, is to use plastic sheeting specially made for lining pools. Pool liners are available in several materials which differ greatly in cost and durability: polyethylene is the cheapest material, but is so short-lived that it cannot really be recommended. PVC or PVC reinforced with nylon fabric is stronger and has a durability of about 10 to 12 years. But by far the toughest, most durable lining material is synthetic rubber, which will easily last for several decades if reasonably

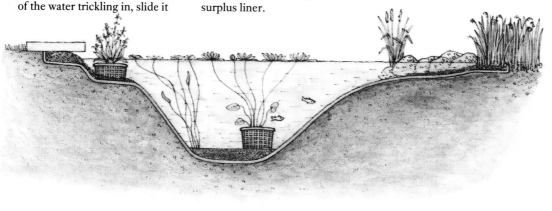

3 Left Try to visualize the completed pool. Make sure the trimmed edge of the liner comes up to the surface, or it will siphon water into the surrounding soil. Secure and protect the edge of the liner by laying stones around the pool's rim packed firmly with soil. You can create a moist area for low-lying plants by extending the liner under the soil. At a few spots, let paving come to the edge of the pool to allow easy access to the water.

cared for. PVC and synthetic rubber pool liners may be expensive, but it is always advisable to use the best quality material available. The additional costs are a minor factor when compared to the frustration and extra work involved in repairing or dismantling and replacing a deteriorated, leaky pool liner after only a few years, just when the pool ecosystem has become stable and well established.

The pool liner needs to be considerably larger than the excavation itself. The depth, length, and breadth have to be considered, and an overlap of about 12in/300mm at the top of the pool is necessary for securing it to the edge. Calculation for an irregularly shaped pool must be based upon a rectangle enclosing the most distant edges of the excavation. To calculate the size of liner you require, use the formula:

Length of liner = twice the depth + length + 2 overlaps
Width of liner = twice the depth + breadth + 2 overlaps

A pool liner should be black or dark brown because these colors look most natural. Under water the dark liner becomes virtually invisible, causing the pool to appear deeper than it really is. Before beginning to dig, you should trace out the outline of the pool using a length of rope or garden hose. This will help you visualize the shape of the finished pool and decide whether the size is adequate and the shape appropriate.

Before filling in the soil or installing plants in containers in your new pool in spring, make certain that the pool does not leak. When you have filled the pool to the planned upper rim with water, mark the level on a partially submerged stone and observe the pool for about a week. If there is no loss of water during that time, you can safely proceed with the installation of your plants in the next season (see page 51). If you plan to spread the soil over the bottom of the pool and plant the aquatics in it directly, you must first empty the pool of water using an electric pump or garden hose as a siphon. Only then can you spread the soil over the bottom of the pool, setting out your aquatics and refilling with water gradually.

Dividing bog plants

Most low-lying and water-edge aquatic plants are herbaceous perennials that require much the same care and treatment as their terrestrial cousins. This includes lifting, dividing, and replanting any plants which have grown too large for their allotted space as well as those which show signs of loss of vigor due to aging. Early spring is the time to deal with any plants needing attention, just as new growth is beginning. Most will need dividing only every three to five years.

After lifting the plants, carefully remove and discard any perennial weeds. The process of dividing low-lying plants and water-edge aquatics is essentially the same as for other herbaceous perennials (see page 159). Before replanting low-lying plants, you may want to work some well-rotted compost into the soil.

Tidying up

If you have not finished tidying up the water garden, then do so before the low-lying and water-edge plants have grown too large.

LAWN AND FLOWER MEADOW

Sowing

The seed bed will have been thoroughly worked over several days before you start sowing. Any final preparations should be carried out just before sowing, when the soil surface is fairly dry and easily workable. When you have finished, the surface must be free of lumps and stones, worked to a fine texture, carefully leveled, and firmed.

For sowing a new lawn or flower meadow, the most suitable seasons are early spring and early fall. In each season there are advantages and disadvantages. In early spring the soil temperatures are steadily rising and there is a full growth year ahead. The main drawback is that diligent watering will be necessary if the spring and summer happen to be dry. However, if you pay careful attention to the irrigation needs of your new lawn or flower meadow throughout the heat of the summer, it will make rapid, luxuriant growth and be well established by the end of the growth season.

Sowing a new lawn

1 Left Immediately before sowing, rake the prepared bed to create very shallow furrows. Divide the seed and sow half lengthwise and half crosswise to ensure even coverage. A mechanical spreader makes it easy to sow evenly but hand sowing can give good results especially for small areas.

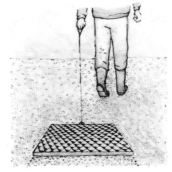

2 Right Rake or draw a ridged rubber doormat over the seed bed to lightly cover the seeds. Do not roll after sowing. If there is no rain within 2 or 3 days, irrigate thoroughly with a lawn sprinkler.

Sowing before early spring is seldom successful: grass seed germinates well only when the temperature does not fall below 46°F/8°C. At all costs be sure to wait until all danger of serious frost is past; the lifting action of freezing soil can tear young seedlings loose, so that they lose root contact with the soil and dry out.

Fertilizing

You may apply a lawn fertilizer as soon as lawn grass starts to grow freely. The nutrients will then be taken up by the plants at once and there is less danger that they will be washed away, out of reach of the grass roots.

There are many different types of lawn fertilizers available and you must always follow the package instructions for timing, rate and frequency of application. Many modern lawn foods are slow-release formulations which allow you to feed only once or twice a year. Such a slow-release sod fertilizer is best applied early in the season.

One of the major differences between the care of a lawn and the care of a flower meadow is that the lawn requires regular feeding; the flower meadow, however, should never be fertilized.

Repairs

Any bare patches in the lawn which have not become green again by now will need to be repaired, either by resowing or resodding.

Mowing

As soon as the outdoor temperatures start to climb toward the 50°F/10°C mark, grass starts to grow and it is soon necessary to mow the lawn. If you have a fine lawn, then cut as soon as the grass is 2in/60mm long. A utility lawn will not need mowing until about 3in/80mm. With any type of lawn, never cut away more than one-third the current height at one mowing. Otherwise you may remove most of the leaf area capable of photosynthesis and even the growing points, so that regrowth may be retarded or the grass plant killed.

After the first mowing, the blades may be gradually lowered to the desired height, and the frequency of mowing increased to suit the speed at which the grass is growing.

BALCONY AND WINDOW BOX PLANTS

Pelargoniums, fuchsias and other balcony or window box plants which you have carried over the winter should be looked after regularly. If you have not already done so, repot them in fresh potting mix. Prune or pinch back any plants that need training to good form. Increase watering as growth begins and give plants as much light and fresh air as possible. Resist the temptation, however, to bring them outdoors too early, unless of course you have time to bundle them all into the house again whenever frosty weather threatens.

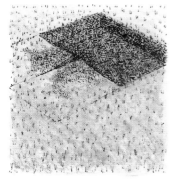   

Repairing a lawn
1 To resow or repair a bare patch in a lawn, remove a sod or two around the worn area, digging out the soil to a depth of 4in/100mm.

2 Loosen the soil and replenish with a mixture of sand, sifted compost, and soil. Repair with a new sod cut to fit the old patch and firm it well; or alternatively, continue preparing the ground for resowing.

3 Before sowing, firm the sand, compost, and soil mix, continuing to fill and firm gently until the soil reaches the level of the rest of the lawn. Sow with a grass seed mixture identical to that of the existing lawn.

4 Cover the seed with the sand, compost, and soil mixture, finely sieved. Water the patch gently but thoroughly if it has been reseeded. If you have resodded it, firm, especially around the edges, and soak liberally.

CHAPTER 3

SPRING

"When, upon orchard and lane,
breaks the white foam of the Spring."

William Watson

White is, more than any other color, characteristic of springtime. One after another the cherry and pear trees, apples, and finally hawthorn open their pale blossoms in our orchards and hedges. It is the pale pink or white of apple blossom – officially the 'Yellow Transparent' apple (also know as 'White Transparent') – which signals the beginning of spring. Other popular early-flowering varieties, however, bloom at the same time, among them 'Idared,' 'Belle de Boskoop,' 'Gravenstein,' 'Discovery,' and 'Red Delicious.' When the first blossoms on several neighboring trees of one of these apple varieties have fully opened and are producing ripened pollen, spring has arrived.

Normally the horse chestnut (*Aesculus hippocastanum*) and the common lilac (*Syringa vulgaris*) cultivars blossom at about the same time as the early apple varieties or, at many locations, about a week later. As spring becomes established, the yellow broom (*Cytisus scoparis*) opens its golden blossoms, to be followed toward the end of the season by a lovely trio of small, flowering trees: the common hawthorn or May tree (*Crataegus laevigata*), the common laburnum (*Laburnum anagyroides*), and the mountain ash (*Sorbus aucuparia*). The average soil temperatures rise during spring from 53°F/12°C to about 60-63°F/16-17°C, close to the optimum germination temperatures for most vegetables and annuals.

THE SPRING GARDEN

With the arrival of full-blown spring you have a complete palette of floral colors at last, and to create a satisfactory design you need to exercise strict discipline in selecting plants and colors that fit into it from the host of flowering trees, shrubs, bulbs and herbaceous perennials, which are now at their exuberant best. The very first roses are breaking into flower, lilacs, clematis, and wisteria flood the garden under billows and cataracts of fragrant mauve blossoms, crab apples in shades of white and pink give the first act of their double feature show, and everywhere there are brilliant tulips in virtually every imaginable shade and color. In choosing varieties of tulip for your garden, you should be guided primarily by your own taste and color scheme because there are so many first-rate varieties available. However, tulips are not permanent residents; because of their transitory nature, you need to plant an interesting, permanent framework of shrubs and climbers, together with herbaceous perennials such as iberis, veronica, and nepeta, which are good companions for tulips, to set the stage for their annual performance.

Flowering trees and shrubs

The earliest of the ornamental crab apples flower at the beginning of spring and it is possible to have a succession of them in blossom for the whole of this season. Their simple, unassuming charm and modest beauty together with their ease of cultivation make crab apples indispensable for the spring garden. Most of them also have the bonus of a second decorative season when their shining red, orange, or yellow fruits ripen in late summer and fall. They are particularly valuable for small gardens.

Generally, the first to flower is *Malus floribunda*, the Japanese crab. It grows to the size of an ordinary standard apple tree, but forms a much denser, spreading crown with an abundance of palest pink blossoms opening from crimson buds. In fall the branches are decorated with yellow and red fruits, no larger than peas. It is hardy to zone 4, tolerant of a wide range of soils and sites, and demands only a sunny, open situation, free from overhead shade of crowding neighbors. Its only weakness is its twiggy nature and the tendency to remain shrubby for several years before developing a trunk. To counteract this tendency, prune away the lower branches each winter until a clear stem has developed, which is long enough to support a crown of the desired height.

A second early-flowering crab is the delightful Chinese tea crab, *Malus hupehensis*. Its large pink-tinted, globular buds open to fragrant, pure white cup-shaped flowers which gradually flatten out to lovely 1½in/40mm broad stars with a center of golden anthers. The blossoms are so numerous that the entire crown is turned into a dense white cloud. It grows into an upright tree, up to 39ft/12m high, with a stiff habit. The small round fruits are pale yellow tinged with red on the exposed side and in the winter its bark is an attractive orange-brown color, becoming cracked with age into large plates. It will grow in any soil and is hardy to zone 4.

The hardy, vigorous *Clematis montana* is ideal for training over walls, archways and fences. With time, the long shoots will hang down to make an enticing floral curtain.

Toward the middle of spring, another Japanese crab, *M. × zumi* 'Calocarpa,' comes into flower. This cultivar assumes a pyramidal habit and remains relatively small, making it particularly valuable for the small garden. In bud, it is a delicate shade of pink which is restricted to the reverse side of the petals. As soon as the flowers open they are pure white. The blossoms are very fragrant, about 1¼in/30mm across and borne in clusters of four to seven. In fall *M. × zumi* is bedecked with showy bright red fruits.

At about the same time, the earliest of the red-flowering crabs, 'Liset,' opens its large single, deep red flowers. This relatively new cultivar is healthy, resistant to scab, and maintains its flower color well. Of upright habit, it is well suited to a formal design and can be fitted into the smallest town garden. 'Liset' will eventually reach a height of 26ft/8m; the foliage is a glossy dark green, and its fall fruits are shiny dark red.

Only a little later, the best of the fruiting crabs, 'John Downie,' breaks into blossom. The merit of this old favorite lies not in the small white flowers but in the elegantly shaped,

A group of pastel-hued tulips is combined skillfully: the delicate pink 'Angelique' and the old favorite white 'Mount Tacoma' are double or peony-flowering cultivars. The taller, pink and green 'Groenland' belongs to the rather unusual group of viridiflora hybrids, which are characterized by the bold green markings on the outside of the petals.

glossy orange and scarlet crab apples, each about 2in/50mm across, which are borne in profuse clusters among the dark green foliage. The tree itself is not shaped like a typical crab apple, but is comparatively erect, with ascending branches and an open habit. 'John Downie' is a superb tree for a small garden; grown as a standard, it will eventually spread up and out to 16ft/5m or more. A small tree of similar upright habit is 'Van Eseltine,' which is one of the most beautiful of crabs when in flower at the end of spring. It is rather like a small, columnar *M. floribunda*, but with double flowers, each about 2in/50mm wide, strawberry red in the bud but opening to a fine rosy pink; they are followed later in the year by little yellow apples. 'Van Eseltine' is so narrow and small that it can be tucked into the tiniest garden. Hardy to zone 4, it will do well in any sunny spot.

The last of the crab apples to flower is generally the superb American cultivar *Malus coronaria* 'Charlottae,' one of the most highly recommended flowering crabs. It has large, semidouble flowers of shell pink, which are deliciously scented like violets. It forms a well-shaped tree, 20-30ft/6-9m high, with a short trunk and a wide-spreading, open crown. In a good year for fall foliage, the large leaves assume a rich, brilliant orange.

All of these crab apples harmonize wonderfully with tulips of all colors, except perhaps the oranges, and they complement tree peonies and lilacs.

In flower the common lilacs, cultivars of *Syringa vulgaris*, are heavenly, with heavy bouquets of deliciously perfumed blossome in delightful colors although, afterward, they are not especially attractive. Their roots are greedy and drain the soil of moisture and nutrients, so they are best kept out of mixed flower borders. The most satisfactory places for them are in the background shrubbery, in an isolated group in the lawn, or in the wilder parts of the garden. Freshly planted lilacs require patience, as some years pass before they produce blossoms of the characteristic quantity and size.

One of the finest double lilacs is *S. v.* 'Katherine Havemeyer,' with large pyramidal trusses of flowers, lavender purple at first, fading to pink. 'Mme Lemoine' is a sumptuous, deliciously fragrant cultivar with large, double white flowers carried in erect, compact clusters; it flowers freely even when young. Deservedly one of the most popular of all, the purple cultivar 'Andenken an Ludwig Späth' bears its single flowers in clusters about 12in/300mm long. It has the darkest flowers of all the lilacs.

All of these *Syringa vulgaris* cultivars, which are hardy to zone 5, need full sun for the best flowers. Any good soil is suitable except a very acidic one, but a heavy fertile loam is what they prefer. A newly planted lilac should be encouraged to form a single sturdy trunk so that it assumes the form of a small tree rather than a large shrub – the shape is more pleasing and it is easier to place and manage among other plants.

Most of the smaller species lilacs are attractive compact shrubs, at most 10ft/3m high. They bear their fragrant flowers over a longer period than the common lilac and possess an unassuming, old-fashioned character that makes them easy to fit into the informal floral design.

One of these species lilacs, *Syringa × chinensis* 'Saugeana,' the best form of the Rouen lilac, is a bush of unexcelled beauty when in flower. It grows to about 10ft/3m and is suitable for planting alone or in groups together with other shrubs such as laburnum, exochorda, spiraea, or viburnum. The hybrid lilac

Robust and sweetly fragrant, 'Andenken an Ludwig Späth' is a popular old lilac cultivar. It looks well planted toward the back of a mixed border featuring pale pink and mauve flowers.

Syringa × *swegiflexa* has 12in/300mm long clusters of flowers. Dark wine red in bud, the slender blossoms assume a delicate pink after opening.

Pink is a frequent and thoroughly welcome color in the spring garden and from no other plant can you expect – and get – more pink than from the aptly named cultivar of the beauty bush, *Kolkwitzia amabilis* 'Pink Cloud.' Few flowering shrubs can compare with its elegance and abundance of blossom and it is certainly one of the best shrubs flowering toward the end of spring. Kolkwitzias are large, up to 10ft/3m tall and just as wide; consequently, they require space. The main stems are erect, but become arching when weighted down by the abundant large, showy clusters of pink, bell-shaped flowers with yellow throats. The graceful shoots bear attractive leaves, which turn to a rich scarlet in fall. The blossoms of 'Pink Cloud' are a deeper pink than the species and it blooms when still a young shrub. The beauty bush is quite easy to grow and thrives in any good soil in full sun. Established plants require little regular attention other than cutting out old, crowded stems as soon as flowering is over. It is well suited for informal planting designs, for example as a background for peonies and bearded irises.

When in flower, the pearl bush *Exochorda* is lovely with snow white blossoms, but after this it is plain. The variety *Exochorda giraldii wilsonii* begins flowering early in the season and is more floriferous than the species. *E. racemosa* 'The Pearl' has blossoms almost 2in/50mm in diameter. *E.* × *macrantha* 'The Bride' is a free-flowering hybrid of Dutch origin with a dense, spreading habit and broadly arching branches. It is a shrub of considerable beauty, producing 4in/100mm long flower clusters at the end of short twigs, each of which carries six to ten blossoms. The pearl bush needs full sun and grows in any well-drained moderately fertile soil. To encourage the best flowering, weak and crowded branches should be cut out as soon as the blossoms have faded.

The tree peonies, hybrids of the Chinese *Paeonia suffruticosa* and *P. lutea*, bear single, semidouble, or double flowers in a wide color range and are choice plants for shrub beds and as feature specimens in mixed flower borders. The true tree peonies are hybrids nearer to *P. suffruticosa*. They grow as upright, deciduous shrubs, in time reaching 6½ft/2m in height and their predominant colors are white through pink to red. The hybrids closer to *P. lutea* are mostly subshrubs and bear flowers mostly in the spectrum white through yellow to gold and orange. In contrast to the *P. suffruticosa* hybrids, their upper shoots die back each winter to woody, persistent lower parts.

Tree peonies are valuable not only for the exceptional beauty of their blossoms, but also for their wonderfully decorative foliage. In the very small city garden, they might take the place of larger flowering shrubs. There are many first-rate hybrids of *P. suffruticosa* including: 'Renkaku' ('Crane's Flight') which has large, very double pure white blossoms, with irregularly cut edges, and is one of the easiest to grow, and the hardy, dependable and wavy 'Kaoh' ('King of the Blossoms'), with red semidouble flowers. Closer to *P. lutea*, the hybrids that are hardy to zone 5 and relatively easy to grow include 'Age of Gold' which has abundant camellialike double flowers with pretty wavy petals of a pale yellow, deepening to gold toward the middle, and 'Chinese Dragon' bearing shining carmine red, semidouble blossoms with elegant wavy, ruffled petals which give a wonderful contrast to the foliage.

All of these tree peonies are demanding. Most of them are hardy to zone 5, but they do best in a sunny, warm and sheltered spot. Young plants in particular should receive some winter protection. Tree peonies grow slowly and need several years before they start flowering heavily. They can, however, reach a very old age. Pruning is restricted to cutting away any dead or frozen shoots in early spring.

The flowers of tree peonies are of much the same spectrum and intensity of color as the tulips and help fill the floral gap between the climax of the spring-flowering bulbs and the spectrum of the colors of the rose season in early summer.

Early roses

At about the time the lilacs have reached their peak, the first roses of the year make their entrance. These are mainly shrub roses falling into two categories: first, the Chinese species roses, mostly yellow, of the group *Rosa xanthina*, *R. hugonis*, *R. primula*, and *R. sericea* together with their lovely, single-flowering hybrids. Second, hybrids between the wild European burnet rose, *Rosa pimpinellifolia*, and various hybrid tea roses, charming, robust roses which all bear names beginning with "Frühling," the German for "Spring," and range in color from pure bright yellow to deep rose-red; most are heavily fragrant. All of these early-flowering roses blossom but once in the season; however, during that time they are without equal for wonderfully clear color, simple, charming form, and rich perfume. Later in the year, their foliage, which is often delicate and fernlike, is attractive and decorative in its own right.

Rosa hugonis, the golden rose of China, shares with *R. sericea* the distinction of being the earliest rose to flower in our gardens. *Rosa hugonis* bears large quantities of dainty yellow, cup-shaped single blossoms carried on short shoots all along the main branches, so that the whole bush seems to be made of floral garlands. The bush can grow to 8ft/2.4m in height and even more in breadth. Its slender, gracefully arching branches are bronze brown in color and densely thorny. It is beautiful even when not in flower, for its leaves have a fernlike texture in appearance and touch, and turn to orange in fall. It grows well even in poorer soils. Try to obtain a plant growing from its own roots; grafted onto a rootstock, this otherwise hardy and robust rose is often short-lived.

Perhaps the showiest of this group of yellow-flowering shrub roses is *Rosa xanthina* 'Canary Bird', another of the very early flowering shrub roses. It forms a large arching bush, about 6½ft/2m tall and just as wide. The dark brown stems are only sparsely armed with thorns and the fresh green foliage has the same ferny quality as the others in this group. The single, canary yellow flowers are about 2in/50mm in diameter and are carried on graceful, hanging lateral shoots. Like *R. hugonis*, 'Canary Bird' is subject to sudden dieback if grafted.

If you have space for only one rose from this group, then 'Golden Chersonese' is the best choice. It makes a fine, well-formed shrub, about 6ft/1.8m tall, hard and robust. It is decidedly upright in habit, which allows planting even where space is limited. The typical, dainty fernlike foliage is borne on thin, wiry, and thorny shoots. The numerous, small deep buttercup yellow, sweetly scented blossoms are held closely along its branches. It is tolerant of a wide range of soils.

Very different in overall appearance from these early, small-flowering oriental roses, the *Rosa pimpinellifolia* hybrids open their larger, showier blossoms a week or so later, toward the end of spring. 'Frühlingsgold,' one of the oldest and most popular, is often the earliest of this type to flower. Probably no other garden rose is so hardy, dependable, and easily grown. Its semidouble flowers are rich butter yellow in color, 4in/100mm across, with showy golden stamens and are powerfully and sweetly fragrant. The thorny, arching branches grow to 8ft/2.5m in height and are covered with attractive foliage.

With its gracefully arrayed, clear yellow blossoms and ferny foliage *Rosa xanthina* 'Canary Bird' is a beautiful early-flowering shrub rose, perfect for a mixed spring border.

'Frühlingsgold' blooms only once, but during that time it is magnificent; the entire shrub is smothered in flowers. An underplanting with a dark blue perennial, such as *Veronica austriaca teucrium* 'Royal Blue,' is strikingly effective, as is a combination with one of the tree peonies. 'Frühlingsmorgen' is one of the most delicately beautiful of the single roses. The exquisite blossoms are large – 4in/100mm across – cherry pink blending to pale primrose yellow at the center and are richly scented. The bush is of upright habit, growing to more than 6ft/1.8m. The foliage is dark gray-green. It starts flowering early and is occasionally a repeat-flowerer.

The last of this group is a dual-purpose rose: 'Maigold' can be grown equally well as a large shrub or as a climber. It is vigorous, growing 10ft/3m, and extremely prickly; however, both blossoms and foliage are of exceptional beauty. The leaves are a glossy, rich green, a perfect foil for the clusters of deep buff-yellow, semidouble flowers, which open from lovely orange-red buds. The flowers are deliciously fragrant.

Climbers

Wisteria sinensis is the most spectacular plant of all those that flower during the spring. Trained on a wall, a pergola, or allowed to scramble up a large tree, its mauve-colored honey-scented blossoms can easily be the floral climax of this season. Buy your plant from a reputable nursery, to be sure that you receive a reliably flowering clone.

Wisteria sinensis is an extremely vigorous climber and needs strong support as well as pruning twice a year, which, more than anything else, is the key to success (see pages 18 and 87). Given free rein, a wisteria can grow as high as 64ft/20m

When laden with its heavily scented mauve flowers, *Wisteria sinensis* is one of the showiest climbers. It requires regular pruning, but grows rapidly once established.

and easily spread that far or farther horizontally. Its growth is remarkably rapid, if given a warm sunny spot and plenty of water. It is not choosy about soil, which need not be rich.

The only other deciduous climbing plants that are able to compete with the wisteria for extravagant beauty and vigorous growth are the clematis species and cultivars. There are dozens, flowering in a myriad of colors and shades and continuing in succession from now until frost. They come in a range of sizes from scarcely over 3ft/1m up to robust giants clambering to heights of 33ft/10m and higher.

One of the earliest is *Clematis macropetala.* The plant itself is a small one, rambling to a height of about a metre or two 3-6ft/1-2m before cascading toward the ground, but the nodding china blue flowers are large and strikingly beautiful. They open from plump dark buds to hang among the attractive fresh green foliage and are followed by decorative silky seed heads. It is a charming plant for twining up a trellis on for rambling through small, open shrubs. A good combination is to grow it next to the hardy herbaceous peony – *Paeonia mlokosewitschii* – itself a bearer of attractive jade green foliage – whose large goblets of clear sulphur yellow open at the same time as the china blue clematis, making an unforgettable picture.

Clematis montana and its few cultivars are among the largest and most vigorous of the genus. It grows quickly to a height of 19½ft/6m in any reasonable garden soil, flowers quickly after planting and is satisfied with almost any exposure; it even tolerates some shade.

The type species has pure white flowers; but the one most commonly seen in gardens is the Chinese form *C. montana* 'Rubens.' It is similar to the type but has pink or rosy red flowers produced somewhat later. They are about 2½in/60mm across. One of the finest clematis, 'Rubens,' grows to 29½ft/9m high. The cultivar 'Alexander' is an extremely fine form with sweetly-scented, creamy white flowers. Somewhat less vigorous, growing only 19-26ft/6-8m high, 'Elizabeth' has large, soft pink, vanilla-scented flowers. The Dutch cultivar 'Tetra-rose' is a superb lilac-rose clematis with large, fleshy blossoms, each about 2¾in/70mm in diameter. It can cover a wall space up to 19ft/6m high.

All of these early clematis can do without regular pruning. They flower on last year's growths, so should pruning be necessary, do so immediately after flowering.

PLANTS FOR SPRING

Blue and mauve
Rhododendron cultivars
Syringa × *chinensis* 'Saugeana'
S. josikaea
S. vulgaris cultivars
Clematis macropetala
C. 'Lasurstern,' 'Sir Garnet
    Wolseley'
Wisteria sinensis
Aster alpinus cultivars
Aubrieta 'Blue Emperor,' 'Dr
    Mules,' 'Neuling'
Iris bearded cultivars
Nepeta × *faassenii*
N. 'Six Hills Giant'
Veronica gentianoides
V. austriaca teucrium 'Royal
    Blue,' 'Shirley Blue'
Myosotis cultivars
Hyacinthoides hispanica cultivars
Hyacinthus orientalis cultivars

White and cream
Cornus florida + *C.f.* 'White
    Cloud'
C. 'Eddie's White Wonder'
Cotoneaster racemiflorus songoricus
    (*C. multiflorus* 'Calocarpus')
Davidia involucrata
Exochorda giraldii wilsonii
E. × *macrantha* 'The Bride'
Fothergilla major
Fraxinus ornus
Halesia carolina
H. monticola 'Vestita'
Malus tschonoskii
M. 'John Downie'
M. × *zumi* 'Calocarpa'
M. hupehensis
Paeonia suffruticosa 'Renkaku,'
    'Godaishu'
Prunus laurocerasus cultivars
Rhododendron cultivars
Skimmia japonica
S. japonica reevesiana
Syringa vulgaris 'Mme Lemoine'
Viburnum × *carlcephalum*

Weigela 'Candida'
Rosa sericea
R. pimpinellifolia
Clematis montana 'Alexander,'
    'Superba'
C. 'Duchess of Edinburgh'
Convallaria majalis 'Grandiflora'
Dicentra eximia alba
D. formosa 'Silversmith'
D. spectabilis alba
Iberis sempervirens 'Findel,'
    'Snowflake'
Iris bearded cultivars
Papaver orientale 'Perry's White'
Smilacina racemosa
Hyacinthoides hispanica 'White
    Triumphator'
Hyacinthus orientalis cultivars
Narcissus poeticus
Trillium grandiflorum
T. undulatum
Tulipa cultivars

Yellow and orange
Berberis linearifolia 'Orange
    King'
Cytisus × *beanii*
C. decumbens
C. kewensis
Genista lydia
Laburnum × *watereri* 'Vossii'
Paeonia lutea cultivars
Rhododendron cultivars
Weigela middendorffiana
Rosa primula
R. 'Golden Chersonese'
R. hugonis
R. pimpinellifolia
    'Frühlingsanfang,'
    'Frühlingsgold,'
    'Maiwunder,' Maigold'
Rosa xanthina 'Canary Bird'
Epimedium perralderianum
Iris bearded cultivars
Paeonia mlokosewitschii
Trollius europaeus
T. 'Earliest of All,' 'Lemon

Queen,' 'Orange Globe'
Cheiranthus cheiri cultivars
Erysimum × *allionii* cultivars
Narcissus cultivars
Trillium erectum luteum
Tulipa cultivars

Red and pink
Cornus florida 'Cherokee Chief'
Daphne cneorum
D. × *burkwoodii*
Enkianthus campanulatus
Kolkwitzia amabilis 'Pink Cloud'
Malus coronaria 'Charlottae'
M. floribunda
M. 'Liset,' 'Van Eseltine'
Paeonia suffruticosa 'Kaoh'
Rhodendron cultivars
Syringa × *swegiflexa*
S. vulgaris 'Charles Joly,' 'Mrs
    Edward Harding'
Weigela 'Abel Carriere,' 'Bristol
    Ruby,' 'Newport Red'
Rosa pimpinellifolia
    'Frühlingsmorgen,'
    'Frühlingszauber,'
    'Frühlingsduft'
Clematis montana 'Elizabeth,'
    'Rubens,' 'Tetrarose'
Dicentra eximia
D. formosa 'Adrian Bloom,'
    'Bountiful,' 'Luxuriant'
D. spectabilis
Iris bearded cultivars
Paeonia officinalis 'Crimson
    Globe,' 'Mollis,' 'Rosea
    Plena,' 'Rubra Plena'
Papaver orientale 'Aladdin,' 'Ali
    Baba,' 'Beauty of Livermere'
Podophyllum hexandrum majus
Primula japonica
P. sieboldii
Hyacinthoides hispanica
Hyacinthus orientalis
Trillium erectum
T. sessile
Tulipa cultivars

Scented plants
Daphne × *burkwoodii*
D. cneorum
Fraxinus ornus
Malus coronaria 'Charlottae'
Rhododendron cultivars
Rosa pimpinellifolia cultivars
Skimmia
Syringa × *chinensis* 'Saugeana'
S. josikaea
S. vulgaris cultivars
Viburnum cultivars
Akebia quinata
Clematis montana 'Alexander'
Convallaria majalis 'Grandiflora'
Paeonia officinalis cultivars
Cheiranthus cheiri cultivars
Erysimum × *allionii* cultivars
Matthiola incana cultivars
Hyacinthus orientalis cultivars
Narcissus cultivars

**Plants for bees
and butterflies**
Cotoneaster species
Fraxinus ornus
Malus species
Rosa species
Alyssum saxatile
Aster alpinus
Aubrieta cultivars
Nepeta × *faassenii*
Veronica cultivars
Iberis sempervirens
Dianthus gratianopolitanus
    cultivars
D. plumarius cultivars
Cheiranthus cheiri cultivars
Erysimum × *allionii* cultivars
Matthiola incana cultivars
Myosotis cultivars
Allium species

SPRING TASKS

TREES AND SHRUBS

The care of newly planted trees

A dry spell during the spring can seriously retard or even kill young trees before they develop enough new roots to fend for themselves. If sufficient rain does not fall, give them a really deep and thorough soaking once a week while the drought lasts.

Keep the soil around young plants free of invasive weeds, especially perennial weeds and grass, which steal precious moisture and nutrients. After the first growth of annual weeds has been removed and the soil is sufficiently moist, warm, and loose, a 2-2¾in/50-70mm layer of mulch may be spread over the planted area.

Deadheading rhododendrons and lilacs

Rhododendrons seldom require any pruning, but they should always be deadheaded immediately after the flowers fade. The new shoots which will produce blossoms next year start to develop just behind the old flower trusses soon after the blooms wither. Common lilac cultivars blossom more abundantly each year if they are deadheaded.

Deadheading heaths, heathers, and lavenders

Deadheading annually is normally the only pruning which is required, in order to keep these plants compact, vigorous, and heavily flowering. Winter-flowering heaths should be trimmed now, immediately after flowering; they are generally compact in habit and seldom require more than a gentle trimming.

Lavender bushes are pruned in much the same way. Some gardeners prefer to cut away the old flower stems in early fall in order to maintain a tidy appearance during winter; where winters are severe, it is a good idea to leave the old flower stems until the beginning of spring; they help to protect the foliage from winter damage. At either season, cut away the dead flower heads and about ¾-1¼in/20-30mm of the previous season's growth in order to stimulate dense new growth, which will blossom well later in the year.

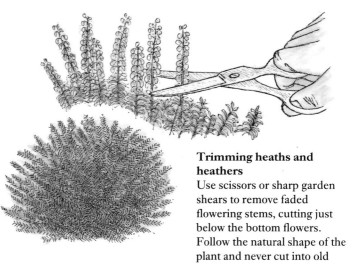

Trimming heaths and heathers
Use scissors or sharp garden shears to remove faded flowering stems, cutting just below the bottom flowers. Follow the natural shape of the plant and never cut into old wood.

Deadheading rhododendrons
Gather up the faded flower clusters between your forefinger and thumb and carefully snap them off. Do not use shears, as you risk injuring the fragile young buds growing at the base of the flowers. Deadheading should be done before the energy-wasting and unsightly seed pods begin to form.

Planting container trees and shrubs

It is best to finish planting trees and shrubs before the onset of summer, so that root and shoot growth coincides with the normal growth period. Container-grown plants have a fully intact root system, which ensures a high success quota after planting; but the young plants must still send out new roots into the surrounding soil in order to obtain sufficient moisture to satisfy the needs of increasing leaf and shoot growth. Any planting which you cannot finish now is better postponed till late summer or early fall. At that time, substantial new root development still takes place without the ever-increasing demands of the aerial parts of the plant for water and nutrients which are typical of the spring and summer seasons.

Taking softwood cuttings

Cuttings may be taken now from the new, fast-growing tips of many shrubs. To ensure success the cuttings must never suffer from loss of water. Take the cuttings during the early morning before water loss due to transpiration has begun; cut only a few sprigs at one time and set them in a polyethylene bag or jar of water immediately. Once a cutting wilts, it will no longer develop roots. Dip the cuttings in a fungicide powder – a rooting hormone is not needed – and plant them in a rooting medium as quickly as possible, covering the pot with a polyethylene bag to maintain a humid atmosphere. (For details on taking and rooting cuttings, see page 156).

ROSES

Pruning

Pruning to keep the middle of your rose bushes open and accessible to light and fresh air also helps prevent pests and diseases. Cut out overcrowded, badly situated shoots, especially any which cross or grow inward toward the center of the plant. Such light, corrective pruning can be done now and any time throughout the growth season.

Fertilizing

If you have not yet fertilized your roses, do so now. Use any good brand name rose food which is rich in potassium but contains no more than 7-9 percent nitrogen. Follow the package instructions exactly and scatter no more than the recommended amount. Work the fertilizer lightly into the soil and water in well. In mixed borders or where roses are underplanted with a groundcover, you may want to use a liquid plant food.

CLIMBERS

Pruning

Early-flowering clematis species and hybrids may need tidying up. Should they become straggly and bare at the base, overcrowded, or too adventuresome, then prune back species such as *C. alpina*, *C. montana*, and *C. macropetala* as well as several of the early, large-flowering hybrids as soon as their flowers have faded. Remove about one-third of the shoots, cutting them back hard to within 2-3ft/600-900mm of the ground (see page 17).

Watering

Climbers growing on walls may need watering long before other plants show any signs of lack of water, since soil at the base of a wall is often the driest in the garden, particularly if it is frequently in rain "shadow" or the wall is high. Drought coupled with sun and drying winds, especially those from the east and northeast can do irreparable damage to young, freshly planted climbers. Water wall plants deeply and thoroughly before they start to wilt. After soaking the soil, allow it to dry somewhat before loosening the surface and applying a thick layer of mulch to help slow evaporation.

Tying in

Many climbing plants need early and continuous training in order to establish and maintain a sound framework of branches which give maximum coverage to their allotted space. The pruning and tying in of new growths ensures that the climber grows where you want it. New shoots should always be trained into place and tied early, while they are still pliable. If you allow them to grow too long and to become woody, they may be broken or bent while fitting them in the required position.

Each shoot should be given room to develop, which means selecting the strongest and tying it into place at an early stage. At the same time, cut out weak shoots to prevent overcrowding. Side shoots may also be trained in the desired direction; space them out to allow easy access to light and air. Always train the climber to grow as close to its support as possible by cutting back unruly, outward-pointing growth and encouraging laterals to grow where you want them.

To tie a shoot to its support, use a strong but pliable twine or plastic-covered wire and, starting from the bottom, bind each shoot firmly but allowing for growth without constriction. Use a figure eight loop to prevent the shoot rubbing from on the support.

Annual climbers

All annual climbers can now be sown outdoors, where they are to grow. Any tender or half-hardy annual climbing plants sown earlier indoors may be planted outdoors as soon as the mountain ash or hawthorn starts to blossom. Harden them off properly and allow them to become accustomed to the outdoor conditions gradually (see *annuals* on pages 48-49).

Before planting out or sowing your climbers, it is good practice to incorporate as much compost as possible into the soil as well as a mineral or organic slow-release plant food, to be sure that the plants get off to a good start.

HERBACEOUS PERENNIALS

Dividing

As a general rule, most herbaceous perennials need to be dug up and divided every four or five years, otherwise many of them will weaken, tire and eventually fail altogether. Dividing perennials almost always successfully restores the plants to their original healthy vigor.

The best time to divide any perennial is shortly after the plant has finished flowering. Deadhead the plant after the blossoms have faded; a few days later lift and divide it into small clumps, each with two or three stems. The strongest young plants originate from the outer portions of the old plant; the degenerated, woody central part can be discarded. Replant the divisions immediately in enriched soil and water well (for division techniques, see page 159).

Weeding and mulching

Open spaces between perennials, particularly in newly planted borders, should be kept weedfree and the soil loosened. It is much easier to keep weeds in check now before they overrun and smother slower-growing plants. After hoeing and loosening the soil, work in a slow-release, mineral or organic fertilizer. Your plants will need nutrients for developing new stems, leaves, and flower buds during the coming months.

Once the soil has warmed up, spread a thick layer of mulch to cover the surface between the plants. This should suppress the germination of annual weed seeds and eliminate the need for hoeing and hand weeding for the rest of the season (for mulching tips see page 152).

Staking

Continue staking and tying up of all perennials which threaten to become top-heavy. Position the stakes and other supports in place well before the plants have reached their ultimate height. Always try to preserve the plant's natural appearance and tie up regularly as described on page 31.

ANNUALS AND BIENNIALS

Direct sowing of annuals

Continue sowing both hardy and half-hardy annuals outdoors where they are to grow. Summer-flowering annuals are useful and versatile, capable of providing rich carpets of brilliant color in beds of their own, of filling gaps in newly-planted borders of shrubs or herbaceous perennials, or of complementing the color schemes in your mixed borders. They are robust and grow quickly to flowering size if they have sunshine, for as many hours of the day as possible. In many cases, certainly with the faster-growing species, direct sowing can be more satisfactory than transplanting seedlings. The plants will be healthier and bloom earlier and for longer, since the shock of transplanting is entirely eliminated. There is also much less work involved: sowing seeds is much easier than transplanting the equivalent number of young seedlings. However, you must have a bed of soil free of weed seeds for this method to be fully satisfactory. One minor disadvantage is that the directly seeded areas will be void of floral color for a short time during the 6 weeks or so before the annuals reach maturity. With clever planning, however, there should be plenty of floral interest elsewhere.

Sowing biennials

Some time between the opening of the lilac's blossoms and the appearance of the golden laburnum or the snowy hawthorn is the time to start sowing the first biennials. The first of the biennials to be sown are those which grow slowly, such as hollyhocks (*Alcea*), Canterbury bells (*Campanula*), sweet William (*Dianthus*), foxgloves (*Digitalis*), honesty (*Lunaria*), and mullein (*Verbascum*). The plants should attain a good size before winter sets in, but they should not become so large that they flower prematurely in the fall, nor so lush and soft that they are unable to withstand the cold of winter.

Biennials should never be sown directly where they are to flower; they rarely ever perform well when set out among other plants while small. Sowing procedures for biennials, both indoors and out, are the same as for annuals.

Hardening-off annuals

A week or two before planting outdoors your indoor-grown annuals, start to harden them off. Until now they have been protected from drying wind, fluctuating temperatures, and strong sun, and they need to be introduced gradually to their new outdoor environment. Avoid subjecting them, at any one time, to more than one set of new conditions that may check growth.

Ideally, plants should be moved first from the warm, sheltered, humid greenhouse to a cooler, but still sheltered cold frame. After a

Sowing annuals outdoors
1 Into prepared soil made weed-free, fine and crumbly, work a slow-release or organic fertilizer and humus material evenly to a depth of 6-8in/150-200mm.

2 Work out your planting plan, arranging the annuals according to their various colors and heights. Outline the areas with white sand, powdered chalk, or flour.

few days, the cold frame may be opened for progressively longer periods, at first during the day only, but later at night as well. As soon as the plants have adjusted to direct sunlight, they may be moved out into the open and should be sufficiently hardened off to recover rapidly from the shock of root disturbance they experienced during transplanting.

If your plants are growing in the house, first move them outside to a shady, sheltered area such as a porch or under a tree during the day. If it turns chilly at night, move them back inside. After two or three days, give them half a day of sun, then a full day, always increasing the exposure gradually. However you harden the young plants off, be sure that they always have enough water.

Planting out annuals

Once they have hardened off, young plants of hardy annuals may be planted outdoors in the beds where they are to flower whenever the weather conditions are favorable. It is advisable to wait until the laburnum and hawthorn are in full bloom before planting outdoors any more tender half-hardy annuals.

As a rule of thumb, the ideal temperatures at planting time should be something like: daytime ground temperatures averaging about 50°F/10°C, daytime air temperatures between 59-68°F/15-20°C; night-time air temperatures not lower than 41°F/5°C.

The day before setting out, water the plants well to minimize transplanting shock. If possible, choose a cloudy day or plant soon after rain or late in the afternoon. The soil in the bed should be moist, but never so wet that it cakes or compacts. After transplanting water every day for about a week until well established. As a rule, annuals do not need irrigating later except when very dry.

BULBS

Fertilizing

Spring-flowering bulbs must be fertilized while their foliage is still fully green. If you have not yet fed the bulbs which are to remain in place permanently, then do so now. Dress with any quick-acting (artificial, granular or liquid) balanced fertilizer which is relatively low in nitrogen but rich in potassium and phosphorus.

Deadheading

Some of the smaller species of spring-flowering bulbs, such as *Scilla*, *Leucojum*, *Galanthus*, *Muscari*, and *Chionodoxa*, set seed readily and can spread to form extensive clumps within a few years, creating lovely sheets of springtime color. They should not be deadheaded; each flower can be allowed to set seed pods, which, in most cases, lie close to the ground and seldom disturb the orderly appearance of your beds. The larger bulbs, such as tulips, narcissus, hyacinths, and the other

3 Scatter the seed over the surface of each area. Rake in lightly or cover with a thin layer of potting mix. Very fine seed should not be covered.

4 Water with a fine spray, moving the nozzle in a circular motion and taking care not to wash away the seed or to make puddles. Keep the soil moist until the seeds germinate.

5 Once at least two pairs of leaves have developed, thin out crowded areas and fill gaps by removing or transplanting seedlings.

6 Until the flower buds form, fertilize every two weeks with a high-nitrogen liquid fertilizer. Sprinkle afterward to wash it off the foliage.

taller spring-flowering ones should always be deadheaded as soon as the flowers fade before they start to make seed pods. All of these hybrids and species increase underground by forming new bulbs – or bulblets. Each plant should use as much energy and nourishment as possible in the formation of these new bulbs. Seed production means less is available for strengthening the bulbs and forming next year's flower buds.

Presprouted begonias and dahlias

Continue potting up presprouted tuberous begonias and dahlias as soon as they break into active growth. Plants that have already been growing in pots should be hardened off gradually in preparation for planting out. Forced dahlias, tuberous begonias and cannas should not be planted out, however, until all danger of frost is past. It is safer to wait until the laburnum and hawthorn are in full bloom before setting these sub-tropical plants out in the garden.

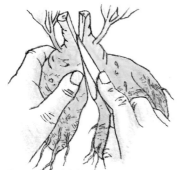

Dividing dahlias
Cut old tubers with a sharp knife, with a bud or shoot attached to each division.

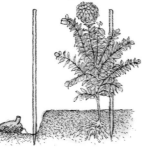

Planting tall dahlias
Set the tuber in a 6in/150mm deep hole, with its bud next to a stake and cover with good soil.

Planting gladioli
In mixed flower borders, group corms 6–8in/150–200mm apart in flat bottomed holes 5–6in/

120–150mm deep. For cut flowers, plant in individual holes at the same depth.

Planting out dahlias and gladioli

Gladiolus corms and unsprouted dahlia tubers may be planted outdoors now. They are among the easiest plants to grow: they like full sun and a warm location, sheltered from buffeting winds but without pockets of dank, stagnant air, and thrive on good, rich, well-cultivated soil with plenty of humus. In fact, any soil where vegetables grow well suits them perfectly, which is probably one reason why both are so common in cottage-style gardens. If you grow them primarily for flowers, then your vegetable garden is still the best place for them. Planted in orderly rows, they will provide cut flowers until fall.

Although gladioli need as much warmth as dahlias for their best performance, they are not nearly so sensitive to cold; consequently you can start planting gladiolus corms earlier in this season, as soon as the apples and lilacs start to blossom. Wait about two weeks until the yellow broom, laburnum, and hawthorn start to flower, before setting dahlia tubers, so that there is no danger of the young shoots being caught above ground by a late frost.

In mixed borders, gladioli should be placed in irregular groups among sun-loving herbaceous perennials. Their spiky, upright leaves and flower stalks contrast dramatically with plants of a broader, more diffuse or transparent habit. To assure continuous flowers, make successive planting every two weeks or so until midsummer.

Other tender bulbs

There is a wonderful group of summer-flowering bulbs which for the most part require the same soil and growth conditions as the gladioli and dahlias and, like them, these nonhardy bulbs and corms are adapted to a dry, frostfree dormant period and should be planted out during the spring and lifted again as soon as the foliage has died back in late summer or fall. Give these sun-loving plants the warmest, best sheltered position in your garden.

Acidanthera has large, scented white flowers, each with a maroon-colored eye. Planting depth: 4-6in/100-150mm.

Galtonia, the summer hyacinth, has tall spikes of up to 30 pendulous, creamy white bells. Planting depth: 4-6in/100-150mm.

Homeria, the Cape tulip, should be planted in a tight group. Each sweetly fragrant, coral pink flower lasts one day, but several are open at one time. Planting depth: 2-2¾in/50-70mm.

Hymenocallis festalis, the Peruvian daffodil, needs plenty of water during the growth season and a fertile loamy soil. Planting depth: 3in/80mm.

Ornithogalum, the South African chincherinchee, produces a long succession of pure white blossoms. Planting depth: 2-3in/50-80mm.

The dramatic *Sprekelia*, also known as the Jacobean lily or Aztec lily, is a most decorative plant, with its large, deep crimson blossoms. Give it a hot location at the base of a sunny wall. Planting depth: 1½-2½in/40-60mm.

The Mexican *Tigridia* or tiger flower, is available in a variety of colors from white to yellow, orange, and crimson. It produces several showy flowers in succession; each one lasts only a few hours in the morning. Planting depth: 2-3in/50-80mm.

THE WATER GARDEN

Planting aquatics

As soon as the water temperature starts to rise, the main planting time for water lilies and other aquatic plants begins. Aquatics are best moved when actively growing and not during their dormant period.

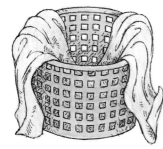

2 Right Fill the container with soil to within about 1in/25mm of the rim. Trim away excess lining material.

4 Right Cover the surface with gravel or small stones to prevent soil from being washed away. Soak or water the basket to remove air and firm the soil.

Planting aquatics in containers

1 Left Line a basket with clean burlap or newspaper to prevent soil from seeping out.

3 Left Plant the aquatic with the roots well spread and the growing point above the surface.

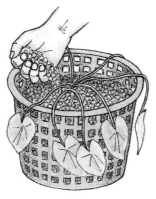

It is important to remember that no more than half of the water surface should be covered. A pond without a reflecting surface loses one of its loveliest attributes. Buy too few rather than too many water lilies and other large aquatics with floating leaves. Nearly all aquatics, except for the free-floating species, are better planted in containers than in soil spread over the bottom of the pool, which is really only practical in one that is concrete. For a plastic-lined pool it is best to use the plastic containers specially designed for aquatic plants which effectively restrict the spread of tougher, more invasive species and prevent them from crowding out tamer neighbors. The soil in such containers will have to be renewed from time to time, but lifting baskets for division or replacement of water plants is much easier and less disruptive than digging around at the bottom of the pool.

Should the pool be empty when the lilies arrive, plant in their final positions, but then only run enough water in to cover the crowns by 4in/100mm. Wait a few days for the water to warm up and growth to start before letting in a little more water. Wait again for it to warm up before filling the pool to the top. Always avoid subjecting water lilies and other aquatics to the shock of cold, deep water, particularly if they have already started active growth.

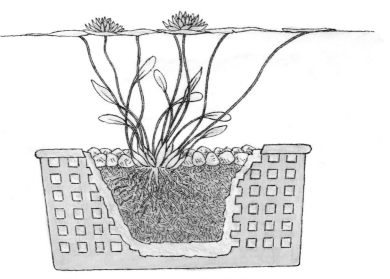

Above A container 12 × 12 × 8in/300 × 300 × 200mm holds 4gal/18l of soil, which is sufficient for many aquatics and smaller water lilies. Any good fertilizerfree garden soil is suitable. Larger containers will nourish plants longer but, remember, waterlogged soil is heavy and all containers have to be moved at some time.

Planting sites
Build up the sides of the pond with soil to create different levels to suit a wide variety of aquatics, water-edge and low-lying plants. Replace the water very slowly to avoid muddying, and in stages in order to acclimatize the plants gradually. Do not introduce fish or water snails for at least a week.

Treat water-edge plants in the same way as water lilies. Plant them in basket containers 6-8in/150-200mm in height, so that the soil surface is at the proper depth underwater to suit the species. A container 10in × 10in × 6in/250mm × 250mm × 150mm can be planted with two or three plants. Do not mix different species in the same container. The more rampant plants, *Typha*, for example, or *Hippuris*, *Butomus*, or *Potamogeton*, should always be confined in containers, or they may overtake the entire pool.

Submerged oxygenators
Be sure to plant enough submerged oxygenating plants. During their rapid growth, they take carbon dioxide and dissolved mineral salts from the water. This competition for essential nutrients starves the algae, which are unable to compete with the higher plants. Once the oxygenators have appropriated all the available food, the algae simply disappear.

Submerged oxygenating aquatics are mostly supplied as bunches of unrooted cuttings, which will quickly develop new roots. To plant, simply stick the cuttings into the soil to a depth of about 2in/5cm. Ideally, these submerged plants should be planted in groups in plastic containers; they will soon creep over the sides and take root in the debris on the pool bottom.

Alternatively, several strands of cuttings may be bound together at their lower ends, tied to a small stone or other weight, and dropped into the pool where they will quickly root in the bottom mud and begin to spread freely.

Submerged aquatics often have very individual requirements. It is always advisable to plant a mixture of different underwater plants. Those species which find your pool conditions more suitable will eventually become dominant.

Dividing aquatics
Every few years lilies and most other aquatic plants need to be pulled out and divided in much the same way as hardy herbaceous perennials. The usual practice is to divide water lilies about every third year, otherwise the lily pads may become congested and climb up above the water rather than floating serenely on the surface. If leaf size begins to diminish and flowering becomes sporadic, the soil in the containers may be exhausted or the roots overcrowded.

Aquatics are generally best divided in spring or early summer. Remove the water lily from its container and select the strongest growth, which should be cut away cleanly with a sharp strong knife. If the cut surface is large, dust with charcoal to prevent rotting before replanting in fresh soil.

LAWN AND FLOWER MEADOW

Sowing

There is still time to sow a new lawn or flower meadow, but plan to finish sowing before the beginning of early summer, otherwise it is better to wait until early fall. Grass seed germinates best at cooler temperatures and the onset of hot and dry conditions in summer makes frequent watering of newly sown lawns a necessity.

Mowing height and frequency

In spring and summer lawn grasses make their strongest growth, which means frequent mowing. For most utility lawns a weekly mowing is sufficient. The mowing height should normally be around 1¼-1½ in/30-40mm. A really fine lawn, however, will need to be cut two or three times every week, at a height of ¾-1¼in/20-30mm if it is to retain its luxuriant texture. Grass should never be shortened by more than one-third its current height at one cutting. If the lawn has not been mown for a while, reduce the grass gradually to the desired height. Too rapid a reduction in height or mowing too short means excessive loss of leaf mass, which robs the grass of too much strength. In such a situation other weeds have a chance to encroach. When cut at the proper height and frequency, the lawn should have the same dark green color after mowing as before.

Weed control in lawns

Frequent and regular mowing at the proper height, repeated feeding with a fertilizer containing a high concentration of nitrogen, and abundant watering guarantee the desired composition and quality of a lawn. A well coordinated program of feeding, watering, and mowing is your best assurance of a weedfree lawn, much more effective in the long run than any chemical weed killer. Dressing with a high-nitrogen lawn fertilizer at the recommended rate, combined with copious watering whenever necessary, encourages the luxuriant growth of both grass and any weeds that are already present. But because of their different growth habits, grasses and broadleaf weeds respond very differently to mowing. A grass plant always holds its growth point quite close to the ground where the blades of the lawn mower cannot reach it; a broadleaf weed, particularly if encouraged by heavy feeding, carries its growth points well above mowing height. Consequently, with each mowing, the weeds become progressively weaker as they lose most or all of their potential growth buds. In contrast, turf grasses are well-adjusted to frequent mowing, and regular mowing actually encourages the formation of a thick mat of turf in which there is no room for new weeds to germinate and grow.

Unfortunately, there are also a few sinister creeping lawn weeds that do not always respond to this treatment. They may require using a lawn herbicide.

Converting a lawn to a flower meadow

If you are thinking of converting a lawn to a flower meadow, now is the time to act – or, rather *not* to act. A lawn is composed of very few grass species to the exclusion of all other plants and is essentially a monoculture. A flower meadow contains a wide range of broadleaved flowering plants as well as a variety of taller, mostly clump-building grasses of an entirely different species composition.

To achieve and maintain a flower meadow, reverse all the rules for lawn care. Never fertilize a flower meadow; the key to a meadow full of colorful blossoms is to starve the soil rigorously. Mow it once or twice at the most three times a year. Rake up and remove all grass clippings. The first cutting should be delayed until after the first flush of meadow flowers has faded, generally at some time in early summer. Do not water; native species can fend for themselves. Watering only encourages less robust species which are not really adapted to the normal environmental conditions in your garden.

Eventually, the fine turf grasses will disappear, to be replaced by coarser, clump-forming tall grasses and 'weeds' or wildflowers which will gradually infiltrate the bare patches arising in between. Once this stage has been reached, you can interfere to a certain extent and deliberately introduce plant species which are suitable to your location. Flowering bulbs may be planted earlier, but it is mostly useless to sow seed of a flower meadow mixture until there are open areas between the grass plants. If you are impatient, many of the perennial flowering plants can be cultivated in small pots and planted out in the meadow. But here as well, success is more likely if you wait until the turf grasses have started their retreat.

THE PATIO AND BALCONY

Annuals in window boxes

Now is the best time to start preparing your window boxes, tubs, and other containers for the summer season. Hardy annuals can be planted at once; with any of the more tender plants, you should wait until all danger of frost is past.

Window boxes and other containers should be as large as possible so that a maximum of root space is available; annuals are hungry and thirsty and grow best when their roots have access to abundant stores of nutrients and water. Renew the soil entirely each year, whenever the planting is changed. Use any good peat-based potting mix, preferably one which contains plenty of loam or clay to prevent shrinkage and to ensure that water will be taken up quickly if the soil should ever become dry. The potting mix must be able to store sufficient water and nutrients and release them as the plants need them. It must be heavy enough to give the roots secure anchorage but still hold enough air so that the roots can breathe. For the best results, mix in a slow-release fertilizer before planting your annuals.

Tender plants

Wait until the hawthorn and laburnum are in full bloom before planting any tender plants such as pelargoniums, fuchsias, begonias, dahlias, cannas, heliotrope, and lantanas in window boxes and other containers. If you move the planted containers out earlier, provide protection against night frosts or move them indoors again should need arise. Any overwintered balcony plants should be hardened off gradually before they assume their final position outside.

A miniature water garden

Even if your gardening area is limited to a modest patio or balcony, there is no reason why you need to deny yourself the pleasure of a water garden. Any small container capable of holding water is a potential water garden, as long as it is at least 12in/300mm deep.

A large cask or beer barrel, cut in half, or an old wooden tub can easily accommodate one of the dwarf water lilies, one or two other small aquatic plants, a handful of submerged oxygenating plants, to help keep the water clear, as well as two or three of the less robust water-edge plants. If you have enough space, you can even combine two, three, or more such tubs with other containers planted with appropriate dwarf shrubs and herbaceous perennials to give a complete miniature landscape.

Suitable small aquatic plants are:

Water lilies – *Nymphaea* × *daubeyana*, *N. pygmaea* 'Alba,' *N.* 'Helvola.' Shallow-water aquatics – *Hydrocharis morsus-ranae* (frogbit), *Hydrocleys nymphoides* (water poppy). Submerged oxygenators – *Callitriche hermaphroditica* (starwort), *Crassula recurva* (pigmy weed), *Fontinalis antipyretica* (willow moss). Water-edge plants – *Acorus gramineus* (dwarf sweet flag), *Butomus umbellatus* (flowering rush), *Mimulus ringens* (blue monkey flower), *Typha minima* (dwarf reed mace). Floating plants – *Azolla caroliniana* (fairy moss).

Repotting and fertilizing container plants

Container plants should be repotted just before they break into new growth or, if tender, when they are moved outside. Until the plants have reached their ultimate size, they should be potted into containers which are only an inch or so (a few centimeters) larger than their present root ball. Smaller specimens should be repotted annually; larger container plants need repotting only every three years or so, but the top ¾-1¼in/20-30mm of soil should be renewed each year. The roots should be pruned when repotting.

Creating a miniature water garden

Be sure that the container is absolutely clean before spreading an 3¼-4in/80-100mm layer of good heavy garden loam over the bottom. Plant a miniature water lily together with a careful selection of other aquatics and water-edge plants, each of which should not be able to grow so large as to obscure the sight of the water or over-run the other plants.

After planting, cover the entire exposed soil surface with a generous layer of clean coarse gravel and then slowly fill with water. Plant a couple of bunches of one of the less vigorous species of submerged oxygenating plants and, if you wish, a small portion of floating plant.

Always use a durable potting mix: a good one contains a high proportion of loam and less peat than most brand name potting composts. Mix in a suitable time-released fertilizer with the soil. This saves feeding for the next six to eight weeks. With all other container plants, weekly fertilizing with an appropriate dilute liquid fertilizer may begin as soon as new growth is evident.

CHAPTER 4

EARLY SUMMER

"Tell you what I like the best–
    'Long about knee-deep in June,
'Bout the time strawberries melts
    On the vine – some afternoon
Like to jes' git out and rest,
    And not work at nothin' else!"

James Whitcomb Riley

The most gentle of all the seasons, early summer makes her appearance with the fragrant blossoms of tall bearded irises, elder, and English dog rose (*Rosa canina*). They break into flower at the beginning of this season, with the heavily perfumed black locust (*Robinia pseudoacacia*) and the sweetly scented mock orange (*Philadelphus*).

The creamy white flowers of European elder (*Sambucus nigra*) are carried in large, flat-topped clusters; they have a powerfully sweet scent which is attractive to large numbers of pollinating insects, particularly flies and beetles. The English dog rose has lovely, single flowers appearing in clusters of up to four blossoms; they are 1½-2in/40-50mm across and vary in color from almost white to shades of pink and even deep red. Their sweet scent disappears once they are fully opened. Too wild for the garden, it is the parent of a host of lovely garden roses, many of which have inherited its sweet perfume.

The common privet (*Ligustrum vulgare*) flowers toward the middle of early summer and finally, at the end of the season, the broad leaved linden (*Tilia platyphyllos*) opens its fragrant blossoms, much to the delight of every beekeeper. At about the same time the earliest strawberries and sweet cherries ripen, to bring the first fruit harvest of the year.

THE EARLY SUMMER GARDEN

This is the season with the longest days of the entire year, with relatively high temperatures, humidity, and plentiful sunshine – ideal growing weather for all garden plants. In open sunny sites roses are at their loveliest, their beautifully billowing blossoms and sweet scents filling the garden with color and fragrance. Many of the best are remontant, or repeat-flowering, and it is their second performance later in the year (see early fall) that makes them so valuable, especially in the smaller garden.

In gardens having the right conditions, rhododendrons are still in their prime. They generally grow best with some protection – under high old trees, for example – which shelter them from drying winds and scorching direct sun. The soil needs to be deep, cool, moist, and rich in acidic humus. Water often plays an important role with rhododendrons, since a pond or lake exerts a moderating influence on the microclimate – extremes of temperature in summer and winter are effectively dampened. A pond also helps to raise the humidity of the air, which will always improve the performance of rhododendrons and other woodland plants. Later in the year, when the flowers have faded, rhododendrons can appear somewhat formless shrubs that need to be relieved by contrasting lines, shapes, and textures. Choose plants with a scale appropriate to your setting. A single slender conifer or a small group of birches, for example, can provide vertical lines and there are several choice trees and shrubs that have strong horizontal lines.

Plants with horizontal accents

The dogwoods (*Cornus* species) are at their best in early summer. The type species of *Cornus alternifolia* makes an attractive small deciduous tree for a solitary position on moist soil; its grows to 19ft 8in/6m. Its horizontal-spreading branches are in distinct tiers but the clusters of small creamy white flowers appearing in early summer are not at all showy. In the wild form, the leaves are light green and turn dark violet and red in fall before they drop to reveal the shining, purple-brown bark, and the strongly horizontal winter silhouette can be very effective. Much showier than the species is the cultivar 'Argentea,' with its smaller silver-variegated leaves and similar growth habit. It forms a dense bush up to 10ft/3m tall.

Cornus controversa, the pagoda dogwood, has nearly horizontal branches arranged in regularly spaced tiers, which form the characteristic silhouette of a Chinese pagoda. In gardens it seldom exceeds 33-40ft/10-12m although it is a rapid grower under favorable conditions. When it reaches sufficient size, it flowers profusely in early summer with abundant small creamy white flowers. They are held in flat clusters of 4-6in/100-150mm in diameter, which rise well above the bright green foliage all along the spreading branches. The flowers are followed by shining blue-black berries, soon eaten by birds, and the leaves change in fall to soft yellow, pink, purple, or glowing red before dropping. The winter silhouette of *C. controversa* is even more striking than that of *C. alternifolia*. Plant *C. controversa* so that the trunk and branches are protected from strong winter sun, to avoid damage due to extreme differences between night and morning temperatures.

Reflecting water is a perfect complement to the colorful masses of the rhododendrons, and the upright arum lilies and slender spikes of iris leaves make a good contrast of form.

In all other respects, the pagoda dogwood is sturdy and hardy to zone 4. It is best planted under the protective crowns of large old conifers; however, because of its striking habit, it should not be wedged in among other shrubs.

C. controversa 'Variegata' is a magnificent little tree for a prominent position in your garden. This form has long, narrow leaves, often with unequal sides and more or less deformed and twisted, but wonderfully variegated with an irregular yellowish white border. It has the same overall habit as the type species, but grows somewhat more slowly and is not so robust. With time, it will grow to 15ft/4.5m tall and 10ft/3m breadth.

The kousa dogwood, *Cornus kousa*, blooms later than other flowering dogwoods, after its foliage is already well developed. Its attractive relatives *C. florida* and *C. nuttallii* bloom two weeks earlier and are rarely spoiled by late frosts. All three species have large, beautiful flowers which are not really flowers at all; their tiny, true flowers are crowded together in a tight, buttonlike central cluster which is surrounded by large attractive bracts – leaves camouflaged to look and function like flower petals. Each creamy white flower of the kousa dogwood has four pointed bracts, which in the wild Japanese species are 1¼-2in/30-50mm long. The flowers are borne well above the foliage, along the upper side of the horizontal branches, so profusely that the foliage almost disappears in a sea of white. In the natural variety *C.k. chinensis*, the bracts are much larger and showier, 2-3in/50-70mm long and ¾in/20mm wide. This grows as a big multistemmed shrub or as a small tree, reaching about 25ft/8m – even more if grown in some shade. There are also two choice cultivars: 'China Girl' is a robust bush, growing up to 13ft/4m tall with large attractive leaves and profuse cream colored flowers about 3½in/90mm in diameter. 'Milky Way' is in every respect like 'China Girl' except the blossoms are milky white.

The flowers of the kousa dogwood are followed in the early fall by red fruits, which hang below the branches like big strawberries and, together with the vivid fall color of the leaves, make a brilliant show. Even after the leaves finally drop, the spreading horizontal branches remain attractive all winter long. Any of the kousa dogwoods, especially one of the *Chinensis* cultivars, deserves a choice, moderately sunny spot in your garden. It is a tree of remarkable beauty, all the more valuable because its floral show comes at a season when the selection of refined flowering shrubs is relatively limited.

Equally refined, but much less showy, the Japanese *Magnolia sieboldii* is one of the few Asiatic magnolias which flower after the foliage has fully developed. Its blossoms open, a few at a time, over several weeks, long into summer. The flowers possess an exquisite and highly sensual beauty: they are fragrant, nodding, alabaster white cups which face outward from the horizontal branches rather than downward, to reveal a ring of crimson stamens which contrast so well with the petals. *M. sieboldii* will grow to 10-13ft/3-4m high and just as wide to form a small, spreading tree or large shrub. Deciduous, its oval leaves are dark green above and downy blue-green below, and are 4-6in/10-15cm long.

The oriental snowbells, sometimes known as storaxes, are small trees, refined and graceful in appearance and hardy to zone 5. The hardier of the two species, *Styrax japonica*, the Japanese snowbell or snowdrop tree, has dark green leaves which angle upward from the horizontal branches, while the waxy white flowers hang below in clusters of three to six, giving parallel green and white tiers, a lovely effect echoed in reverse by *Viburnum plicatum* 'Mariesii,' which also flowers in early summer. *S. japonica* forms a wide spreading tree, with a slender trunk up to 30ft/9m tall. In northern areas it does best in a warm, sheltered spot, shaded from the morning sun and protected from late frosts. The closely related *S. obassia*, the big leaf storax of fragrant snowbell, makes an entirely different impression. Its remarkable leaves are up to 8in/200mm in diameter and nearly round, but abruptly pointed and very showy. This species has a more upright pyramidal habit and grows taller than *S. japonica*. Its white fragrant flowers are carried in 6in/150mm drooping clusters at the ends of the branches. Each bell shaped flower is about ¾in/20mm long.

In their early years, storaxes are often slow to become established and may require some winter protection, but once settled in, they grow vigorously. Their routine needs are minimal and they require no regular pruning.

The most splendid of all the horizontal-growing shrubs is *Viburnum plicatum* 'Mariesii,' a beautiful deciduous flowering shrub from the Orient. The large flat clusters of white flowers are carried in two rows along the top sides of the branches, well above the leaves; they are so profuse that the branches seem to have been draped with white lace tablecloths. The shrub remains in flower for two to three weeks. This broad, distinctly horizontal shrub grows 6½-10ft/2-3m tall and can reach

10-15ft/3-4.5m in breadth. The dark green foliage changes in fall to shades of dark red to violet brown. The shrub is almost never bothered by pests and all it really requires is sufficient moisture in the soil; therefore it can be situated to advantage along a stream or at the edge of a garden pool.

Hardy ferns

It is worth giving thought to plants that will provide light airy textures and bright fresh foliage color to contrast with the ponderous masses of the season's blossom. The hardy ferns are ideally suited to moist areas of the garden. Most need acidic soil, rich in humus, light shade, and a cool spot protected from wind and sun. The fern's dainty filigree lightens up even the darkest planting. Their unique grace and delicacy of form makes them perfect for shady spots and woodland conditions. They grow in various shades of green and the variety of forms and textures of their fronds ensures that there is always plenty of interest and contrast. In milder regions, ferns such as *Blechnum*, *Polypodium*, and *Polystichum* will almost always retain their greenery throughout winter until their new fronds unfurl in spring. Some hardy ferns make invaluable ground-cover plants. Other species, the clump-forming ferns such as *Athyrium*, *Dryopteris*, and *Polystichum*, deserve to stand alone so that their beautiful geometry is not obstructed from view.

One of the daintiest and prettiest of all the hardy ferns, *Adiantum pedatum*, the common maidenhair, is a deciduous species with matt green leaves. It grows well in shady, sheltered nooks where the soil is permanently moist but well-drained. It requires a period of winter cold and does not do at all well in warm climates. It must have shade, for the filmy leaves are easily scorched by direct sun. The short creeping rhizomes send up delicate pale bronze fronds in early spring. The fronds are roughly shaped like a fan and may be up to 12in/300mm wide and 12-16in/300-400mm long.

The lady fern, *Athyrium filix-femina* is a highly variable deciduous species which prefers to grow in light, dappled shade. It is one of the easiest ferns to grow and under favorable conditions will spread slowly, but it is always graceful. Its fresh green fronds commonly reach a length of 36in/900mm; they are sword-shaped and repeatedly divided to create a lovely lacy effect. In a large garden it is suitable for planting in groups; in smaller gardens, however, it is better used as a solitary specimen. By keeping the soil constantly

In a sunny glade the soft green of ferns, including the shuttlecock fern, *Matteuccia struthiopteris*, is set off by the tall, colorful candelabra primula, *P. japonica*.

moist during the heat of summer, the lady fern can be persuaded to keep its foliage green well into fall before it starts to wither.

The Japanese painted fern, *Athyrium goeringianum* 'Pictum,' is unique among ferns because of the color of its fronds; they are of a beautifyl soft gray green subtly stained with wine purple along the midribs. Sword-shaped and doubly-divided, they are usually 24in/600mm long and about 8in/200mm wide. This fern has an attractive, compact habit. Watering during dry periods will prolong its beauty into fall, when the leaves will die back to the ground with the first night frost.

The long-lasting foliage and graceful arching stems of Solomon's seal, *Polygonatum* × *hybridum*, make a striking architectural effect. It grows well in shade, where its pale, belllike flowers look best.

Polystichum aculeatum, the hard shield fern, is one of the most elegant hardy species. Its graceful, daintily cut fronds are about 24in/600mm tall and up to 6in/150mm across at their widest. Young fronds are at first yellowish green, but change to a rich shining green later. The hard shield fern is one of the last ferns to unroll its new fronds. Old plants growing on a favorable spot can form clumps of 4ft/1.2m in diameter. This is one of the most valuable ferns for the evergreen garden; the fronds glisten all winter long.

Flowering herbaceous perennials

A number of herbaceous perennials, which are valued primarily for their bold and beautifully structured foliage can make an impressive contribution in your garden throughout the months of summer. At this time of year some of them bear attractive, often refined flowers that create variety and interest in the lower levels of a woodland design. Their flowers are mostly white or quite pale and contrast well with brighter colors.

The Solomon's seals (*Polygonatum*) are graceful plants for any lightly shaded sites where the soil is rich, deep, and moderately moist. Their splendid foliage confers the feeling of natural woodland to any planting plan. The arching leafy stems grow from slowly spreading underground rhizomes and the plant is attractive from the time the shoots break the surface, especially when planted to rise from a carpet of low ground cover. The flowers are green-tipped white bells which hang from the leaf axils in a row of clusters beneath the main stalk and parallel to it. Few plants are easier to grow and they can remain undisturbed in one place for many years.

A hybrid form, *Polygonatum × hybridum*, is the usual Solomon's seal grown in gardens. This gracious and lovely plant is a strong grower and reaches a height of 36in/900mm. *P. multiflorum* is perhaps not so showy, but is nevertheless a charming plant. Its pea green stalks shoot up rapidly in early spring and soon arch over as they reach a height of 24-32in/600-800mm. The white, bell-shaped flowers, somewhat constricted at their middles, are about ³⁄₄in/20mm long and hang in clusters of two to five. *P. odoratum* is a plant for the connoisseur of scented plants. It grows up to 18in/450mm tall and carries its pendulous blossoms singly or doubly along the underside of the distinctly angled stems. A similar, deliciously scented and related plant is *Smilacina racemosa*, commonly known as false Solomon's seal.

Rodgersias are outstanding ornamental foliage plants and are well suited for growing in marshy ground or along watersides, but they will succeed just as well wherever there is deep, fertile, moist soil and full sun or dappled shade. Large plants with dramatic foliage and attractive tall feathery spikes of flowers, they can convey the impression of space and depth when positioned properly. They are effective with ferns and Japanese primulas and are hardy to zone 7.

Rodgersia aesculifolia will grow 2-5ft/0.6-1.5m in height and has crinkled, bronze green leaves like a horse chestnut, up to about 18in/450mm across, usually with seven leaflets which spread from the tops of the leaf stalks. The creamy white flowers are in wide pyramidal spikes, up to 5³⁄₄ft/1.7m high and are most effective against a dark background. *R. pinnata* is a variable species; it will easily grow to a height of 3¹⁄₄ft/1m or more. The leaves are lustrous dark green with six to nine leaflets. The flowers are creamy pink, but there are other forms with flowers ranging from white to almost red, and the darker the flower, the darker the leaves. The cultivar 'Superba,' for example, has brilliant pink flowers and foliage of a striking burnished dark green. *R. sambucifolia* is similar to *R. pinnata* but is a smaller, neater plant with elegant flower plumes in creamy white, up to 3¹⁄₄ft/1m tall. Its large, matt green leaves have seven, nine, or eleven leaflets which, except for the terminal one, are in widely separated pairs.

For brighter colors among the moisture-loving herbaceous perennials there are many wonderful species, such as hemerocallis and primulas and their cultivars, which are perfectly

A handsome clump of *Hemerocallis lilio-asphodelus* spills over a border of *Euonymus fortunei*, together with creamy 'Buff Beauty' roses. Perennials with good foliage are important in sunny, open sites, too, and the fresh green of the strap-shaped hemerocallis leaves remains after the flowers have faded.

suited for sunny or light shaded areas in the garden. The tall Candelabra primulas include some of the best species for planting in moist soil in light shade, among them the crimson rose *Primula beesiana* and *P. pulverulenta*, orange *P. bulleyana*, yellow *P. helodoxa*, and *P. japonica* in shades of red, rose, and white. The Sikkimensis group of primulas includes many deliciously fragrant species, such as the yellow *P. sikkimensis*, *P. alpicola* in white and yellow, and the sulphur yellow *P. florindae*. A short, variable species with mostly pastel shades of rose is *P. sieboldii* whose foliage dies back after the flowers fade. These primulas flower at the same time as rhododendrons and, if you choose colors with care, can look well together. However, primulas grow best on a moist, more nearly neutral soil.

PLANTS FOR EARLY SUMMER

Blue and mauve

Buddleja alternifolia
Clematis × durandii
Hydrangea macrophylla 'Blue Wave' (correctly *H.m* 'Mariesii Perfecta')
Rhododendron cultivars
Syringa josikaea
Clematis 'Lasurstern,' 'Perle d'Azur,' 'Mrs Cholmondely'
Anchusa azurea 'Loddon Royalist', 'Royal Blue', 'Little John'
Aster alpinus
A. tongolensis 'Berggarten,' 'Leuchtenberg,' 'Napsbury'
Campanula carpatica 'Blaue Clips,' 'Karpatenkrone'

C. persicifolia 'Grandiflora Coerulea'
Centaurea montana 'Grandiflora,' 'Parham'
Delphinium cultivars
Erigeron 'Adria,' 'Schwarzes Meer'
Geranium himalayense 'Gravetye'
G. 'Johnson's Blue'
Iris bearded cultivars
Linum narbonense
Lupinus hybrids
Polemonium foliosissimum
P. reptans 'Blue Pearl'
Salvia nemorosa 'Ostfriesland,' 'Mainacht,' 'Blauhügel'
Scabiosa caucasica 'Blauer Atlas,' 'Clive Greaves,' 'Nachtfalter'

Thalictrum aquilegiifolium
Veronica spicata incana
Allium giganteum
Iris sibirica cultivars
Myosotis palustris

White and cream

Chionanthus virginicus
Cornus alternifolia and *C.a* 'Argentea'
C. controversa and *C.c.* 'Variegata'
Cornus kousa and *C.k. chinensis*
Crataegus crus-galli
C. persimilis 'Prunifolia'
Deutzia × magnifica
D. × rosea 'Campanulata,' 'Grandiflora'

D. scabra 'Candidissima,' 'Watereri'
Erica cinerea 'Alba Minor'
E. tetralix 'Alba Mollis'
Hydrangea macrophylla 'White Wave'
H. petiolaris
Lonicera maackii
Magnolia sieboldii
Philadelphus 'Albâtre,' 'Belle Etoile,' 'Avalanche,' 'Beauclerk,' 'Virginal,' 'Manteau d'Hermine'
Photinia villosa
Potentilla fruticosa 'Abbotswood'
Rhododendron cultivars
Viburnum plicatum 'Mariesii'
Rosa species and cultivars
Actinidia arguta
A. deliciosa (A. chinensis)
Clematis 'Mme LeCoultre,' 'Henryi,' 'Marie Boisselot'
Lonicera periclymenum
Aconitum septentrionale 'Ivorine'
Armeria maritima 'Alba'
Aruncus dioicus
Aster alpinus 'Albus'
Astrantia major
Campanula carpatica 'White Clips,' 'White Star'
C. persicifolia 'Grandiflora Alba'
Cerastium tomentosum columnae
Crambe cordifolia
C. maritima
Delphinium cultivars
Dianthus plumarius cultivars
Dicentra eximia alba
Dicentra spectabilis alba
Dictamnus albus
Erigeron hybrids
Gypsophila repens
Iris bearded cultivars
Lupinus hybrids
Monarda 'Snow Maiden'
Paeonia lactiflora hybrids
Polygonatum multiflorum
P. odoratum

Linum narbonense

Primula sieboldii 'Snowflakes'
Rodgersia aesculifolia
R. pinnata 'Alba'
R. sambucifolia
Scabiosa caucasica 'Miss
 Willmott'
Smilacina racemosa
Tiarella wherryi
Trillium grandiflorum
Eremurus himalaicus
Aponogeton distachyos
Hottonia palustris
Menyanthes trifoliata
Sagittaria latifolia
S. sagittifolia

Yellow and orange
Cytisus decumbens
Genista lydia
Genista tinctoria
Potentilla fruticosa cultivars
Rhododendron cultivars
Rosa species and cultivars
Clematis tangutica
Lonicera caprifolium
Lonicera × *heckrotti*
Achillea 'Golden Plate,'
 'Moonshine,'
 'Schwefelblüte'
A. tomentosa
Alchemilla mollis
Anthemis tinctoria 'E.C. Buxton,'
 'Grallagh Gold,' 'Wargrave'
Corydalis lutea
Digitalis grandiflora
Helianthemum 'Golden Queen,'
 'Praecox,' 'Wisley Primrose'
Hemerocallis cultivars
Iris bearded cultivars
Linum flavum 'Compactum'
Lysimachia nummularia
Lysimachia punctata
Eremurus stenophyllus bungei
Iris pseudacorus
Orontium aquaticum
Primula alpicola
P. bulleyana

P. florindae
P. prolifera (P. helodoxa)
P. sikkimensis
Trollius europaeus 'Superbus'

Red and pink
Cytisus purpureus
Daphne × *burkwoodii* 'Somerset'
Deutzia × *elegantissima*
D. 'Mont Rose'
D. × *kalmiiflora*
D. × *rosea*
Erica cinerea 'Eden Valley,' 'P.S.
 Patrick,' 'Atrosanguinea
 Smith's Variety,' 'Velvet
 Knight'
E. tetralix 'Con Underwood,'
 'Hookstone Pink'
Rhododendron cultivars
Syringa reflexa
S. × *swegiflexa*
Rosa species and cultivars
Clematis 'Bees Jubilee,'
 'Kardynal Wyszynski,' 'Nelly
 Moser,' 'Comtesse de
 Bouchaud'
Lonicera × *brownii* 'Dropmore
 Scarlet'
Armeria maritima cultivars
Aster alpinus 'Happy End'
Astrantia major 'Rosea'
Centranthus ruber and *C.r.*
 'Coccineus'
Dianthus carthusianorum
D. gratianopolitanus cultivars
D. plumarius cultivars
Dicentra eximia
D. spectabilis
Dictamnus albus purpureus
Digitalis × *mertonensis*
Dodecatheon meadia
Erigeron 'Foersters Liebling,'
 'Rotes Meer'
Geranium endressii 'Wargrave
 Pink'
G. macrorrhizum 'Ingwersen's
 Variety'

G. × *oxonianum* 'Rose Clair'
Geranium psilostemon
 'Bressingham Flair'
Helianthemum 'Cerise Queen,'
 'Fire Dragon,' 'Henfield
 Brilliant,' 'Rose Queen,'
 'Wisley Pink'
Hemerocallis cultivars
Heuchera cultivars
Incarvillea delavayi
Iris bearded cultivars
Lupinus hybrids
Lychnis chalcedonica
Monarda 'Cambridge Scarlet,'
 'Croftway Pink,'
 'Morgenröte,' 'Prairie Glow'
Paeonia lactiflora cultivars
Papaver orientale 'Beauty of
 Livermere,' 'Catharina,'
 'Carnival'
Rodgersia pinnata 'Superba'
Thalictrum delavayi 'Hewitt's
 Double'
Allium cernuum
A. christophii
A. oreophilum
Eremurus robustus
Butomus umbellatus
Primula beesiana
P. japonica
P. pulverulenta
P. sieboldii

Scented plants
Buddleja alternifolia
Calycanthus floridus
Chionanthus virginicus
Daphne × *burkwoodii* 'Somerset'
Deutzia × *elegantissima*
D. × *magnifica*
Lonicera maackii
Magnolia sieboldii
Philadelphus cultivars
Photinia villosa
Rhododendron cultivars
Rosa species and cultivars
Actinidia arguta

L. caprifolium
L. periclymenum
Lonicera × *heckrottii*
Crambe cordifolia
Dianthus plumarius cultivars
Dictamnus albus
Paeonia hybrids
Polygonatum odoratum
Smilacina racemosa
Tiarella wherryi
Aponogeton distachyos
Primula florindae
P. sikkimensis

**Plants for bees and
butterflies**
Buddleja alternifolia
Crataegus crus-galli
C. persimilis 'Prunifolia'
Erica cinerea cultivars
Erica tetralix cultivars
Lonicera species
Philadelphus cultivars
Photinia villosa
Rosa single-flowered species and
 cultivars
Armeria cultivars
Astrantia major
Aster alpinus cultivars
A. tongolensis
Centaurea montana
Dianthus cultivars
Dictamnus albus
Digitalis species
Erigeron cultivars
Geranium cultivars
Helianthemum cultivars
Lysimachia species
Polemonium foliosissimum
P. reptans
Salvia nemorosa cultivars
Scabiosa caucasica cultivars
Thalictrum species
Allium species
Butomus umbellatus
Primula species

EARLY SUMMER TASKS

TREES AND SHRUBS

Pruning flowering shrubs

Many of the regular tasks started in spring can be continued into early summer. Pruning of spring-flowering shrubs after their blossoms have faded and deadheading of lilacs, rhododendrons, and, of course, roses, for example, are typical jobs which you should take care of whenever necessary.

Many popular deciduous shrubs, which bear their blossoms on wood that was produced during the previous growth season are best pruned as soon as they finish flowering. If you wait until winter to prune these shrubs, you will effectively cut away most of the flower buds. So, if any of your deciduous shrubs that flower in spring and early summer are showing signs of exhaustion, aging, or overcrowding, prune them, as soon as their flowers have faded. They will repay you with vigorous new growth that will blossom profusely next year.

Shrubs such as *Deutzia*, *Exochorda*, and *Spiraea*, which produce new growths from the lower parts of the stems, are simple to prune: cut the old wood that has already flowered back to the first strong new shoot, maintaining the natural shape and symmetry of the plant. If your shrub is older, prune about one-fourth of the oldest stems to ground level each year. *Forsythia* and *Kerria*, so treated, retain their youthful vigor, flower abundantly, and never lose their natural habit.

Broom (*Cytisus scoparius*) and other shrubs which do not regenerate well from old wood should not be cut back so hard. Start while the plants are small and, once the flowers have dropped, prune the flowered wood back to where young growths are developing.

Hedge trimming

Formal deciduous hedges may be trimmed in early summer. However, where birds are nesting in a hedge, it is better to postpone trimming until the fledglings have left their nests. Hedging shrubs that normally receive their first trimming of the year during this season include berberis, hornbeam, cotoneaster, beech, privet, and blackthorn. Some of the faster-growing species may require two or more clippings each year in order to maintain dense growth.

When pruning a formal hedge, either keep the sides parallel or taper each side slightly inward toward the top, about 4in/100mm from vertical for each 3ft/1m of height. Shorten the new growths of this season only, so that the hedge is a uniform dense color after clipping. The top of a newly set hedge is normally not pruned in early summer during the first 4 to 5 years.

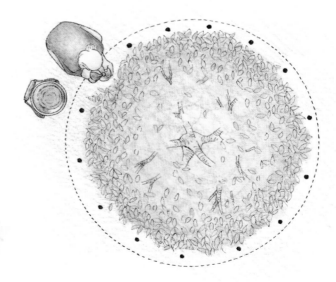

Fertilizing trees
Most of the active feeding roots of a tree lie in the area just below the drip line – the outer edge of the foliage or outer fringe of the crown.

Use a sharp implement to bore holes 12-18in/300-450mm deep and 18-24in/450-600mm apart in a circle. Insert a quick-acting balanced fertilizer and water the tree thoroughly.

Deadheading

Continue deadheading rhododendrons and lilacs (see page 46) in order to ensure abundant flowers next year. The majority of other flowering shrubs do not require systematic deadheading. Any shrubs that bear decorative fruits or berries which provide food for garden birds should, of course, be left untouched.

Fertilizing trees

Well-established ornamental trees do not usually require annual feeding; however, large specimen trees standing in an area of lawn, close to the street, or on other exposed or restricted locations may need occasional fertilizing to maintain health and vigorous, youthful growth. Any trees that show signs of mineral deficiency or unsatisfactory growth should be fertilized as soon as possible. Feeding trees and shrubs should be completed by the middle of early summer, before the linden trees and privet bushes flower, so as not to affect adversely the ripening of any newly formed wood. Plants which receive late doses of fertilizer may continue to produce new, soft growths long into summer, which then do not have sufficient time to harden off before winter. To fertilize trees properly during the growth season the nutrients must quickly pass the roots of lawn grass, herbaceous perennials, and any other voracious neighbors, into the soil depths where the tree roots can absorb them at once.

Watering and mulching

During dry periods give newly planted trees and shrubs a thorough soaking once a week for as long as the drought lasts.

If you have not already spread a mulch around your new trees and shrubs, then do so now, but remember: you should apply a mulch only if the soil is adequately supplied with moisture. If the soil is dry, water well, then wait a day or two before loosening the surface, after which you can spread the mulch material.

Softwood cuttings

Many shrubs and subshrubs can be propagated easily from softwood cuttings taken in early summer. Suitable species include *Berberis, Caryopteris, Cornus, Corylopsis, Cotinus, Cotoneaster, Deutzia, Euonymus, Exochorda, Hibiscus, Kolkwitzia, Laburnum, Lavandula, Lespedeza, Ligustrum, Lonicera, Potentilla, Ribes, Rosmarinus, Salix, Santolina, Syringa, Viburnum, Weigela.* It is perfectly feasible at this time of year to propagate enough plants for a hedge from hedge shearings. (See page 156 for advice on cuttings.)

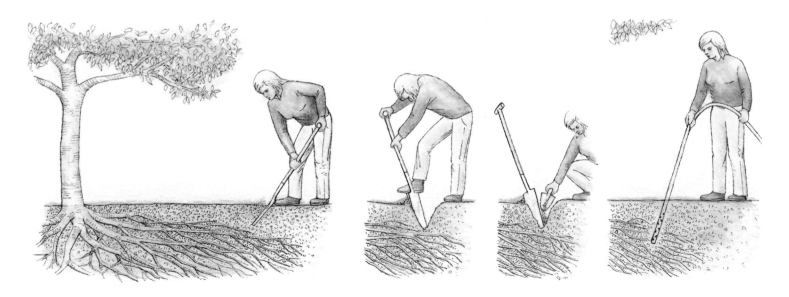

Alternatively, make holes by driving a spade into the ground under the drip line at an angle with the tip directed toward the trunk to avoid severing roots. Press the spade forward and apply the fertilizer behind the blade. You can also apply fertilizer directly to the roots with a fertilizer lance inserted to about 24in/600mm; this attaches to a garden hose.

ROSES

Fertilizing

Unless your soil is poor in nutrients or so sandy that rapid leaching (washing away) is a problem, two or three modest applications of a suitable fertilizer are sufficient to satisfy your roses' needs. However, the timing of fertilizer applications is important. Give the plants the nutrients when they need them most, just after they have completed one burst of blossoms and are about to make new growth for the next flush. As soon as your roses have opened their first flowers, it is time to apply a second dose of fertilizer. Make sure the soil is moist before applying any dry fertilizer, in order to avoid damaging the roots. Water the roses the day before you plan to fertilize. On the next day, lightly scratch the soil surface and spread a suitable balanced rose food around the bushes. Try to keep the fertilizer away from the base of the plant and concentrate most of it in the area around the foliage drip line (the ground below the outer edge of the foliage). It is most important to water the fertilizer thoroughly.

Watering

Roses are deep-rooted plants and, once established, require much less watering than many other ornamentals. However, newly planted roses, whose root systems are not yet fully developed, are quicker to suffer from lack of water than older, established bushes. A less than adequate supply of water will reduce vigor and impair the production of blossoms. Prepare to water your roses during any prolonged dry weather periods throughout the flowering season.

Try to water during the morning hours, so that the foliage is dry before evening. Avoid wetting the leaves as much as possible and never splash them with muddy water as fungal spores from the ground may get to the leaves that way. Irrigate thoroughly and always give enough to soak the soil to the full depth of the root zone; this means a water penetration to at least 16-18in/400-450mm. Do not water again for several days, until the soil has dried out somewhat. Less thorough, more frequent watering does not penetrate very far below the soil surface, the feeder roots are encouraged to grow in the shallow, moist, upper zone. Concentrated close to the surface, they are subject to injury during cultivating, are easily burned by fertilizers, and are extremely susceptible to damage if this thin soil layer ever dries out.

To see if your watering has penetrated deeply enough, conduct a simple test to determine your soil's ability to absorb water. Water your roses as normal or for an arbitrary amount of time; then, a day later, dig down to see how far your watering penetrated. If you determine, for example, that 30 minutes of irrigation was only sufficient to wet the top 8in/200mm of soil, you will need to double your watering time in order to penetrate the entire root zone.

Water penetration varies, of course, according to soil type. A sandy

Deadheading hybrid teas and floribundas
Cut back to a strong well-placed bud or young shoot, no more than one-third of the way down the stem.

Deadheading climbers
Cut away faded blossoms to a bud halfway down the short flower shoot.

soil may require less water than a heavier soil to be moist enough to satisfy the roses' needs, but it will also dry out more quickly and you will have to water again sooner. For example, you may have to water your roses about every week in sand, every week-and-a-half in loam, but only every two weeks in clay. Daytime temperatures, sunlight, wind, and the presence or lack of a mulch will also have an effect.

Cutting flowers

Deadheading of faded rose blossoms and cutting flowers for the vase are, in a sense, both a kind of summer pruning; done correctly, each helps to maintain a well-shaped, healthy bush and encourages all repeat-flowering roses to produce a bountiful new crop of large, well-formed flowers. When cutting roses for the house never cut a flower stem longer than really necessary for your arrangement and do not take more than one or two long stems from any single bush at one time. Because the leaves supply the energy needed to build up the plant and to produce new blossoms, it is best not to cut away more than one-third of the flowering stem. As with deadheading, always cut back to a strong, outward facing bud. All faded blossoms of most display roses, certainly of the floribundas and hybrid teas, should be cut away regularly and always as soon as possible. This prevents the rose from squandering energy in forming hips and conserves its resources for the production of new flowers. Continual deadheading also removes a possible source of fungal diseases and keeps the bushes looking neat and tidy. Any withered blossoms on freshly planted rose bushes are best removed with only very little stem, in order to retain as much foliage as possible. In most cases, summer pruning is limited to cutting flowers and deadheading; if both are carried out conscientiously, no other pruning will be necessary till winter.

Obviously, wild roses, *Rosa rugosa* cultivars, and any other roses that are grown for their beautiful display of hips in fall should never be deadheaded.

CLIMBING PLANTS

Tying in
Continue tying and training climbing plants as they grow and produce new shoots.

Pruning of spring-flowering clematis
Spring-flowering clematis may be pruned as soon as their flowers have faded to maintain an orderly appearance. Species of clematis that blossom in the spring on short shoots produced during the previous summer, such as *Clematis montana*, *C. alpina*, and *C. macropetala*, are normally left unpruned for several years, or receive only enough trimming to keep them orderly and in their allocated space. If mature plants become overcrowded or threaten to outgrow their space, cut back the side shoots to within a few inches of the main framework immediately after flowering, leaving one or two buds, which will soon produce strong new growths that will bloom again next spring. Alternatively, these species may be given a renewal pruning every few years.

The large-flowering clematis hybrids such as 'Lasurstern,' 'Nelly Moser,' 'Henryi,' and 'Mme LeCoultre' also produce blossoms in the spring on wood ripened during the previous summer. They often flower again in late summer or fall, so pruning requires some forethought. The best method is a regimen of renewal pruning. As soon as the spring flowers have faded, cut back one-fourth to one-third of the old shoots to within 12-24in/300-600mm of the base. Vigorous new shoots will grow to produce an abundant crop of flowers next spring, while the unpruned shoots will blossom a second time later this year.

Annual climbers
Now that no more dangerous frosts are to be expected, plant outdoors any annual climbing plants that you have started from seed. Even the tender tropical and subtropical species, such as *Cobaea scandens*, *Ipomoea tricolor* 'Heavenly Blue,' and the moon vine, *Calonyction album*, will make rapid headway, as the daytime and – equally important – nighttime temperatures continue to rise. There is still time to sow in place any of the most rapidly growing species, such as *Phaseolus coccineus*, the scarlet runner bean, or *Humulus scandens*, the Japanese hop. They will quickly clothe any screen, trellis, or fence for which you want temporary coverage.

All of these annual climbers need support from the start. Their rapidly growing shoots are often slender and fragile at first. Once they have reached their supports, they will need no further assistance other than an occasional tucking in.

Watering
Climbers on house walls often suffer from lack of water, so be alert for signs of dryness. Such climbers will require watering sooner and more often than other plants which grow in the open. When you irrigate, be sure that the water penetrates deeply, in order to encourage the roots to grow far into the soil. Frequent, but insufficient, shallow watering does more harm than good because it encourages the active roots to remain near the surface, where they are especially vulnerable to drying out.

HERBACEOUS PERENNIALS

Weeding and mulching
Keep the soil between the plants in your beds and borders loose and free from weeds at all times. Weeds not only detract from the beauty of your herbaceous perennials, they compete for water, nutrients, and light. Be sure to cultivate the beds as early in the season as possible; this minimizes the harm that weeds – and your weeding – are likely to do to the growing herbaceous perennials. It is best to cultivate lightly, only loosening the tip ⅓-¾in/10-20mm of soil. This is deep enough to combat most annual weeds without damaging the roots of your ornamentals. In addition to controlling weeds, cultivating loosens and opens the soil, easing the way for air and rain to reach the plants' roots. Loosening the surface soil also interrupts the capillary link between the lower, wetter soil and the air above, thereby reducing water loss due to evaporation.

Mulching works in much the same way to reduce direct evaporation losses from the surface, but it not only protects the soil surface from drying out, it also prevents compacting and erosion from rain or watering and keeps the upper soil cool during the summer. So, if you need to hoe after rain in order to break up the surface crust or to combat weed seedlings, then you need to mulch. Now that the soil is warm, mulch whenever there is sufficient moisture in the soil.

For weed control, the mulch must be so thick that weed seedlings cannot grow through it on their own stored food. After you have cleared weeds from the herbaceous border, apply an organic mulch 2-4in/50-100mm deep. This cuts off light from the soil surface and makes it impossible for most weed seeds to germinate. If a uniform mulch is maintained over the herbaceous borders, most problems with annual weeds can be eliminated within two or three years.

Continue staking

Throughout the summer continue staking and tying up tall herbaceous perennials as they grow and always well before they are so large that they are in danger of falling over. (See page 31.) Once the shoots have been bent or broken, the damage is irreparable.

Cutting back

Some herbaceous perennials which normally flower only once in the spring can be coaxed into producing a second flush of blossoms later in the year. Delphiniums, for example, can be cut back to about 12in/300mm in height after their flowers have faded. When the new growths begin to show, cut back the old stalks even further, to within 4in/100mm of the ground. Fertilize well, water regularly and you will be rewarded with a second crop of flowers in the fall.

Essentially the same treatment can be used to produce a second flowering from a number of perennials that flower in spring and early summer, including: *Centaurea montana* (mountain knapweed), *Chrysanthemum coccineum* (painted daisy), *Erigeron* (fleabane), *Lupinus* (lupin), and *Nepeta* (catmint). Even if they fail to flower a second time, the fresh new foliage they produce is much more attractive than spindly seed stalks.

Similarly, *Digitalis purpurea* and several other garden plants that are normally biennials can be induced to stay for at least another year if you cut them back nearly to the ground after flowering. In the wild or woodland garden, however, a few flower stalks of the best foxgloves should be left standing to ripen and scatter seed.

Deadheading

Regular deadheading stimulates many perennials to continue producing new blossoms and helps to maintain a compact form. However, even if no new flowers are to be expected, continue to cut off dead flower heads; as a result your perennials will be stronger, healthier, and much neater in appearance.

Use small pruning shears to make a clean cut just above a leaf or leaf pair. Cutting flowers for decorating the house achieves much the same effect as deadheading and should be done in the same way. In the more natural garden, where some plants are encouraged to spread, you can leave standing some seed stalks of the most desirable plants of species like columbines, for example, to ripen seed and to become naturalized.

Extending the flowering period

The flowering period of several of the most popular and colorful herbaceous perennials can often be prolonged by means of a simple trick: take, for example, *Phlox paniculata* which normally flowers only once during late summer. Just shorten about one-third of the stalks by about 4in/100mm before the flower buds start to form; this will induce the formation of new branched shoots. While the intact stalks flower at their usual time, the new growths will blossom about three weeks later. In a year with a long summer, phlox may even produce a third set of flowers: if the initially unshortened stalks are cut back by a third of their length as soon as their first blossoms have dropped, they will often produce a new set of flowers. Other herbaceous perennials which respond well to this persuasive treatment include the hardy asters, helenium, and coreopsis.

Perennials that die down

Bleeding heart (*Dicentra spectabilis*), oriental poppies (*Papaver orientale*), Virginia bluebells (*Mertensia virginica*), and other perennials that die down in summer after flowering leave patches of bare soil and unsightly gaps in the flower beds. Mark the places where they grow now, before they disappear entirely, so that you can avoid injuring the roots and crowns of the slumbering plants when weeding or digging.

Plant late-developing perennials in front of or behind those which disappear to camouflage the empty spaces. Use plants that sprawl, such as perennial baby's breath (*Gypsophila*) or sea lavender (*Limonium*), or others that grow tall enough to hide the vacant spots, such as tall veronicas, hardy asters or chrysanthemums.

ANNUALS AND BIENNIALS

Last sowings of annuals

There is still time to sow fast-growing annuals in the garden; indeed, a good remedy for any bare spots that appear in your borders would be to sow such annuals as zinnia, marigold, calendula, nasturtium, California poppy, annual candytuft (*Iberis umbellata*), summer forget-me-not (*Anchusa capensis*), or the ever dependable cornflower (*Centaurea cyanus*).

Planting

If you want an instantaneous solution for empty patches, buy annual plants from the nursery. If you are careful to select vigorous, well-grown plants, there is no reason why you should not get good – and quick – results.

Any annuals grown from seed and raised under glass should also be planted out as soon as possible. For most annuals, early summer is the last possible date for planting out seedlings if they are to make a good showing.

Fertilizing
Should the plants have weak growth, fail to flower well, or show signs of mineral deficiency, then give them a boost with a dose of quick-acting fertilizer, preferably in liquid solution. Choose a balanced mineral-based fertilizer, rich in phosphorus.

Sowing biennials
Finish sowing biennials during early summer so that you will have vigorous young plants in time to be set out in fall for scent and color next year. Now is the best time to sow: hollyhocks, daisies, Canterbury bells, wallflowers, foxgloves, Siberian wallflowers, honesty, forget-me-nots, Scotch thistles, brown-eyed Susan, and pansies. Biennials can be sown equally well in a nursery bed or in boxes.

BULBS

Gladioli
Continue to plant gladiolus corms at intervals of 10 to 14 days to give a continuous supply of blossoms for cutting. As soon as the shoots appear above ground, give them a modest dose of any balanced fertilizer that is relatively rich in phosphorus. Apart from occasional hoeing and watering during periods of drought, gladioli will require very little attention. Fertilize a second time once the foliage has fully developed, when each corm will start to produce daughter corms. Tall varieties should be tied carefully to their stakes as soon as the flower stalks have started to stretch up. When the flowers open, the old corm is exhausted and a third dose of fertilizer helps to strengthen the young daughter corms. To encourage the further development of the new corms, cut the flower stalks early, always leaving as many leaves on the plant as possible, and deadhead any flower stalks that remain.

Dahlias
Any dahlias which have not yet been planted should be put in as soon as possible. Once they start to grow, tall dahlias should be tied to their supports. Feed growing dahlias every two weeks with a good balanced liquid fertilizer.

WATER GARDEN

Planting
Water lilies and other aquatics can still be planted as long as the daylight hours continue to increase. Now that the water has warmed up, all aquatic plants will grow rapidly and most newly planted water lilies should bloom during the first year. Try to complete planting all aquatic plants before the end of early summer. Any water lilies planted later would not have enough time to become sufficiently established to survive the following winter. (For planting techniques, see page 51.)

Aeration
If fish are present make sure that aeration is adequate. Submerged oxygenating plants will normally generate enough oxygen for them, provided you have not overstocked your pool. However, as the water temperature increases, the amount of dissolved oxygen sinks and on hot days the fish may sometimes be seen gulping air at the surface.

You can provide aid either with an air pump, which bubbles air directly into the water, or with a recirculating water pump, which can feed a fountain or a waterfall or just keep the water gently in motion. A fountain or waterfall can aerate the water quite effectively and also make an attractive feature in its own right.

Should quick relief be necessary during an especially hot spell, an air pump equipped with an aerating stone that delivers lots of fine air bubbles is most effective. If you are caught without any kind of pump, then direct a fine spray from the garden hose onto the water surface for as long as necessary.

Removing dead leaves
To maintain good water quality remove dying leaves of water lilies and other large-leaved aquatics whenever you see them. Cut them off; do not pull or the whole plant may come away too! If they are far from the pool edge and hard to reach, use a long-arm pruner.

An occasional thinning of submerged oxygenators whenever they become too dense also helps, since the nutrients otherwise released when the plants die back for the winter would only aggravate the algae problem next year.

Algae
A certain amount of algae is a natural, even desirable component in a well-balanced pool, as long as algae do not multiply so strongly that they become an unsightly nuisance. When filamentous algae appear they should be pulled out by hand or twirled out on the end of a stick or branch before they envelop underwater plants completely. Do this repeatedly. If you pull them out regularly, they will eventually cease being a problem.

Microscopic algae may be a more serious problem, but the best remedy is to be patient and do nothing as they will eventually die or be eaten by microscopic pond life. The worst mistake of all is to attempt to solve the problem by exchanging the water in the pool. This simply prolongs the problem by introducing additional nutrients, which then leads to a renewed explosive growth of algae.

LAWN AND FLOWER MEADOW

Mowing lawns

Grass is growing rapidly, so you must time mowing according to the weather and composition of your lawn grass mixture. Although cutting frequency depends on such factors as lawn type, soil fertility, and moisture, your best guide is always the height of the grass itself: at cutting time it should – ideally – be no more than ½-¾in/15-20mm above the recommended height for your type of lawn. That means the finest lawns will now probably need mowing twice a week, while a utility lawn will need cutting once a week or every 10 days. If watering is not possible during prolonged dry spells, raise the height of the cut somewhat and mow less often. To avoid weakening the grass, never reduce the height by more than one-third its length at any time, regardless of how often you mow.

Fertilizing lawns

Pale, off-colored grass that is not growing vigorously at this time of year probably needs nitrogen. If you fertilized your lawn with a fast-acting lawn fertilizer, you may now apply a dressing of nitrogen-rich complete lawn fertilizer. The nutrients contained in a balanced fertilizer do much more than make the grass greener; they produce a dense grass in which neither weeds nor moss can obtain a toehold. The deep green color is, of course, more attractive, but just as important is the increased resistance to drought and disease. Some lawns, however, go dormant when fertilized in summer.

After spreading the fertilizer, be sure to water it. If possible, water the lawn thoroughly whenever necessary during periods of drought, always wetting the soil to a depth of at least 6in/150mm.

Lawn repair

In cool areas this may be a suitable time to repair any faulty patches which appear in the lawn. Ugly bare patches can be reseeded or returfed. Whichever method you choose, try to repair with a grass mixture identical to that in your present lawn. (For repair methods, see pages 120 and 161.)

Mowing flower meadows

In the flower meadow some of the tall grasses are flowering, as are the ox-eye daisy (*Chrysanthemum leucanthemum*), meadow clary (*Salvia pratensis*), vetch (*Vicia cracca*), and meadow cranesbill (*Geranium pratense*). A flower meadow needs cutting only twice – at the most three times – each year.

However, not only the frequency, but also the timing of cutting is of the utmost importance, for together they determine the species composition of the meadow. Cutting at different times in following years effectively hinders the development of a flora suited to a particular mowing schedule and favors only one group – the grasses. So, once you have settled on a schedule for mowing, stick to it each year.

The usual practice is to mow the meadow after each main flowering period, which most often means that the meadow will be cut for the first time after the grasses, ox-eye daisy, and meadow clary have blossomed. You can then be sure that the foliage of all the spring-flowering bulbs has died back on its own, which ensures a rich display of narcissus, crocus, and snake's head fritillary next spring.

If you wish to grow a variety of meadow plants that bloom in succession throughout spring and summer, then you should divide the meadow into sections and cut the different areas at different times. This plan also reduces the amount of work necessary at any one time and helps keep your "hay harvest" within manageable limits.

PATIO AND BALCONY

Planting

Window boxes, tubs, and other containers should be planted as soon as possible; the weather conditions in early summer are so settled and warm that it is safe to plant even the most tender plants outdoors. If you plan to purchase nursery-grown plants, then do so as quickly as possible to take advantage of the better selection.

When planning and planting your window boxes and containers for the balcony, do give some thought to color schemes and always choose colors which are appropriate to the background. Against a red brick wall, for example, try various shades of blue, from soft powder blue to rich deep blue, together with white blossoms, set off by foliage plants with silvery gray or variegated leaves. In front of a neutral gray wall you might concentrate on deep blues and purples, rich reds and pink, while a white-painted wall will demand the boldest of floral colors, scarlet, gold, yellow, and deep green foliage. Should your house wall be of dark-colored brickwork, try pastel pinks and blues together with white or a planting entirely in shades of yellow.

It pays to incorporate a special time-released fertilizer into the potting mix when planting window boxes and other containers. It will eliminate the necessity of fertilizing again for the next six to eight weeks.

Moving out and repotting

Very tender container plants that are to spend the summer outdoors on the patio or balcony should be brought out as soon as possible, so that they can recover from the long winter months in the sunroom or basement. Choose a still day with an overcast sky to move them outside and place in a shady, sheltered spot to prevent sunburn and wind damage to their still tender leaves. After a few days, they can be moved to their final positions.

1 Place one hand over the top of the pot, fingers on either side of the plant.

2 Turn the pot over and tap it against a hard edge to loosen the root ball.

3 Lift off the pot gently, holding firmly onto the plant and root ball.

Removing large plants from pots

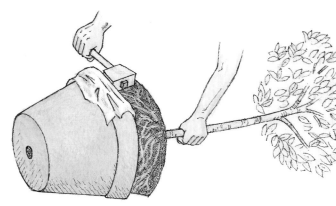

Let a large container dry out slightly and lay it on its side. Hold the plant by the stem and,

protecting the rim with a cloth, tap the rim with a hammer while pulling the plant steadily.

Alternatively, you can force a jet of water through the pot by sticking the nozzle of a hose

through the drain hole. This pushes the root ball out as you pull.

The best time to repot container plants is early in the growing season, just as they start to break into growth. Small plants that are still increasing in size should be repotted each year. Larger specimens can be allowed to grow in their containers for two, three, or more years before they need repotting again.

When deciding whether a plant needs repotting or not, look at the state of the roots; if they have filled the container and are just beginning to spread on the outside of the soil ball, then repot. If you wait until the plant becomes rootbound, growth will slow down or stop completely and, even with increased watering and fertilizing, the plant will eventually lose vigor and die. Always repot before the roots have become coiled around and around at the bottom of the container or have grown through the drainage holes. A container plant that has not yet reached its final size may be moved on to a new container that is so

Repotting
1 Shave off ¾-1¼in/20-30mm around the root ball with a sharp knife to remove old soil and prune the roots. Unwind and cut any encircling roots.

2 Place drainage material over the bottom of the container and cover with new soil. Replace the plant so that the top of the root ball rests about 2in/50mm below the rim of the container.

3 Gradually fill in with new soil and, with a stick, work it into the space between the container and root ball; firm it to the same degree as the old soil.

4 Cover the top of the root ball with a thin layer of soil. Saturate the new soil and the root ball, allow to drain and place the plant in a shady place for a day or two.

much larger that there is a space ¾-2in/20-50mm between the root ball and the container. Repotting large shrubs in heavy containers is no easy job and you may need extra help for moving and repotting them. Large plants that have reached their final size may be repotted in a container of the same dimensions, but the root ball will need to be reduced by cutting away ¾-1¼in/20-30mm from each side.

Because removing and exchanging the soil in large containers is a formidable, even costly job, it is advisable to defer it as long as possible by doing everything to keep the soil in good condition. A good alternative to complete repotting is to topdress the plants annually. The plants remain in their containers and only the top 2-2¾in/50-70mm of soil are carefully removed and replaced with fresh soil.

Soil which is to remain in containers for several years without replacement needs to be of a more permanent composition than that in pots or window boxes which is renewed frequently. The organic components of most potting mixes, such as compost, peatmoss, or leaf mold, decompose in time, causing the mixture to shrink, become pasty, and impervious to water and air. When mixing soils for long-term use in containers, therefore, reduce the amount of organic material to no more than 10 per cent by bulk. At the same time increase the coarse mineral component by the same amount. This may be sharp sand or better still a porous substance such as crushed brick or lava, perlite, calcined clay or real soil. A mixture of this type is less able to absorb nutrients than one with a higher organic content. This can be remedied easily by judicious fertilizing. It pays to incorporate a time-released fertilizer into the soil mixture.

Feeding and watering
Container plants will need more frequent fertilizing than those in garden beds. A little, given often, is the rule. In general, throughout the growing season, all well-established and actively growing container plants should receive a weekly feeding with an appropriate dilute liquid fertilizer. To avoid the buildup of damaging salts from both water and fertilizer, always water thoroughly. Each time a container plant is irrigated, some water should flow through the drain holes, carrying excess salts with it.

All container plants need more watering than those planted in the open ground, where the roots can grow down or outward into moist soil. Conscientious watering is the most important task in the patio or balcony garden. Observe your plants daily and inspect the soil regularly to determine when and how much water they need. During warm weather, water evaporates rapidly from the soil; at the same time, the plants are growing fast and require a constant supply of water at their roots. You must be prepared, therefore, to water as often as once or even twice a day.

If you are unable to provide such regular daily attention, then you might consider installing an automatic watering system. There are several different systems available on the market, ranging from sophisticated computer-controlled models to simple, but equally effective and dependable mechanical systems. You will be astonished at the improved performance of balcony and patio plants that have a guaranteed, optimal supply of moisture as the result of an automatic watering system.

CHAPTER 5

MIDSUMMER

"Brightly the sun of summer shone
Green fields and waving woods upon
    And soft winds wandered by.
Above, a sky of purest blue,
Around, bright flowers of loveliest hue
    Allured the gazer's eye."

Anne Brontë

Midsummer, when temperatures are at their highest, begins with the flowering of the honey-scented small-leaved linden or lime, *Tilia cordata*. The small-leaved linden usually flowers a little later than the broad-leaved linden, *T. platyphyllos* (whose first flowers mark the end of early summer). The former has neat heart-shaped leaves (about 2½in/60mm long and as wide), dark shining green above and silvery grey-green beneath. The yellowish-white flowers are borne conspicuously apart from the leaves, making more of a show than most other lindens. They spray out from their long green bracts in large bunches of a dozen or so.

The small-leaved linden makes an attractive pyramidal tree, up to 170ft/30m in height; it has a dense crown which gives excellent shade. It grows well in any weakly acidic to neutral soil that is not too dry. For insects, particularly the honey bee, *T. cordata* is an important source of nectar and on a lazy, warm, humid day, the humming of honey bees busily working the fragrant linden blossoms is one of the most welcome sounds of midsummer. However, like most lindens, *T. cordata* often suffers from aphids, which excrete a sticky drip, honeydew, that can blacken the leaves and drop onto everything below.

The warm atmosphere of midsummer is capable of holding immense quantities of moisture. When rain falls it often comes in the form of thunderstorms with localized heavy rainfall. So, one area may have a sudden downpour while others nearby receive no rain at all. Because of this the gardener should pay attention to water needs during midsummer, especially of lawns and newly acquired plants.

THE MIDSUMMER GARDEN

There is a special magic to the midsummer garden, bound up with memories of those carefree days of childhood which always seem to be followed by mysterious twilight, when pale flowers, scarcely noticed during the day, suddenly assume a luminous, ghostly glow. The midsummer garden is a picture-book old-fashioned cottage garden, fragrant and pure, yet voluptuous and romantic. As so many nineteenth-century painters recognized, it is the light and heat from the midsummer sun that gives this season's garden its ambiguous mood. The light can be bright and intense, but the heat can produce a haze, softening the colors and contours which become fuzzy and lack definition. Distant trees are milky blue, not green, and the sky is not pure deep blue but rather a continuum of tints of bluish white, bluish gray and hazy yellow. The flower colors in the garden are transformed.

A skillful gardener takes into account the quality of the light when choosing and placing plants for color. He or she is aware of the way light transforms the colors of flowers, and plans color schemes to work with rather than against its prevalent moods. Whereas brilliant reds, fiery oranges, bright yellows, and strong blues work perfectly in the intense summer sunlight of a southern location, these colors can be garish and vulgar in the hazier, less pure light of more northerly regions where softer pastel floral colors, against a background of misty silver and gray foliage, seem more appropriate.

For a garden of subtle colors and textures, choose pale mauve erigerons, lavender blue campanulas, and, of course, lavender itself and the gentle pink of sidalcea and centranthus. Add the more dramatic pink-and-white spikes of acanthus and liatris, all surrounded by billowing clouds of white baby's breath; you could introduce more white and cream and just a touch of palest yellow to enliven the composition and keep it from being too sugary sweet. Underneath and toward the front, create a carpet of woolly, silver-leaved lamb's ears to link the border with the surrounding paving, making a pleasant transition.

Most plants of the midsummer garden revel in full sun and thrive on any well-drained soil; many of them prefer a soil with at least some lime and ask for little else.

Mainly blue-flowerers

A garden which includes a wide range of soft blues shading into pale violet is always peaceful and harmonious. Blue-flowering shrubs are relatively rare at this season but one such shrub is the butterfly bush, *Buddleja davidii*, sometimes known as summer lilac whose strong, honeyed scent attracts butterflies. It is one of the easiest shrubs to grow and fits perfectly into a sunny mixed border, where it combines well with herbaceous perennials.

The vibrant splashes of color in the midsummer garden, like the purple *Salvia*, yellow *Achillea*, and red *Rudbeckia* here, are best surrounded by soft colors and textures, with misty silver and grey foliage and shadowy depths as background.

Buddleja 'Empire Blue' has powdery lavender blue flowers, probably the closest to a true blue to be found among the buddleias (which range from purple to pure white). The color of its blossoms against the silvery green foliage makes an attractive show and combines well with smaller plants in the midsummer border. The equally handsome cultivar, *B.* 'Fascination,' bears long graceful somewhat open trusses of soft orchid pink. Both 'Empire Blue' and 'Fascination' make vigorous growth and flower dependably and profusely; well grown, they easily attain a height of 6-10ft/2-2.5m each year. To make the best show, cultivars of *B. davidii* need to be cut back hard each year in early spring (see page 29).

A second group of blue-flowering shrubs, the deciduous ceanothus hybrids can be grown in mixed borders just as successfully as the buddleias. *Ceanothus*, the California lilac or buck brush, is an exclusively North American genus. Unfortunately, most of the evergreen species are too tender for northern gardens, where even the hardiest need the protection of a sheltering wall to survive winter frosts. The deciduous species, however, are much hardier. Even if they do freeze during a cold winter, they can be treated like buddleias, being pruned back almost to the ground each year in early spring.

Together with the buddleias, deciduous ceanothus hybrids provide you with a complete palette of blue, lavender, violet, and purplish blue. *C.* 'Gloire de Versailles' is the best known: it carries its bushy panicles of powder blue flowers for many weeks during midsummer and fits well into misty pastel color schemes. It grows to a height of 3-4ft/0.9-1.2m. There are also choice hybrids with much deeper colors, such as 'Topaz,' which is a rich indigo blue, and 'Henri Desfossé,' which is similar to 'Gloire de Versailles' but a darker blue. For richness of color and sheer abundance of blue blossoms, there are no other shrubs which can compete with the ceanothuses. California lilacs are tolerant of summer drought and even tend to live longer when kept fairly dry, so avoid placing a ceanothus near plants that require extra summer watering.

Whether you are looking for a tiny blue-flowered alpine jewel or a towering herbaceous perennial in blue or pink for the back of a mixed border, consider first the versatile bellflowers, members of the genus *Campanula*. There are nearly 300 species to choose from to give flowers from early spring until well into fall. *C. lactiflora*, for example, one of the tall bellflowers, has long been a popular cottage-style garden plant.

The original wild form has starlike flowers of very palest blue, which are carried in large branching clusters on stalks up to 4ft/1.2m high. There are several good cultivars in better shades of blue, as well as forms in pink and white, all of which are generally preferable to the species. Undoubtedly, the old favorite 'Prichard's Variety' is the best of the lavender blue forms; with a height of 2ft/600mm, it is also one of the smaller cultivars. The charming 'Loddon Anna' is a pale pink-flowering form, which retains more of the vigorous growth of the wild form, growing to about 3ft/900mm tall; *C.l. alba* is much the same in cool pure white. All three campanula cultivars are elegant and congenial companions for lilies, delphiniums, and roses, particularly for the old-fashioned roses that bloom only once a year.

Campanula lactiflora needs plenty of room; in a large group of at least five plants it will make a soft cloud bank of misty color, a lovely foil for flowers of more defined or dramatic shapes, such as the trumpets of *Lilium regale*. Planted with a silvery gray carpet of *Stachys byzantina* at its feet, the resulting picture can be peaceful, cool, and refreshing, a welcome sight in the hot days of midsummer. After planting, leave campanulas to grow three or four years undisturbed before dividing and replanting.

All lavenders flower at the height of midsummer and there is no plant more evocative of the old-fashioned cottage-style garden. Lavender 'Hidcote' boasts the darkest flowers, of an intense shade of violet. The equally popular 'Munstead' bears violet-blue flower spikes and there is also a white-flowering form 'Nana Alba.' All three varieties flower freely and make compact, dense shrubs, about 16in/400mm high. They are more suitable for the smaller garden than the original wild species, *Lavandula angustifolia*, which is much taller and laxer in habit. Although commonly known as English lavender, *L. angustifolia* is of Mediterranean origin and all lavenders should be planted with that climate in mind. The smaller cultivars can be used as solitary shrubs toward the front in mixed borders and to make neat, low hedges; a lavender hedge is an excellent foreground to a rose bed, giving structure as well as harmonious color.

Stokes' aster, *Stokesia laevis*, is a charming, often overlooked blue-flowered perennial, from the southeastern USA, where it grows in warm, sunny pine woods. Though not really an aster, its flowers betray a close relationship with cornflowers. The best form for gardens is 'Blue Star' which blooms from midsummer well into fall; its flowers are about 4in/100mm in diameter, the outer petals clear, light blue and the centre a creamy white. Even the unopened flower buds are conspicuous due to the long, finely-toothed bracts that surround the bud. The flower stems arise to a height of 18in/450mm from a dense rosette of narrow, overlapping leaves, which are smooth, firm in texture, and medium green. These basal rosettes are evergreen and quite attractive during the winter months.

Stokes' aster combines well with other species with attractive winter foliage; in summer, it is especially lovely with gray-leaved plants, for example, *Achillea* 'Moonshine' which has silvery foliage and pale yellow flowers. It is an excellent plant for the front of a border, where it mixes well with low, sun-loving species. Rugged, adaptable, and remarkably free of pests and diseases, it needs little more to thrive than a dryish, fertile, well-drained soil and a warm location in full sun. A heavy soil that remains wet for long periods is fatal.

Mauve or lilac flowers

Mauve or lilac is a common color among wildflowers and, not surprisingly, of many old-fashioned cottage-style garden flowers. Used with discretion it can serve as a link between pale blue flowers and pink.

The North American perennial *Erigeron*, fleabane, is similar in appearance to the asters, but has threadlike petals, and blossoms long before the first hardy asters. Erigerons are available in several excellent mauve-colored garden forms, as well as in many shades of pink and blue. There are many good hybrids, some single flowered, others semidouble or double, and it is best to select them after you have seen them in flower. One of the best is 'Strahlenmeer,' which flowers in pale mauve and grows to 30in/750mm. Only about half as tall, 'Mrs F. H. Beale' also has blossoms of mauve. The flowers of 'Märchen-land' and 'Foerster's Leibling' are semidouble and soft pink, as are those of 'Charity.' 'Prosperity' is a pale sky blue and 'Dunkelste Aller' ('Darkest of All') is, as the name implies, a deep lavender blue. Fleabane is very easy to grow and free-flowering on any fertile, well-drained soil.
well-drained soil.

For the flower border, there are several valuable ornamental alliums. Some are boldly geometrical, with large perfectly spherical flower heads, others are much more relaxed with loose tousled heads of hanging flowers. The Mediterranean species *Allium carinatum pulchellum* has dusty lilac bells, at first drooping in the bud, then turning upward after pollination. They dangle from the ends of slender stalks which rise 12-18in/300-450mm above the bluish green grassy foliage. The flowers look lovely among gray and silver plants such as artemisias. *A.c. pulchellum* sets seed abundantly and will sow itself freely, even in cracks in paving stones, where it looks lovely.

From deep pinks to pure whites

The pastel pink tones are the most typical colors of the traditional cottage-style garden, and what could be better in this season's garden than the pink itself, with its delicious, heavy, clovelike scent? This almost legendary plant has been cultivated in cottage-style gardens for hundreds of years.

The stately aristocratic-looking *Lilium regale* is one of the easiest lilies to grow. For the best visual effect, plant the bulbs in groups of at least five, about 12in/300mm apart.

The cottage pinks, sometimes known as sops-in-wine, are all derived from the European species *Dianthus plumarius*. They are gray-leaved perennials, 10-12in/250-300mm high with candy pink, wine red, or white flowers, often fringed and laced in delicate patterns. There are countless varieties, some old, such as 'Dad's Favourite' with double white flowers, each beautifully laced with maroon, or 'Mrs Sinkins' with fringed double flowers which are powerfully fragrant, but also many improved modern hybrids that flower for as long as two months if regularly deadheaded. First rate varieties of cottage pinks with pink-colored flowers include 'Maggie,' 'Pike's Pink,' and 'Altrosa'. There are also first class mixtures available which can easily be grown from seed. One such seed mixture, 'Highland Hybrids,' for example, features single flowers varying in tint from white to deep pink, some with maroon centers.

Try to choose pinks not only for good flower color and fragrance, but also for quality and color of foliage and vigor. Even when pinks are not in bloom, their blue-gray foliage is attractive in pastel border schemes, as an edging in beds or as a carpet under roses. The evergreen leaves maintain their glaucous color all winter long if grown in well-drained soil.

The long classically beautiful trumpets of *Lilium regale* are creamy white, with sulphur yellow centers and the backs of the petals are shaded rose-purple. This lily is a perfect partner for plants that flower in soft pastel tones of pink, blue, or lilac. It grows to a height of about 40in/100cm. A single bulb normally produces up to eight trumpets, but a strong, well-grown bulb can carry as many as twenty-five flowers, each 4-6in/100-150mm long. The flowers are deliciously scented. *L. regale* is hardy to zone 4 and easy to grow in any well-drained soil with frequent topdressings of ripe compost during the growth period, needing just sun and protection from wind and late frosts. It is a good companion for other border plants, such as the artemisias, gypsophilas, or tall nepeta, preferring to have its bulbs and young emergent shoots under their protective cover. Lilies look excellent rising from such an underplanting of silver gray foliage, which makes a good foil to the flowers and partially disguises the stalks after the flowers have dropped.

Plants with a long flowering season

Centranthus ruber, red valerian or Jupiter's beard, is hard to beat for a long period of showy flowers. Being very drought-resistant, it will grow in the poorest, most alkaline soil, indeed virtually anywhere except in damp shade. A herbaceous perennial, 20-24in/500-600mm tall, with fleshy blue-green leaves, its minute fragrant flowers are carried in dense terminal clusters above the foliage. The wild form, which is the one to plant in a cottage-style garden, has pink flowers, but the forms *coccineus* with deep rosy red flowers and *albus* with milky white blossoms, are also useful. Red valerian seldom lasts longer than five years and does not transplant well when large. It is a good idea to raise new plants regularly from seed, and indeed, red valerian often seeds itself freely.

Helianthemum species, rock roses, and their cultivars will cascade splendidly down steps or over low walls to display their masses of jewellike flowers to advantage. Each day's crop of blossoms drops before evening, but is followed for many weeks by equally plentiful masses of new flowers. Only on a cloudy day will they remain closed.

Helianthemums are mostly low evergreen shrublets which grow no more than 12in/300mm high, but can spread out to 24in/600mm or more. They flower in a range of white, pink, yellow, orange, red, and bronze. The species *H. apenninum* flowers white, but the subspecies *H.a. roseum* has clear pink blossoms; both have handsome gray foliage. Excellent pink-flowering hybrids are 'Rosa Königin' ('Rose Queen') and 'Wisley Pink' which have attractive gray, evergreen foliage. 'Wisley Primrose' is a lovely pale yellow cultivar and the white varieties are 'Wisley White' and 'The Bride' ('Snow Queen'). A carpet of white-flowering rock roses planted beneath lavender 'Hidcote,' or a sea of pink helianthemums dotted with misty islands of feathery silver artemisias makes an elegant, cool corner in a sun-drenched yard. Helianthemums prefer a light soil with much lime. A fully sunny site is a must; in shade they sulk and die.

The hardy geraniums or crane's bills are invaluable. These versatile garden plants produce flowers in great profusion for weeks on end during the summer months. Many are also excellent ground-cover plants, well able to suppress any annual weeds under their thick carpet of attractive foliage. In fall the geranium leaves often color well, extending the decorative

The warmth of the rosy red *Centranthus ruber* 'Coccineus' is accentuated by the pale pink flowers of *Lavatera thuringiaca* 'Barnsley' and the cool, pale mauve tones of the vigorous evergreen horned violet, *Viola cornuta* 'Lilacina'.

The pale pink blossoms of
Geranium sanguineum striatum,
with their filigree crimson veins,
rise above the attractive foliage.
It has a long flowering season,
continuing into late summer.

effect beyond the flowering period. One of the most charming, *Geranium sanguineum striatum (G.s. lancastrense)*, bears light pink flowers with crimson veins and has deeply divided dark green leaves. This natural variety of the bloody crane's bill has numerous blossoms (which open anew daily) carried on 8-12in/200-300mm stems rising well above the dense foliage.

The *Sidalcea malviflora* hybrid 'Elsie Heugh' is a perfect long-flowering plant for the front of a pastel summer border. Lavishly covered with pretty miniature hollyhocklike flowers of pale shimmering pink rising from well-formed clumps of attractive foliage, it thrives in any good soil, but prefers a relatively acidic soil. It likes full sun, but not dry conditions. As soon as the flowers fade, the flowering stems should be cut partway back to encourage a second crop of flowers. 'Elsie Heugh' will thrive if dug up, divided, and replanted every four or five years, whenever it shows signs of tiring.

Just a few flowers of palest yellow can be a refreshingly welcome contrast near lavender blue and mauve plants. A fine plant for this purpose is *Achillea* 'Moonshine,' one of the yarrows, which perfectly combines pale sulphur-yellow flowers with soft silvery gray, feathery foliage. In flower, 'Moonshine' carries its bold flat heads of tiny flowers on graceful branching stems about 24in/600mm tall, well above the foliage, and is also a valuable foliage plant, making large mounds of soft silver.

White-flowering plants
Sometimes two colors do not work well together in the flower border and need to be separated. White flowers are the answer, and massed white also serves as the best background for more dramatic floral events. *Campanula lactiflora alba* is good for both purposes, but the gypsophilas – filmy, atmospheric plants of an open habit – can provide the best backdrop of all.

Gypsophila paniculata, popularly known as baby's breath, is a hardy perennial from Siberia. It dies back completely each winter but grows quickly in late spring to form a huge bushy mound 40in/1m or more high and just as wide. During midsummer it is covered in a haze of tiny, white, slightly scented flowers. It is good for concealing areas left bare by spring bulbs or oriental poppies which die back completely after flowering. There is a double-flowering form, G. 'Bristol Fairy,' which flowers over a much longer period. For spilling over the front edge of the border there is also a compact pink-flowering form 'Rosenschleier' ('Rosy Veil'). It associates well with gray-leaved plants.

All gypsophilas are taprooted and cannot be moved once they are established, so choose their spots carefully. They need deep, fertile soil with plenty of lime. If cut down after the first flush of flowers has faded, gypsophila may produce a second crop of blossoms in early fall.

Accent plants
To counteract the hazy effects of pastel colors, it is a good idea to introduce a few bold accent plants, either with strong vertical lines or with bold, ornamental foliage. An excellent herbaceous perennial which combines both attributes is *Acanthus hungaricus*. It has handsome, deeply indented leaves of dark dull green, 2-3ft/600-900mm long. They are narrower than those of the better known *A. mollis* and they make an impressive mound of foliage out of which rise the imposing 3½ft/1m tall spikes of hooded white or pale pink flowers, each

The airy flowers of *Gypsophila paniculata* 'Bristol Fairy' set off bolder colors, such as red *Potentilla* 'Monsieur Rouillard' and bright blue *Polemonium foliosissimum*.

attractive. If the flower spikes are to remain vertical, it is essential that it stands in full sun; otherwise the spikes will twist and bend toward the light. *L. spicata* is a long-lived plant and can remain undisturbed for years. Watch out for small rodents; they often develop an appetite for the fleshy rootstocks!

The sea hollies, *Eryngium* species, have stiff leathery leaves with spikes. The leaves and thistlelike flowers have firm, sharply defined outlines, good textures, and arresting colors. They provide a bold structure against a background of mingled colors or a bank of gypsophila. Most sea hollies are at their best in midsummer. *E. alpinum* has the largest flower heads up to 1½in/40mm long. It has light green, heart-shaped basal leaves and stout blue stems, rising to 28in/700mm, each bearing several steel-blue cylindrical flower heads which are surrounded by large lacy ruffs of metallic blue. *E.a* 'Opal' exchanges blue for an exquisite tone of silvery-mauve. *E. bourgatii* has beautiful, deeply cleft foliage; the gray-green leaves are heavily veined with white. The spherical flower heads, up to 1in/25mm in diameter, are steel blue; they are surrounded by spiny silver blue bracts. It remains relatively short, seldom growing taller than 16in/400mm.

Once established, sea hollies require little care, but they resent root disturbance and should not be transplanted without good cause. In cold climates (zone 6 and north), a winter blanket of evergreen branches is advantageous.

Silver and gray foliage plants

A selection of silver and gray foliage plants provides the framework which holds the midsummer border composition together and links it with its surroundings. Also, grays and silvers almost never clash with other colors but make every other color seem brighter and purer.

At the lowest level and toward the front of the border, the silver-leaved lamb's ears is a favorite groundcover plant. The non-flowering cultivar *Stachys byzantina* 'Silver Carpet' is best for its soft woolly white leaves that retain their beauty well into fall. It grows rapidly to make an impenetrable evergreen groundcover, the stems rooting wherever they touch the soil, and never exceeds 8in/200mm. Stachys is prone to mildew so good drainage and full sun are absolutely necessary. Whenever gaps in the carpet appear, stachys should be dug up and divided. If you replant the best pieces, they will grow again quickly to restore the thick silver ground cover.

protected by a spiny reddish purple bract. Acanthus should stand unobstructed, and toward the front of the border, in spite of the considerable height of the flower spikes. It grows best in full sun and needs deep, fertile, well-drained soil.

Liatris spicata, blazing star or Kansas feather, is another striking plant with its narrow, vertical flower spikes. Unlike the solitary acanthus, *Liatris* is best when massed together. In midsummer its basal tufts lengthen to send up tall, slender stems that are densely covered with narrow leaves topped by stiff bottle-brush heads. These are crowded with fluffy, small rose-purple or white flowers that open from the top of the spike downward. The outstanding cultivar *L.* 'Floristan Violett' flowers in a brighter shade of violet and reaches 3ft/900mm, as does the white-flowering version 'Floristan Weiss.' Both make excellent, long-lasting cut flowers. A shorter form 'Kobold' has mauve-pink blossoms and seldom exceeds 18in/450mm. Under dry conditions liatris remains shorter, but is just as

The feathery artemisias are the most valuable and universal of the silver and gray foliage plants for the midsummer border. *Artemisia abrotanum*, known as southernwood or lad's love, has silvery green aromatic leaves and stalks. It is a shrubby, densely bushy plant with fine feathery foliage; the insignificant flowers are small yellow balls. It does well on the poorest of soils, as long as it is warm and well-drained. It grows 3¼ft/1m tall and must be pruned hard every year in early spring to keep it neat, compact, and well-shaped.

Somewhat shorter, but every bit as pungently aromatic, the wormwood or absinthe cultivar *A. absinthium* 'Lambrook Silver' has silver gray, finely divided foliage. Its stems reach 2½ft/750mm by midsummer, when they bear tiny gray flowers on long spikes. At flowering time, the silver color becomes darker. An evergreen, bushy shrublet, 'Lambrook Silver' maintains its attractive form if judiciously shaped and lightly pruned in early spring. It is hardy to zone 6, as is the choice hybrid *A.* 'Powis Castle' which hardly ever flowers, so its leaves retain their beauty throughout the season. More shrublike in habit than the other artemisias, *A.* 'Powis Castle' grows some 24-28in/600-700mm tall.

Ornamental grass

These days no planting plan is really complete without at least one ornamental grass. For the pastel midsummer border, there is a marvelous species *Helictotrichon sempervirens*. Making dense clumps of gracefully arching narrow blue-green leaves, it is well-behaved and noninvasive. Apart from the value of the blue cast of its evergreen foliage, it has fine architectural qualities. The flower stalks may be cut away as soon as they cease to be attractive. Helictotrichon should stand free, so that its form can be admired.

PLANTS FOR MIDSUMMER

Blue and mauve
Buddleja davidii 'Empire Blue,' 'Black Knight,' 'Ile de France,' 'Dartmoor'
Ceanothus × *delileanus* hybrids 'Gloire de Versailles,' 'Henri Desfossé,' 'Topaz'
Hibiscus syriacus 'Ardens,' 'Oiseau Bleu' ('Blue Bird')
Hydrangea aspera sargentiana
H. macrophylla 'Blue Wave'
Lavandula angustifolia 'Hidcote,' 'Munstead'
Aconitum hybrids 'Newry Blue,' 'Bressingham Spire'
Campanula carpatica 'Blue Clips,' 'Chewton Joy,' 'Karpatenkrone'
C. lactiflora 'Prichard's Variety,' 'Pouffe'
Clematis cultivars
Clematis heracleifolia + *C.h. davidiana*
Delphinium hybrids
Echinops bannaticus 'Taplow Blue'
E. ritro 'Veitch's Blue'
Erigeron hybrids
Eryngium alpinum + *E.a.* 'Blue Star', 'Opal'
E. bourgatti
E. × *oliverianum*
E. × *zabelii* 'Jewel,' 'Violetta'
Hosta fortunei cultivars
Liatris spicata 'Kobold,' 'Floristan Violett'
Linum narbonense
Nepeta × *faassenii*
Salvia nemorosa 'Superba,' 'East Friesland,' 'Blauhügel'
Scabiosa caucasica cultivars
Stokesia laevis 'Blue Star'
Thalictrum dalavayi (T. dipterocarpum)
Veronica longifolia 'Blaureisen' ('Blue Giant'), 'Blauer Sommer'
V. spicata 'Saraband' 'Blaufuchs,' 'Blaubart'
V. spicata incana

Allium christophii
A. giganteum
Gladiolus cultivars
Iris laevigata cultivars
Pontederia cordata

White and cream
Buddleja davidii 'Peace'
Calluna vulgaris cultivars
Catalpa bignonioides
Ceanothus americanus
Clethra barbinervis
Deutzia scabra 'Candidissima,' 'Watereri'
Erica tetralix cultivars
E. vagans cultivars
Hibiscus syriacus 'Totus Albus,' 'Diana,' 'Red Heart,' 'W. R. Smith'
Holodiscus discolor
Hydrangea aspera sargentiana
H. paniculata
H. quercifolia
Philadelphus hybrids
Potentilla fruticosa 'Manchu',

'Abbotswood'
Yucca filamentosa
Y. flaccida
Rosa cultivars + species
Clematis cultivars
Hydrangea petiolaris
Lonicera periclymenum 'Serotina'
Anaphalis triplinervis 'Sommerschnee'
Aruncus dioicus
Astilbe hybrids 'Brautschleier' ('Bridal Veil'), 'Professor van der Wielen,' 'Bergkristall'
Astrantia major
Campanula carpatica 'Weisse Clips', 'White Star', 'Zwergmöve'
C. lactiflora alba
Centranthus ruber albus
Leucanthemum × *superbum (Chrysanthemum maximum)* 'Alaska,' 'Beethoven,' 'Christine Hagemann,' 'Gruppenstolz,' 'Julischnee,' 'Wirral Supreme,' 'Saturn'

Rosa 'Alister Stella Gray'

Rosa 'Fantin Latour'

Clematis recta 'Grandiflora'
Delphinium hybrid
Dianthus plumarius hybrids
Echinops sphaerocephalus 'Niveus'
Erigeron hybrids
Gypsophila paniculata + *G.p*
   'Bristol Fairy'
Helianthemum hybrids
Hemerocallis hybrids
Hosta sieboldiana 'Elegans'
Liatris spicata 'Floristan Weiss'
Lysimachia clethroides
Macleaya cordata
Monarda 'Schneewittchen'
   ('Snow Maiden')
Phlox paniculata cultivars
Scabiosa caucasica cultivars
Veronica spicata 'Icicle'

Galtonia candicans
Gladiolus cultivars
Lilium species + cultivars
Tigridia pavonia cultivars
Tritonia cultivars
Aponogeton distachyos
Hydrocharis morsus-ranae
Iris laevigata cultivars
Nymphaea alba
Nymphaea hybrids 'Marliacea
   Albida,' 'Gladstoniana'
N. tuberosa 'Richardsonii'
Ranunculus aquatilis
Sagittaria graminea
S. latifolia
S. sagittifolia

Yellow and orange
Genista tinctoria 'Royal Gold'
Hypericum calycinum
H. 'Hidcote'
H. × *moserianum*
H. forrestii
Koelreuteria paniculata
Potentilla fruticosa 'Elizabeth,'
   'Katherine Dykes,'
   'Goldfinger,' 'Goldteppich,'
   'Klondike,' 'Primrose Beauty'
Santolina chamaecyparissus
Rosa cultivars
Campsis radicans 'Flava'
Lonicera acuminata
L. × *heckrottii* 'Goldframe'
Achillea 'Coronation Gold'
A. filipendulina 'Parker's

Variety,' 'Gold Plate,'
   'Neugold'
A. 'Moonshine'
A. × *taygetea*
Coreopsis grandiflora
   'Badengold,' 'Tetragold,'
   'Sunray'
C. verticillata 'Grandiflora,'
   'Moonbeam,' 'Zagreb'
Digitalis grandiflora
Gaillardia 'Mandarin,'
   'Goldkobold' ('Golden
   Goblin'), 'Kobold' ('Goblin')
Helenium bigelovii 'The Bishop'
Helenium 'Bressingham Gold,'
   'Waltraut,' 'Golden Jugend'
   ('Golden Youth')
Helianthemum hybrids

Hemerocallis hybrids
H. citrina
Ligularia × *palmatiloba*
L. przewalskii + *L.p.* 'The Rocket'
Gladiolus cultivars
Lilium species + cultivars
Tigridia pavonia cultivars
Tritonia cultivars
Lysimachia nummularia
L. punctata
Nymphaea 'Aurora,' 'Sunrise,' 'Moorei,' 'Sioux,' 'Sulphurea'
Nymphoides peltata
Ranunculus lingua 'Grandiflora'

Red and pink
Buddleja davidii 'Cardinal,' 'Fascination,' 'Purple Prince,' 'Royal Red'
Calluna vulgaris cultivars
Ceanothus × *pallidus* 'Marie Simon'
Deutzia × *hybrida* 'Contraste,' 'Mount Rose'
Erica tetralix cultivars
E. vagans cultivars
Fuchsia magellanica gracilis
F. 'Mrs Popple'
Hibiscus syriacus 'Hamabo,' 'Woodbridge'
Rubus odoratus
Weigela 'Eva Rathke,' 'Eva Supreme'
Rosa cultivars + species
Campis radicans
Clematis cultivars
C. 'Kermesina'
Lonicera × *heckrottii*
L. × *brownii* 'Dropmore Scarlet'
Acanthus hungaricus
Astilbe 'Bressingham Beauty,' 'Hyazinth,' 'Fanal,' 'Spinell'
Astrantia major rosea
Campanula lactiflora 'Loddon Anna'
Centranthus ruber +

C.r. coccineus
Dianthus plumarius hybrids
Erigeron hybrids
Gaillardia 'Bremen,' 'Burgunder,' 'Fackelschein'
Geranium endresii + *G.e.* 'Wargrave Pink'
G. × *oxonianum* 'A.T. Johnson,' 'Russell Prichard'
G. sanguineum + *G.s. striatum* (*G.s. lancastrense*)
Gypsophila paniculata 'Flamingo,' 'Rosenschleier' ('Rosy Veil')
Helenium 'Crimson Beauty,' 'Moerheim Beauty'
Helianthemum hybrids
Hemerocallis hybrids
Lychnis chalcedonica
Lythrum salicaria 'Brightness,' 'Robert,' 'The Beacon'
L. vergatum 'Rose Queen,' 'The Rocket'
Monarda 'Adam,' 'Cambridge Scarlet,' 'Prärieglut' ('Prairie Glow') 'Prärienacht' ('Prairie Night')
Phlox paniculata early + midseason cultivars
Sidalcea 'Brilliant,' 'Elsie Heugh'
Veronica spicata 'Barcarolle,' 'Minuet,' 'Heidekind,' 'Rotfuchs'
Allium carinatum pulchellum
A. sphaerocephalon
Gladiolus cultivars
Lilium species + cultivars
Tigridia pavonia cultivars
Tritonia cultivars
Alisma lanceolatum
A. plantago-aquatica
Butomus umbellatus
Eupatorium maculatum 'Atropurpureum'
E. purpureum
Filipendula palmata 'Nana'

Iris laevigata cultivars
I. versicolor 'Kermesina'
Nymphaea 'Charles de Meurville,' 'Conqueror,' 'Escarboucle,' 'William B. Shaw,' 'James Brydon,' 'Rosennymphe'

Scented plants
Buddleja davidii cultivars
Calycanthus floridus
Ceanothus × *delileanus* 'Gloire de Versailles'
Clethra barbinervis
Holodiscus discolor
Lavandula cultivars
Philadelphus hybrids
Rubus odoratus
Tilia cordata
T. platyphyllos
Yucca filamentosa
Rosa cultivars + species
Lonicera heckrottii
L. periclymenum
Clematis heracleifolia
Clematis recta 'Grandiflora'
Dianthus plumarius hybrids
Hemerocallis citrina
Nepeta × *faassenii*
Phlox paniculata cultivars
Galtonia candicans
Lilium species + cultivars
Aponogeton distachyos
Nymphaea alba
Nymphaea 'Escarboucle,' 'William B. Shaw,' 'Marliacea Albida,' 'Moorei'
N. tuberosa 'Richardsonii'

Plants for bees and butterflies
Buddleja davidii cultivars
Calluna vulgaris cultivars
Clethra barbinervis
Erica species + cultivars
Tetradium daniellii (*Euodia danielli*)

T. hupehense (*E. hupehensis*)
Genista tinctoria
Hibiscus syriacus cultivars
Koelreuteria paniculata
Lavandula angustifolia cultivars
Potentilla cultivars
Rubus odoratus
Tilia cordata
T. platyphyllos
Weigela 'Eva Rathke,' 'Eva Supreme'
Rosa single-flowering species + cultivars
Lonicera species + cultivars
Astrantia major
Campanula species + cultivars
Centranthus ruber + forms
Coreopsis cultivars
Echinops bannaticus
E. ritro
E. sphaerocephalus
Erigeron hybrids
Eryngium species + cultivars
Gaillardia cultivars
Geranium species + cultivars
Gypsophila species + cultivars
Helenium hybrids
Helianthemum hybrids
Liatris spicata cultivars
Ligularia species + cultivars
Lysimachia species
Lythrum species + cultivars
Nepeta × *faassenii*
Phlox paniculata cultivars
Salvia nemorosa cultivars
Scabiosa caucasica cultivars
Sidalcea hybrids
Stokesia laevis
Veronica species + cultivars
Allium species
Butomus umbellatus
Eupatorium maculatum 'Atropurpureum'
E. purpureum

MIDSUMMER TASKS

TREES AND SHRUBS

Hedge trimming
Deciding when to trim a formal hedge depends largely on the species planted. More vigorous plants, like hawthorn and privet, or dwarf hedges, such as box, will need pruning every four to six weeks during their growth period, or whenever they start to look messy. Slow-growing hedge plants normally need only one annual trimming, during midsummer. For example, box (*Buxus*), hornbeam (*Carpinus*), beech (*Fagus*), holly (*Ilex*), or cherry laurel (*Prunus laurocerasus*) if cut now, quickly make new growth, and usually retain their neat appearance for the rest of the summer.

Conifers such as yew (*Taxus*), western red cedar (*Thuja plicata*), or lawson cypress (*Chamaecyparis lawsoniana*), for example, should be trimmed only once a year, either in midsummer or late summer, depending on their appearance.

Watering new plants and mulching
Any newly planted trees and shrubs that have not yet had time to develop a deep and wide-reaching root system should be watched carefully for signs of water stress. When necessary, water deeply and thoroughly. If you plan to be away from the garden for a long stretch at this time of year, irrigate new plantings well before departure. Evaporation loss can be minimized by spreading a thick mulch.

Taking cuttings
Midsummer is an excellent time to propagate many woody plants by cuttings either from new softwood or, somewhat later, semiripe wood. There is still time to take softwood cuttings from shrubs such as caryopteris, lavender, santolina, buddleia, etc. Take softwood cuttings from vigorously growing young shoots. The first semiripe cuttings may be taken toward the end of this season, as soon as shoots start to become woody and firm, but are not fully hardened. Many gardeners have the most success with cuttings from semiripe wood; the shoots are thicker and have more stored nutrients than softwood cuttings. Shrubs such as ceanothis, daphne, hypericum, buddleia, and lavender can easily be propagated this way (see page 156).

Foliar feeding against chlorosis
Too much lime in the soil can prevent the roots of some plants, particularly those which prefer an acidic soil, from taking up enough iron to maintain healthy foliage. As a result the leaves turn yellow, although their veins often remain green, a symptom known as chlorosis. The youngest leaves are always the most severely affected. Rhododendrons, camellias, hydrangeas, ceanothus, and chaenomeles frequently show evidence of iron deficiency.

Foliar feeding is the quickest method to remedy any trace mineral deficiency, especially a lack of iron. When chlorosis occurs, the green color can often be restored by spraying a chelated iron preparation over and under the leaves of the affected plants. This treatment should be repeated weekly until leaves have regained their healthy green coloration. However, soil analysis is advisable to reveal what steps are necessary to solve the problem at its origin.

ROSES

Watering
Provide extra water during prolonged periods of hot dry weather; always give enough to saturate the entire root zone (see page 66).

Removing suckers
Most roses are budded onto a rootstock of some wild rose species. Any growth on a grafted rose bush that comes from below the point where the ornamental variety was budded onto the rootstock is a sucker. A sucker is the rootstock plant trying to grow its own leaves and stems. If nothing is done to check this growth, suckers will quickly weaken and eventually replace the named variety. They must be removed as soon as they appear, when it is still an easy job.

No specific identifying characteristics can guide you in recognizing sucker growth. However, one point is certain; the growth will be somehow different from the rose it supports.

Removing rose suckers
Dig down carefully and remove any growth from the rootstock with clippers, or by pulling hard, close to the base so that the sucker comes away cleanly.

Picking and deadheading
Continue deadheading roses as the flowers fade.

Fertilizing
Unless your soil is particularly fertile, repeat-flowering garden roses may benefit from an additional moderate dressing of fertilizer in midsummer, at the time the first flush of flowers is just finishing. This will encourage the production of an abundant second crop of blooms. However, if you live in an area where winter temperatures drop below 12°F/−10°C, you need to consider when to *stop* fertilizing a rose. Dressing with a nitrogen-rich fertilizer too late in the summer promotes succulent new growth which does not have enough time to ripen sufficiently to withstand fall frosts. On no account should roses be fed with a fertilizer containing nitrogen after a date some 8–12 weeks before the first anticipated frosts, which means no more fertilizer after the end of midsummer.

Foliar feeding
Roses growing in alkaline soils may show signs of iron-deficiency chlorosis just like rhododendrons or hydrangeas. Should the leaves, particularly the youngest leaves, show large yellow areas, the rose bushes should be sprayed with a foliar fertilizer containing chelated iron. However, many rose growers also use special complete foliar fertilizers as a helpful supplement to their regular soil fertilizer in order to obtain the quickest growth results. The nutrients in a foliar plant food are taken up through the pores of the leaves and are almost immediately available for the plant's use. More of the nutrients are absorbed on the undersides of the leaves, so direct the spray there.

One word of caution; foliar fertilizers, even if correctly dosed, may cause leaf burn in hot weather. If temperatures rise above 86°F/30°C, do not spray with a foliar preparation, but wait until the weather cools down.

CLIMBING PLANTS

Watering
Observe climbing plants growing on house walls for signs of lack of water. During the hottest days of the year, they may be the first plants in the garden to need extra water. In particular, newly planted climbers which have not had time to develop a deep-reaching root system should be watched closely. When irrigation is necessary, be sure to water deeply.

Tying in
Training and tying in new shoots of clematis, climbing roses, and all vigorously growing climbers continues to be an important task. Whenever you notice any shoots that are heading in the wrong

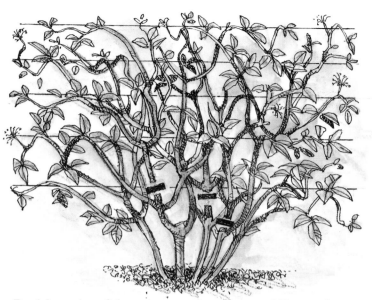

Partial pruning of clematis Cut away one-fourth to one-third of the oldest shoots each year after the first flowering, to a height of 12-24in/300-600mm from the ground. Remove the severed shoots, then water and fertilize the plant to encourage strong new growth. This allows the plant to flower twice.

direction, a bit of tucking in and tying done at once can spare you a confrontation with an impenetrable tangle of unruly tendrils, which can be formed almost overnight during this season of rapid growth.

Pruning clematis
Some of the large-flowering clematis hybrids blossom in spring and early summer on short side shoots from the growths made during the previous year. While the first flush of blossoms is still at its best, new growths are being formed which will flower during late summer and early fall. Consequently, these clematis cultivars are somewhat difficult to prune. This group includes such favorite hybrids as 'Bracebridge Star,' 'Duchess of Edinburgh,' 'Lady Northcliffe,' 'Lasurstern,' 'Mme LeCoultre,' 'Nelly Moser,' 'The President,' and 'William Kennett.'

There are three possible methods for pruning these clematis: annual hard pruning, back to near ground level in pre-spring (see page 17) or similar radical rejuvenation in pre-spring or early spring after several years of largely uninhibited growth. Neither is ideal. The first method means the regular loss of one crop of flowers each year and the second requires enormous quantities of shoots to be removed at one time, which drastically alters the appearance of the planting and reduces the floral effect for a year or two. A third method, an annual

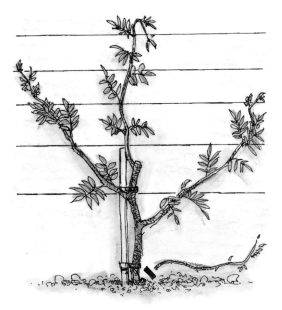

Summer pruning of wisteria
1 In the first year after planting, cut out new growths from ground level, remove any unwanted sublaterals (secondary side shoots). Cut the main side shoots back to 6-9in/ 150-225mm long. Position and tie all the shoots for the plant's framework at approx 45°.

2 During the second summer follow much the same principles: train and tie in the leader shoot and further well-spaced side shoots. Again cut back unwanted laterals and sub-laterals to 6-9in/150-225mm (leaving four or five leaves). Cut away new base shoots.

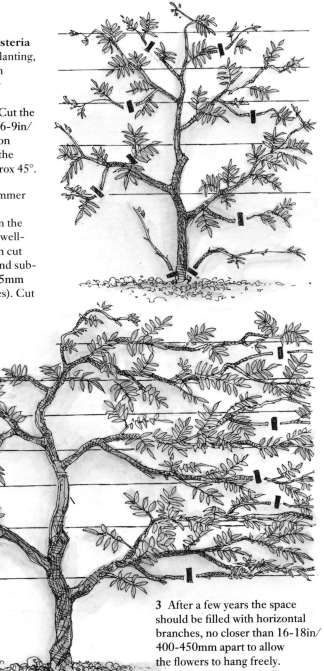

rejuvenation regimen (shown left), is preferable although it is by no means simple to carry out. It does, however, allow two crops of flowers each year. It guarantees that the clematis plant remains young, vigorous, and dense at the base and it hardly changes the appearance of the planting.

Pruning wisteria

If your wisteria is to flower dependably every year and smother your house front with masses of fragrant flowers rather than degenerate into a hopeless tangle, you will need to prune it faithfully, twice each year, once in pre-spring and again in mid- or late summer. Pruning in summer should start in the first year after planting, although it is likely to be minimal. This summer pruning is followed each year, of course, by a second pruning in pre-spring; the purpose of this double pruning is to convert new growths into short flowering spurs instead of allowing them to develop into tangles of leaves and stems.

HERBACEOUS PERENNIALS

Deadheading

It is good gardening practice to cut out faded flower heads whenever you see them, but continual deadheading does much more than improve the appearance of your borders and lengthen the flowering period of your perennials. In some cases it can even ensure the integrity of your planting design and the longevity of selected hybrids.

If a hybrid of, say, *Phlox paniculata* is allowed to set seed, some seeds

3 After a few years the space should be filled with horizontal branches, no closer than 16-18in/ 400-450mm apart to allow the flowers to hang freely. Continue cutting back all new growths to form flowering spurs.

 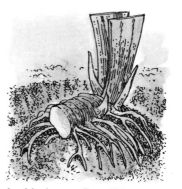 

Dividing and replanting iris
Dig up the entire clump of iris, select and cut off the best rhizome pieces: they should be 4-6in/100-150mm long, with well-developed roots and healthy leaves. Cut off the top of the leaves to reduce water loss and rocking by wind. Set the rhizome on a mound of earth, spread out the roots and partially cover with soil.

may fall and germinate among the parent plants. The seedlings will not be identical with the mother, of course, but probably inferior in flower and much more robust in growth. With time, the offspring, which will go undetected until they flower, may succeed in crowding out the more desirable hybrids and you will be left with a border full of reverted washed-out mauve-colored phlox. Therefore, always be sure to deadhead your perennials soon enough, before any seed can ripen, even if it means losing the last few flowers.

Fertilizing perennials
If your soil is fertile and well-supplied with nutrients, most perennials will be satisfied with occasional dressings of ripe garden compost and will seldom require any other fertilizer. After cutting back or deadheading perennials which will not flower again until next year – peonies are a good example – or after dividing and replanting spring-flowering perennials, give them a generous dressing of ripe compost. However, where the soil is not yet in ideal condition or if your plants have a more fastidious appetite, you may want to resort to some other fertilizer to satisfy their needs.

Herbaceous perennials that have been cut back or deadheaded with the intention of promoting additional flowers should receive a dressing of fast-acting balanced mineral fertilizer, preferably in dissolved form. The goal is to replace the nutrients lost during pruning, to support rapid new growth, and to promote a second flush of blossoms before fall. Only if clear signs of some mineral deficiency are apparent will most other perennials need a topdressing of mineral fertilizer this late in the year.

It is particularly important to know the individual requirements of the plants in your borders; some of them may not need any extra feeding at all and may repay your best intentions with their prompt demise.

Dividing perennials
Many spring-flowering herbaceous perennials can be divided and replanted now that their flowering period is finished. The most favorable time to divide is about two weeks after the last flowers have faded when the plant is ready to develop new roots and vegetative growth is active. Any perennials that have become too large for their location and threaten to crowd out their neighbors, as well as those that failed to give their usual good performance at blossom time or otherwise show signs of ageing or deterioration, are good candidates for division. This may be the case with *Antennaria, Arabis, Armeria, Aubrieta, Campanula carpatica, Chrysanthemum coccineum, Doronicum, Helleborus, Phlox subulata, Primula, Saxifraga,* and *Trollius,* to list just a few. Bleeding hearts (*Dicentra spectabilis*) and oriental poppies (*Papaver orientale*) can also be divided and transplanted in midsummer, or whenever their foliage has started to die back (see page 159).

Work plenty of good compost and a slow-acting organic fertilizer, such as bone meal, into the soil. After a deep soaking, the young plants should get off to a good start. Keep them well-watered during the next few weeks; hoe the soil as often as necessary to combat weak seedlings and break up any crust that forms on the surface. Once the soil around the plants is loose, moist, and without weeds, spread a thick mulch layer in order to reduce work for the rest of the year.

Dividing and planting iris
As they grow and spread outward, bearded irises leave behind in the middle of the clump a mass of barren, woody old rhizomes, which are no longer able to produce flowers or leaves. To keep your iris plants attractive and to maintain their youthful vigor, it is necessary to dig up, divide, and replant them every third or fourth year. The best time to do this is six weeks after the flowers have faded and dropped, just as new rhizomes and roots are beginning to develop.

In preparation for planting, renew the soil where the irises are to be replanted; spade over and work in a moderate amount of ripe compost and some bone meal. Bearded irises grow well on any soil capable of growing vegetables, but perform best on a well-drained, nearly neutral soil.

Always allow sufficient space between the rhizomes for normal growth for the next three or four years. Depending on the variety, plant tall irises about 10in/250mm apart, intermediates at 8in/200mm and dwarf irises about 6in/150mm apart.

Midsummer is also the best time to buy and plant new bearded iris rhizomes from nurseries. New irises are planted in the same way as divisions. Always plant bearded iris in sunny, warm locations, dryish but not arid. They dislike shade and dampness around their roots.

ANNUALS AND BIENNIALS

Recurrent tasks
Most flowering annuals will be in full blossom in midsummer; at the peak of their development, they require very little attention except for regular deadheading to keep them flowering as long as possible. Any annuals that become straggly can be persuaded to remain compact and flower more freely if they are pruned back lightly after their first flush of blossoms has past. Fertilize and water well after trimming to encourage a rapid bounce back.

Exhausted plants can be replaced at any time with new, pot-grown annuals or even with a crop of decorative salads or annual herbs. Keep a reserve supply of these plants, growing in pots, to be tucked in wherever and whenever a suitable space becomes vacant.

Biennials
Seedlings of hollyhocks and other biennials sown during the past weeks should be pricked or potted whenever necessary to keep them growing well until they are planted in the fall where they are to flower. There is still time to sow some biennials, for example *Myosotis* hybrids, *Papaver nudicaule*, *Erysimum* × *allionii*, *onopordum acanthium*, and *Viola* × *wittrockiana* hybrids.

BULBS

Feeding dahlias, gladioli, and summer bulbs
Dahlias are heavy feeders and to flower abundantly for the rest of the summer months they need a topdressing every two weeks with a quick-acting balanced fertilizer, preferably a liquid plant food applied either to the roots or as a foliar feed. By now the dahlias' feeding roots will have invaded the surface soil; stop hoeing, water thoroughly whenever the weather is dry, and apply a surface mulch.

Gladioli and most summer-flowering bulbs and corms should also

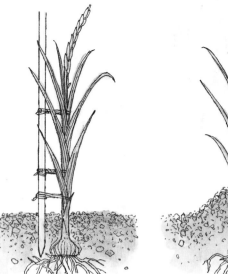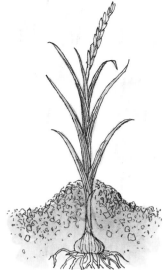

Staking gladioli
Stake gladioli individually, the stake placed well clear of the corm. If the plants are growing in an area for cutting, "hill up" the soil around their bases to give support: make a 4-5in/ 100-130mm mound as soon as plants are 8-10in/ 200-250mm tall.

be given a moderate topdressing of a balanced, quick-acting fertilizer preferably one rich in potassium and phosphorus. This will help them to develop new bulbs and corms for replanting next year.

Staking dahlias and gladioli
If you are growing tall gladioli and large-flowering dahlias, either for cut flowers or purely for their decorative value in the garden, stake and tie them up before they reach a height at which they need support. Gladiolus spikes with crooked stems are of no use for flower arrangement and once they bend over even the most careful staking and tying cannot correct their form. Dahlias are normally staked at planting time to avoid damaging the tubers, so tie in the stems at regular intervals, before the buds of the heavy flowers start to unfold.

Lifting
Most spring-flowering bulbs can grow for many years in one place before they need to be dug up and divided. Daffodils can remain in their borders for four or five years until they become too crowded. However, bedding tulips and hyacinths are usually dug up each year. As soon as their foliage has died back naturally the bulbs can be removed. A few, such as *Muscari* and *Scilla*, may be divided and replanted at once. Most other bulbs should be dried off under cover, then stored in a dry, cool, and airy place for replanting in fall.

Fall-flowering bulbs

Fall-flowering bulbs should be planted in midsummer. Fall crocuses, such as *Crocus sativus, C. speciosus,* and *C. goulimyi,* in many shades of blue or white, as well as the sparkling yellow *Sternbergia lutea* and the pink or white colchicums will bloom for the first time just a few weeks after planting, so it pays to get them into the ground early.

WATER GARDEN

Midsummer maintenance

An established, well-balanced water garden usually requires little attention during midsummer. The general housekeeping tasks which began in early summer should be continued throughout the season.

Remove dead and dying leaves of water plants whenever you see them. Any underwater plants that threaten to take over and crowd out other valuable plants should be partly cut back and removed. In a small pool, it may be necessary to cut away the leaves of some water lilies and other plants with floating leaves as well. Generally they should not be allowed to cover more than one-third to one-half of the water surface.

Continue removing filamentous algae, as soon as they appear, by winding the strands around a stick or branch. Frequently duckweed (*Lemna*) also becomes a nuisance as it spreads out to cover too much of the water surface. Fish out duckweed as often as necessary, with a fine-mesh fishnet and add it to your compost pile. Do be sure, however, not to catch any fish or other creatures in the process. Removal of duckweed from the pond helps indirectly to combat algae as it takes with it many nutrients that would otherwise be available to nourish algae. To leave duckweed unchecked is to court disaster later. The same applies to other free-swimming plants such as fairy moss (*Azolla*), frogbit (*Hydrocharis*), or water hyacinth (*Eichhornia*) although these are seldom as much of a problem as duckweed.

Other plants in the low and water-edge areas which are invasive should be restrained before they can oust their less robust neighbors. Species such as horse tails (*Equisetum*), manna grass (*Glyceria*), mare's tail (*Hippuris*), spearwort (*Ranunculus*), arrowhead (*Sagittaria*), burr reed (*Sparganium*), and cat tails (*Typha*) need watching. Try to hold them within bounds by cutting out encroaching shoots regularly.

Continue weeding the bog area and be on the lookout for windborne nuisances, like seedlings of birch, willow, poplar, maple, or willow herb (*Epilobium*).

Some low-lying plants, if allowed to set seed, can themselves become as much of a problem as any weed. Deadheading is the best prevention, if it is possible to carry it out often enough. Otherwise, remove excess seedlings before they can become a problem. Watch out especially for monkey flower (*Mimulus*) or purple loosestrife (*Lythrum*): lovely as they are, they are also potential weeds.

LAWN AND FLOWER MEADOW

Mowing the lawn

Continue to mow the lawn regularly, but less frequently as soon as summer heat sets in. If you cannot water it, set the lawn mower higher, to cut the grass longer (1-2in/3-4cm) to avoid sunburn. If you plan to be away and cannot make provision for regular mowing during your absence, then adjust the height of the grass gradually, allowing it to grow about 1in/2.5cm longer than usual before cutting.

Watering

Grass first shows its need of water by loss of springiness: when you walk across it, there is no resilience and you can clearly see your footprints in the grass. The next stage of water stress is a change of color: the fresh green takes on a dull gray, almost blue, smoky cast. If drought conditions last even longer, the grass tops begin to turn yellow, then brown. Once brown, the grass is already so weakened that weeds can easily gain a toehold as soon as water is again available.

Ideally you should water as soon as the lawn begins to lose its springy texture or even sooner, but there is little danger, even when the grass has taken on a gray-green hue, if you water at once. However, on no account can you put off watering any longer without damaging the quality of your lawn.

There are no exact rules governing the frequency of watering, but the guiding principle is always to allow the turf to dry out to some extent between waterings to encourage deep root development.

Mowing a flower meadow

Flower meadows are generally mown only twice or perhaps three times a year. This is normally done at the end of flowering phases and depends on the species composition of the meadow. If you have planted colchicums or fall-flowering crocuses, you should schedule mowing so that the grass is relatively short before the flower buds start to break through the soil surface in early fall.

PATIO AND BALCONY

Maintenance tasks

During midsummer the regular maintenance tasks in the patio or balcony garden are mostly reduced to watering, fertilizing, and deadheading. To ensure that your container plants never suffer for lack of water should be your most important consideration. You may find it useful to invest in an automatic watering system. There are various commercial systems that can be put together to suit individual needs. Plants in boxes, tubs, and other containers should be fed weekly with a liquid fertilizer. At this time of year, choose a fertilizer with less nitrogen and relatively more phosphorus and potassium.

CHAPTER 6

LATE SUMMER

"Come, let us stray our gladsome way
And view the charms of Nature;
The rustling corn, the fruited thorn,
And every happy creature."

Robert Burns

Late summer is one of the shortest seasons of the natural calendar. It is a season of transition and change, often with warm, even blisteringly hot, days and clear, cool nights. The mountain ash or rowan (*Sorbus aucuparia*), which has already appeared as a signal plant at flowering time at the end of spring, now heralds this season. Its brilliant red fruits are like tiny little apples borne in numerous dense, flat clusters.

The mountain ash is a small, slender, and graceful tree, reaching 15–20ft/4.5–6m. It has no special requirements for soil or location and will grow virtually anywhere, although it does best in light, sandy soils. A typical pioneer plant, it grows rapidly during its early years and is hardy to zone 4 and tolerant of the most bleak conditions, but it seldom lives longer than about eighty years. For the garden there are selected forms which are superior to the wild form: 'Beissneri' is a choice tree with a dense head of erect branches. Its young shoots are of a dark coral red and the leaflets are more prettily serrated than those of the type. The form 'Edulis' has large fruits that are sweet and edible without pretreatment. 'Sheerwater Seedling' is a neat, vigorous, upright tree with a well-shaped crown and large clusters of orange-red fruits.

Another signal plant of late summer is snowberry (*Symphoricarpos albus*) with its ripe clusters of showy, marblelike fruits, which are large, white, and long-lasting.

THE LATE SUMMER GARDEN

The late summer garden features colorful old-fashioned annuals and exuberant cottage-style garden perennials, with a cornucopia of edible and decorative fruits, vegetables, herbs, and salad plants. Such ornamental species and utilitarian edible plants, mixed more or less at random, was once characteristic of English village or country gardens. Out of this tradition has grown the integrated garden – a cottage-style garden modified and adapted to the situation of the small modern urban or suburban garden. Mixed among the ornamental shrubs, perennials and annuals are plants carefully selected for their double role. These are ornamental plants that also produce edible fruits, or varieties of utilitarian plants selected for their decorative value. Examples of trees in the first group are the mountain ash, the crab apple, notably 'John Downie,' the flowering quince *Chaenomeles* 'Rubra Grandiflora,' and the

European native cornelian cherry (*Cornus mas*). The second group includes fruit trees such as apples, pears, and plums, and vegetables such as artichokes and asparagus, and a multitude of culinary herbs. In contrast to the traditional, "naive" cottage-style garden, in which these plants might have appeared haphazardly placed, the modern version is furnished with the same plants, carefully placed to give a maximum of enjoyment.

Decorative fruits, vegetables and herbs

Late summer is the traditional time of harvest when the countryside begins to be dominated by golden fields of ripe Indian corn. In the integrated garden, the harvest of vegetables and herbs is still in full swing, and now the first apples are ripe enough to pick – early dessert varieties such as 'James Grieve' and the old favorite 'Gravenstein.' Early pears such as 'Williams' Bon Chrétien' ('Bartlett') and 'Clapp's Favourite' should be picked now so that they can attain their perfect juicy ripeness in the house. At the same time delicious greengages, early prune plums, and damson plums – can be picked.

Fruit trees are decorative at flowering time and in late summer when they are heavily laden with ripening fruit. They can be grown as standards, or as semidwarf or dwarf trees, freestanding or trained as cordons or espaliers. Apple trees are particularly versatile, and there are many cherished, well-flavored older varieties and new disease-free ones that are well worth growing. Pear trees are perfect for espaliers on fences or house walls since the best fruit grows on trained trees. They do better than most fruit trees in a lawn and since the fruits are best picked before they fall, there is no problem of fruit drop. Generally grown as standards, plums make graceful, vase-shaped trees. They look lovely along a driveway, but they must be kept away from the sidewalk, so that fruit drop is not a problem. Mostly of an open, irregular form, they make an interesting accent as a lawn tree.

Vegetables, too, can be ornamental. The yellow cup-shaped flowers of squash (zucchini) are large and showy; the plant itself is dramatic in appearance, so give it a prominent position. It is however, prone to mildew and stem borer. Several varieties

The self-seeding annual herb, borage (*Borago officinalis*), looks lovely planted together with red-flowering daisies. Its young cucumber-flavored leaves and bright blue edible blossoms are pleasant in summer salads.

Chinese chives (*Allium tuberosum*) carry their attractive blossoms for many weeks; the flowers have a milder flavor than the leaves. They grow best in deep rich soil, in sun.

of the purely ornamental thistle or acanthus species. If some flower buds are not picked, but allowed to open, you will be rewarded in late summer with enormous blue, fragrant thistle flowers that are much loved by bumblebees. Because they make such spectacular plants, artichokes even deserve a prominent solitary position within a flower border. The plant is shaped like a fountain and will grow to a height of about 4ft/1.2m and spread just as wide.

Asparagus, whose edible spears are harvested as they break through the ground in spring, is not just a luxury crop though the harvest season is short; cutting should cease around the middle of early summer, to allow the plants to develop foliage and store energy for next year's crop. Shoots that are not cut for eating develop into feathery foliage plants, about 3–5ft/0.9–1.5m tall. They form an attractive background in late summer for a brightly colored flower border or make a useful low summer hedge. Asparagus plants will often continue to bear for twenty years or more, so plan a permanent place for them.

Perennial chives with their fresh green spiky leaves and mauve flower heads are highly decorative as are the more exotic garlic chives (*Allium tuberosum*) which have flat straplike leaves that taste of garlic instead of onion. Flat clusters of fragrant white flowers appear in late summer. Like common chives, the blossoms are edible. They are very attractive to bees and to the useful syrphus flies, natural predators whose larvae help control aphids.

Another pungent herb used in oriental cuisine is the garland chrysanthemum (*Chrysanthemum coronarium*), known as shungiku, an annual chrysanthemum with yellow and cream-colored flowers. Stir-fried briefly, it has a strong aromatic flavor. Harvest shungiku while it is still young, but leave a few plants to flower, partly because they are pretty to look at and partly because you may want to eat the spicy blossoms. In flower, shungiku grows from 2–4ft/600–1200mm tall, and will bloom from late summer until killed by frost. The aromatic foliage is dark green and very attractive.

Many well-known herbs are lovely as well as useful. Shiny green sweet basil leaves combine well with many annuals as well as with lettuces, nasturtiums, and vegetables. The purple-leaved variety 'Dark Opal' looks gorgeous with pink-flowering annuals such as sweet alyssum. Basil is a warm-season annual, easily grown from seeds sown indoors, which grows to 24in/600mm in height.

are available, with green or yellow fruits. 'Gold Rush' was developed especially for small gardens. It has beautiful cut leaves with silver splotches and shiny golden fruits.

The artichoke is a giant thistle whose flower buds, when cooked, are delicious either hot or cold. Planted in a mixed border, it has a dramatic, sculptured appearance; the handsome, silvery gray leaves are bold and just as decorative as any

As with many herbs, both the hairy leaves and lovely flowers of borage are edible. The electric blue, starry flowers are as decorative as many strictly ornamental species and are great favorites of honeybees. The plant combines especially well with white flowers, such as *Lavatera* 'Mont Blanc,' or with marigolds or nasturtiums.

The nasturtium is another attractive plant with equally edible leaves and flowers. The tender young leaves have a delicious peppery flavor and the fragrant flowers are gently spicy. The compact dwarf nasturtium (*Tropaeolum minus*) varieties are about 12in/300mm high and can be sown anywhere in flower borders where their bright colors are appropriate.

Annual flowers

Certain flowers are always associated with summer in the simple country garden. Many are colorful annuals, grown by our ancestors from seed gathered every fall to be sown again the following spring. This traditional practice is of no use, of course, with modern hybrid varieties, which never grow true from seed. It is still the best way to maintain the old-fashioned species annuals in the garden.

Annual sunflowers (*Helianthus annuus* varieties), for example, can be grown for years on end from homegrown seed without much loss of floral quality. There is something rustic and altogether wholesome about their enormous sun faces shining high above the garden fence. There are many varieties to choose from, single or double, huge or simply large, in a range of colors from pale yellow and gold to brown and mahogany red. Sunflowers prefer full sun and a deep fertile soil. They can be sown in place outdoors, but if you want a prize-winning giant, you may want to sow early indoors. The flowers are excellent for bees, and if you leave the ripe seed heads in the garden, you will attract finches and cardinals.

Cosmos are graceful border flowers that also attract bees and butterflies. Their finely divided foliage is especially pretty, a lovely foil to the flowers which are produced abundantly from summer till frost. Wonderful flowers for cutting, cosmos are available in many bright clear colors – pink, white, rose, crimson, yellow and orange – depending on the variety and mixture. They vary considerably in their heights and colors, so choose them carefully for your individual color scheme.

Lavatera trimestris is one of the best new annuals to be introduced in recent years. 'Silver Cup' with glowing pink

The old-fashioned cottage-style favorites, cosmos and nicotiana, are two of the most dependable annuals, giving weeks of colorful blossoms throughout the summer.

mallow blossoms, 'Mont Blanc' with glistening white flowers on compact, bushy plants, and 'Mont Rose,' its rose-colored counterpart, are outstanding border annuals, tirelessly flowering till frost.

Nicotiana, flowering tobacco, should never be omitted from the summer garden, but be sure to plant a scented form. The colorful dwarf tobacco varieties that flower in shades of red, pink, white, or green have the advantage that they are open during the daylight hours, but they usually lack the most essential and delightful attribute of nicotiana, its strong, wonderfully narcotic evening perfume. Instead, plant *Nicotiana alata* 'Grandiflora' or *N. sylvestris* for the best scent; both are attractive plants, about 4ft/1.2m tall, with creamy white nocturnal flowers. Their perfume is the best of all plants in late summer. Nicotiana requires a long growth period and lots of warmth; sow seed early indoors or start the previous year.

Left A colorful composition of scented herbaceous perennials for the sunny summer garden. The yellow flowers of yarrow (*Achillea*) are pungently aromatic, as are their leaves when bruised. They are excellent for cutting and drying for winter arrangements. The pure white bells of the summer hyacinth (*Galtonia*) emit a sweet, soft scent. The versatile catmint (*Nepeta × faassenii*) is valuable as a summer ground cover as well as for its lovely hues of blue and gray; both the leaves and flowers are aromatic.

Right Perennial red-hot pokers (*Kniphofia*) and the equally vibrant annual Mexican sunflower (*Tithonia*) combine to give a fiery summer spectacle. For best performance, both require a deep rich soil and the warmth of a sunny sheltered spot.

Scabiosa atropurpurea, the annual scabious, is another fragrant, old-fashioned summer delight. Its long-stemmed purple, crimson, pink, or white pincushion blossoms are most attractive in a border – not least for butterflies – and as long-lasting cut flowers for the house.

Acroclinum and *Xeranthemum annuum* are two of the best "everlasting" flowers, which are not only charming for dried arrangements but are also good in the flower border. Acroclinum, the Swan River everlasting from Australia, is delicate in habit and softer in color and texture than the better-known strawflower (*Helichrysum bracteatum*). Its flowers are semi-double, in pale shades of pink with golden yellow centers. Xeranthemum, the pretty paper flower, is seldom seen but is easy to grow. The flowers are single or semidouble, in white or shades of lilac or pink. They flower for weeks on end in late summer. Both species of everlastings can be sown in full sun, where they are to flower.

Erigeron karvinskianus is a perfect annual for growing in nooks in a wall or in cracks and crevices along steps. This Mexican species can become a weed if it finds your garden to

its liking, seeding itself with abandon in paving cracks. Nevertheless, its small daisylike flowers are so naively charming that it should be welcomed in every garden. It blossoms all summer in various shades of pink and white on airy, wiry 12in/300mm stems.

Tithonia rotundifolia, the Mexican sunflower, is a tall, robust, and dramatic annual, easy to grow where there is plenty of heat in summer. Tithonia flowers in vivid orange-scarlet or chrome yellow and is a good cut flower for fiery-hot floral arrangements.

Perennial flowers
Late summer is also the season for the extrovert herbaceous perennials from the Compositae family, such as *Helenium*, *Coreopsis*, *Heliopsis*, and *Rudbeckia*, most of which originated in the plains and prairies of North America. All of them are sturdy species with brightly colored, rather straightforward blossoms mostly in brazen shades of yellow, gold, or red. They are plants that make good companions to the summer-flowering annuals and homely vegetables in an integrated garden plan. All associate well together and are best when grouped in

irregular masses, as if naturalized, rather than formally planted, but they also look good in enormous pots. At a time when few plants of European origin are in flower, these healthy children of the sunny prairie are highly valued for their contribution to late summer flower borders. Varieties of helenium are particularly useful as "bridge" plants, flowering as they do together with the last of the tall phlox and lasting till the first of the fall chrysanthemums.

Coreopsis verticillata 'Grandiflora' is a beautiful mound-shaped plant, about 18in/450mm high and somewhat more across, with masses of fine, ferny foliage. It is much daintier than many of the other composites now in flower. The rich golden blossoms are borne for many weeks during midsummer and late summer; they are like small daisies, about 2in/50mm in diameter, produced in great profusion on thin, graceful stalks.

The monardas, known as bergamot, bee balm, or oswego tea, have pleasantly aromatic leaves which can be used to brew a refreshing summer tea with a taste somewhere between anise and lemon. They are closely related to the culinary mints, with which they share a tendency to spread if they find your garden fits their requirements. Their flowers are curiously constructed: each has a central cone from which emerge rings of curved, claw-shaped tubular flowers. Among the best cultivars are 'Cambridge Scarlet' with brilliant red flowers which emerge from a maroon center; 'Croftway Pink' with bright rosy pink flowers which are splendid together with blue or white blossoms; and 'Beauty of Cobham' which blooms in a softer, paler pink, wonderful as a partner to deep purple flowers. Monardas prefer a moist, deep, rich soil in full sun.

The tall perennial *Phlox paniculata* has the same preferences for moist soil and a sunny location. It can be found in virtually every country garden in the USA, where no perennial border is complete without several of the fragrant phlox varieties. Phloxes flower in shades of white, pink, red, purple, and lavender, often with a central eye of a contrasting color. Not a plant for a refined or elegant planting design, phlox fits perfectly into more informal flower borders, but choose your colors carefully. For sheer massing of color, phloxes are unexcelled at this season, but mildew can be a big problem. Many phloxes have a quiet, delicate perfume that is so typical of the cottage-style garden in late summer.

Many varieties of the tall perennial phlox (*Phlox paniculata*) emit a fresh sweet scent as they open. Among the best white-flowering cultivars are the robust 'Alba Grandiflora' as well as 'White Admiral,' 'Pax,' and 'Mount Fujiyama,' which is the whitest phlox of all. Phlox grows best in a fresh deep soil, rich in humus.

PLANTS FOR LATE SUMMER

Blue and mauve
Buddleja davidii 'Black Knight,' 'Dartmoor,' 'Empire Blue,' 'Ile de France,' 'Purple Prince'
Caryopteris × clandonensis 'Arthur Simmonds,' 'Heavenly Blue,' 'Kew Blue'
C. incana
Ceanothus × delileanus 'Gloire de Versailles,' 'Henri Desfossé,' 'Topaz'
Hibiscus syriacus 'Oiseau Bleu' (*H.s.* 'Blue Bird')
Lavandula angustifolia 'Hidcote,' 'Munstead'
Perovskia abrotanoides
P. atriplicifolia
Clematis 'Kathleen Wheeler,' 'Perle d'Azur,' 'Mrs Cholmondeley'
Aconitum 'Bressingham Spire'
A. napellus
A. paniculatum
Aster amellus 'Sternkugel,' 'Veilchenkönigin' ('Violet Queen'), 'Moerheim Gem'
A. × frikartii 'Mönch,' 'Wunder von Stäfa'
A. sedifolius 'Nanus'
Baptisia australis
Calamintha nepeta
Ceratostigma plumbaginoides
Clematis heracleifolia + *C.h. davidiana*
C. integrifolia 'Hendersonii,' 'Olgae'
Delphinium cultivars
Echinops bannaticus 'Blue Globe,' 'Taplow Blue'
E. ritro 'Veitch's Blue' + *E.r. ruthenicus*
Erigeron hybrids
Eryngium tricuspidatum
E. × tripartitum
Gentiana asclepiadea
G. dahurica

G. septemfida lagodechiana
Liatris spicata 'Floristan Violet'
Nepeta 'Six Hills Giant'
N. × faassenii
Scabiosa caucasica 'Clive Greaves,' Moerheim Blue,' 'Nachtfalter'
Thalictrum delavayi (T. dipterocarpum)
Veronica longifolia 'Blauriesen' ('Blue Giant'), 'Blaue Sommer' ('Blue Summer')
Iris laevigata
Pontederia cordata

White and cream
Aralia elata + *A.e.* 'Variegata'
Buddleja davidii 'Peace,' 'White Profusion'
Clethra alnifolia
C. barbinervis
Hydrangea paniculata

'Grandiflora'
Potentilla fruticosa 'Abbotswood'
Sophora japonica
Yucca filamentosa
Y. flaccida 'Ivory'
Rosa cultivars
Clematis 'Huldine,' 'Marie Boisselot'
Lonicera periclymenum 'Serotina'
Anaphalis triplinervis 'Sommerschnee'
A. thunbergii 'Professor van der Wielen'
Astrantia major
Centranthus ruber 'Albus'
Cimicifuga racemosa
Delphinium cultivars
Erigeron hybrids
Filipendula kamtschatica
Gypsophila paniculata 'Schneeflocke' ('Snowflake'), 'Bristol Fairy'

Hemerocallis hybrids
Hosta 'Royal Standard'
H. plantaginea 'Grandiflora'
Leucanthemum × superba (*Chrysanthemum maximum*)
Liatris spicata 'Floristan White'
Monarda 'Snow White'
Phlox paniculata cultivars
Physostegia virginiana 'Summer Snow'
Scabiosa causasica 'Miss Willmott,' 'Loddon White'
Galtonia candicans
Alisma plantago-aquatica
Aponogeton distachyos
Nymphaea hybrids

Yellow and orange
Hypericum calycinum
H. 'Hidcote'
H. × moserianum
Koelreuteria paniculata

Hosta plantaginea

Potentilla fruticosa 'Goldfinger,'
  'Gold Star,' 'Primrose Beauty'
Santolina chamaecyparissus
Rosa cultivars
Campsis radicans 'Flava'
Clematis tibetana vernayi (*C.
  orientalis*)
C. tangutica
Lonicera × *heckrottii* + *L.* × *h.*
  'Goldflame'
Achillea 'Coronation Gold'
A. filipendulina 'Altgold,' 'Gold
  Plate,' 'Parker's Variety'
Alcea ficifolia
Coreopsis grandiflora 'Sunray'
C. lanceolata 'Goldfink,'
C. verticillata 'Grandiflora,'
  'Moonbeam,' 'Zagreb'
Gaillardia hybrids
Helenium hybrids
Helianthus decapetalus 'Capenoch
  Star,' 'Soleil d'Or,' 'Maximus
  Flore Pleno'
Heliopsis hybrids
Hemerocallis hybrids
H. citrina
Kirengeshoma palmata
Kniphofia 'Bressingham Comet,'
  'Green Lemon,' 'Lemon Ice,'
  'Limelight'
Ligularia dentata + *L.d.* 'Orange
  Queen,' 'Desdemona'
L. przewalskii + *L.p.* 'The
  Rocket,' 'Gigant'
L. 'Gregynog Gold'
L. × *palmatiloba*
Oenothera missouriensis
O. tetragona var. *fraseri* + *O.t.*
  'Hohes Licht,' 'Sonnenwende'

A cottage-style garden mix of
roses, tall pink hollyhocks (*Alcea
rosea*), silver-leaved *Stachys
byzantina* and rose campion
(*Lychnis coronaria*), and wine red
Allium sphaerocephalon.

Rudbeckia fulgida deamii + *R.f.
  sullivanti* 'Goldsturm'
R. laciniata 'Golden Glow'
R. nitida 'Herbstsonne', 'Juli
  Gold'
Solidago 'Golden Gate,' 'Golden
  Shower,' 'Ledsham,' 'Leraft,'
  'Strahlenkrone'
Nymphaea hybrids
Nymphoides peltata
Ranunculus lingua 'Grandiflora'

Red and pink
Buddleja davidii 'Fascination,'
  'Royal Red'
Calluna vulgaris 'Carmen,'
  'County Wicklow,'
  'J.H.Hamilton,'
  'Alportii'
Ceanothus × *pallidus* 'Marie
  Simon'
Fuchsia magellanica gracilis
F. 'Riccartonii'
Hibiscus syriacus 'Hamabo,'
  'Woodbridge'
Lespedeza thunbergii
Rosa cultivars
Campsis radicans
C. × *tagliabuana* 'Mme Galen'
Clematis 'Ernest Markham,'
  'Gipsy Queen,' 'Nelly Moser,'
  'Ville de Lyon,' 'Mme Baron
  Veillard'
Acanthus hungaricus
A. mollis
A. spinosus
Anemone × *hybrida* 'Superba'
A. hupehensis 'Praecox,'
  'September Charm,'
  'Splendens'
A. tomentosa 'Robustissima'
Astilbe × *arendsii* 'Cattleya,'
  'Bressingham Beauty,'
  'Hyazinth'
Astilbe japonica 'Red Sentinel'
A. thunbergii 'Straussenfeder'
  ('Ostrich Plume')

Astrantia major rosea
Centranthus ruber + *C.r. coccineus*
Erigeron hybrids
Gaillardia hybrids
Helenium hybrids
Hemerocallis hybrids
Kniphofia 'Bressingham Flame'
Lavatera thuringiaca
Lychnis coronaria
Monarda 'Adam,' 'Croftway Pink,'
  'Prärieglut' ('Prairie Glow'),
  'Prärienacht' ('Prairie Night')
Phlox paniculata cultivars
Physostegia virginiana 'Bouquet
  Rose,' 'Summer Spire'
Alcea rosea
Allium sphaerocephalon
Cyclamen hederifolium
Alisma plantago-aquatica
Butomus umbellatus
Eupatorium purpureum
E. maculatum 'Atropurpureum'
Iris laevigata 'Rose Queen'
Nymphaea hybrids

Scented plants
Buddleja davidii cultivars
Clethra alnifolia
C. barbinervis
Sophora japonica
Yucca filamentosa
Rosa cultivars
Clematis tibetana vernayi
Lonicera × *heckrottii*
L. periclymenum 'Serotina'
Clematis heracleifolia davidiana
C. integrifolia 'Olgae'
Hemerocallis citrina
Hosta plantaginea 'Grandiflora'
Phlox paniculata cultivars
Galtonia candicans
Aponogeton distachyos
Nymphaea hybrids

Plants for bees and butterflies
Buddleja davidii cultivars
Calluna vulgaris cultivars

Caryopteris incana
C. × *clandonensis* cultivars
Clethra alnifolia
C. barbinervis
Hibiscus syriacus cultivars
Hypericum species
Koelreuteria paniculata
Perovskia abrotanoides
P. atriplicifolia + *P.a.* 'Blue Spire'
P. 'Blue Haze'
Sophora japonica
Rosa – single-flowered cultivars
Aconitum species
Alcea ficifolia
Aster amellus cultivars
A. × *frikartii* cultivars
A. sedifolius
Astrantia major + *A.m.* 'Rosea'
Baptisia australis
Calamintha nepeta
Centranthus ruber
Coreopsis cultivars
Echinops species + cultivars
Erigeron hybrids
Eryngium species
Helianthus species + single-
  flowered cultivars
Heliopsis helianthoides scabra
  hybrids
Leucanthemum × *superbum*
  (*Chrysanthemum maximum*) –
  single-flowered cultivars
Liatris spicata
Ligularia species + cultivars
Monarda hybrids
Nepeta × *faassenii*
Oenothera species + cultivars
Phlox paniculata cultivars
Rudbeckia species + cultivars
Scabiosa caucasica cultivars
Solidago hybrids
Veronica longifolia cultivars
Allium sphaerocephalon
Butomus umbellatus
Eupatorium purpureum
E. maculatum 'Atropurpureum'

LATE SUMMER TASKS

TREES AND SHRUBS

Pruning

Deciduous shrubs that blossom on the previous year's wood and have finished flowering may need pruning now. Species such as *Buddleja alternifolia*, *B. globosa*, *Philadelphus* cultivars, tamarisks, deutzias, lilacs, and weigelas may need pruning annually or every two or three years to keep them within bounds and retain their shape. When such shrubs become crowded with unproductive shoots at the base, carry weak or damaged wood, or show signs of declining vigor, they should be pruned, about two weeks after their flowers have faded, not in winter or early spring.

Generally pruning consists of thinning out enough worn out, old branches and weak, crowded younger ones to ensure that those remaining receive adequate light and free circulation of air. At the same time any overlong branches may be cut back to a lower, strong, and well-placed new shoot. When pruning, always aim to preserve the natural habit of the shrub and do not spoil its balance and symmetry. If necessary, shorten any remaining shoots that are too long by cutting back to the main stems that you are retaining.

Never prune lavender now, as this stimulates new growth that usually does not have enough time to ripen well enough to withstand winter frost. Many tidy gardeners cut away the old, faded flower spikes

Pruning summer-flowering shrubs

Thin out and open up an overcrowded shrub by cutting out about a quarter of the old stems, as well as any weak new ones, at ground level. Then, if necessary, shorten some shoots

by cutting back to where they join the well-situated branches that you wish to retain. Thinning out (*above*) preserves the shrub's general form and balance. Merely shortening branches will only produce several new shoots from the uppermost buds.

in late summer or early fall to maintain a neat appearance. But if you live in an area with cold winters, it is a good idea to leave these old flower stalks until early spring, for they give the evergreen foliage some protection from severe winter weather.

Taking cuttings

A large number of shrubs can be easily propagated by means of cuttings taken now from semiripe wood (see page 156). Such popular shrubs as box, ceanothus, and lavender are typical for this group of woody plants for which cuttings from semiripe shoots are almost always successful. Semiripe cuttings may be made as soon as this year's shoots have started to become firm at the base but are not yet woody. Late summer is also an excellent time to root cuttings taken from the nonflowering shoots of many species of *Erica* and *Calluna*.

Planting and transplanting evergreens

In late summer planting time commences for conifers and for most of the broadleaved evergreens, with the possible exception of the more tender species, which are generally better planted in early spring. Digging and transplanting necessarily reduces the root system and severely limits the plant's ability to absorb enough water to replace that lost during transpiration. To reduce water stress as much as possible, transplant only when top growth is firm and mature and the soil is warm enough to encourage speedy growth of new roots.

If, by late summer, growth of new shoots has ceased you may plant now; otherwise wait until early fall. The new shoots should always be sufficiently hardened to withstand transplanting with a minimum of distress. (See page 115 for advice on transplanting conifers and other evergreen shrubs.)

When you buy new conifers and broadleaved evergreens they will always come either in containers or with root balls wrapped in sacking. It is important that the soil around the roots is never allowed to dry out. To ensure that the soil is thoroughly moist, soak the entire root ball with water before planting. After planting, continue watering regularly until new roots have become well established. (See page 153 for planting techniques for container plants and plants with balled roots.) Now is a good time to plant all evergreen hedges.

Hedge trimming

Many formal hedges can still be trimmed during late summer. Conifers and slow-growing evergreen species such as yew and holly, which are usually trimmed only once each year, can be pruned toward the end of this season or at the beginning of early fall. Faster-growing species such as privet may also require monthly trimming up to the end of early autumn to keep them dense and tidy. You may also prefer to give formal hornbeam or beech hedges their annual pruning now. However, deciduous hedges requiring more radical

Shaping formal hedges
The illustrations show the untrimmed state, with cuts to achieve the shape required and, on the right, the skeletal or winter form of a deciduous hedge where, at first, the overall form is difficult to see.

To achieve a dense trapezoid shape in the first year after planting, cut back any vertical and lateral branches that are too long. The remaining leaf buds will be stimulated into growth and start to branch in the following spring.

In the second and third years cut back the long upward-growing stems to stimulate the growth of the side wood. Trim side branches to encourage the branches to thicken. The final hedge shape is gradually appearing.

cutting back may be left till the winter (see page 147).

Whatever sort of hedge you are pruning, be sure to shorten only the new growths; do not cut back into old wood for normal maintenance pruning. If new growth has been weak, it may be better to delay pruning somewhat in order to allow the leaves to absorb nourishment as long as possible; this strengthens the plant and encourages better roots. Normally, however, try to complete this year's trimming by the end of this season, especially if you live in an area with cold winters. Hedges trimmed too late may produce new growth which cannot ripen sufficiently to withstand the first heavy frosts.

ROSES

Deadheading and watering
In the rose garden, deadheading and watering continue to be the most important regular tasks, both of which promote further flowering and help keep roses free from diseases such as mildew.

Fertilizing
After midsummer, roses should no longer be fed with fertilizers rich in nitrogen, which stimulates continued production of new growths. New canes formed so late in the season cannot ripen sufficiently before winter and such soft, succulent growth is much more subject to winter damage than firm, well-ripened shoots.

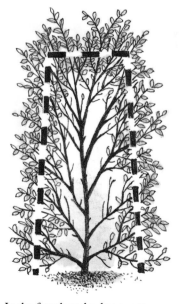

In the fourth and subsequent years side growth is held back and the hedge trimmed to achieve a good symmetrical shape. Upward growth can gradually be allowed to achieve the desired height.

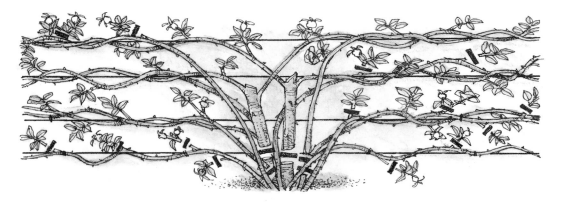

Pruning rambler roses
If there are enough replacement shoots growing from ground level to retain a good framework, cut out all the old canes completely close to ground level, leaving about six new stems. If there are not enough new stems, or if an old stem has a strong new shoot growing from it, cut the old stem away just above the junction. Tie up the replacement shoots, spreading them out evenly.

If you live in an area with cold winters, dress your roses with a potassium fertilizer that does not promote new growth but helps ripen woody tissues. About six weeks before the first frosts are expected, scatter a handful of sulfate of potash or two handfuls of wood ashes per square yard/meter over the soil surface and hoe in lightly. Any phosphorus and potassium or potassium and magnesium fertilizer can also be applied according to package directions.

Pruning ramblers
Rambler roses, such as the old favorites 'American Pillar' and 'Dorothy Perkins,' differ from other climbing roses in flowering only once a year, in one great flush during early summer, on side shoots of long canes which grew during the previous year. Each year after flowering, ramblers produce vigorous, long, and comparatively slender new canes from the base of the plant, and these and the old canes can become hopelessly entangled, making pruning necessary.

Fortunately, ramblers are simple to prune although you may need to untie the stems from their supports in order to sort them out more easily; remove some older canes to make room for renewal growths. Wherever there is sufficient space for their growth, ramblers may be allowed to grow for a few years without pruning; in this way you can obtain a lovely, less orderly, more natural effect.

CLIMBING PLANTS

Tying in
Continue to tie in and train new growths of clematis and other rapidly growing climbing plants whenever you spot a loose, errant end.

Pruning wisteria
The new lateral shoots of wisteria should be pruned now as soon as possible if you have not completed this already; only if you do so can you be sure of abundant flowers next year and avoid a hopeless tangle of barren vines. Shorten all laterals now to two or three leaves in order to divert energy into the formation of flower buds (see page 87).

Planting clematis
Clematis can be planted equally well in late summer or early spring. Their roots range deeply and need a fertile soil, well prepared to a depth of at least 20in/500mm. To avoid injuring the roots, insert a stake before planting to lead the clematis to its support. Slant the root ball toward the support and sit the plant about 4in/100mm deeper in the ground than it grew in the pot.

HERBACEOUS PERENNIALS

Deadheading
Continue deadheading herbaceous perennials as their flowers fade. However, since plants flowering after midsummer are unlikely to bloom a second time if cut back, consider whether the plant might look better if left alone. If the old flower stalks are unsightly, it is generally better to cut them away, unless they will provide some protection to overwintering plants. Some freely flowering perennials, such as coreopsis, gaillardia, centranthus, and shasta daisies, should be cut back hard immediately after flowering so that strength can be gathered for next year.

Planting
Now is a good time for planting all herbaceous perennials that flower in spring and early summer. The soil is warm and conditions are favorable for rapid growth of new roots; well-established plants will be able to withstand the winter months and will give you a better first

season's display than those planted in the spring.

You may also plant peonies in late summer. Prepare the planting site very well, for once they become established, peonies can remain for many years in one spot, steadily increasing in size and beauty from year to year. Peonies are heavy feeders and require a deep fertile soil, rich in humus, so work lots of ripe compost into the top soil layer, to a depth of about 24in/600mm. The planting depth is important, as peonies will not flower if planted too deeply. The top of the peony root should be covered with no more than 2in/50mm of soil.

Dividing

Summer-flowering herbaceous perennials that have become over-crowded or are showing signs of decline may be lifted and divided after they have finished blooming (see page 159). There are a few exceptions to this rule, such as bergamot (*Monarda*) and scabious as well as the ornamental grasses and ferns, which are better left until early spring. Hellebores, which flower in winter and into spring, can also be divided now, so that they can become reestablished before winter sets in.

ANNUALS AND BIENNIALS

Sowing hardy plants

Some hardy annuals can be sown now, in the beds where they are to flower, for early blossoms next year. Suitable ones include: *Calendula officinalis* (pot marigold), *Centaurea cyanus* (cornflower), *Echium plantagineum* (bugloss), *Eschscholzia californica* (California poppy), *Iberis amara* (rocket candytuft), *I. umbellata* (candytuft), *Lobularia maritima* (sweet alyssum), *Nigella damascena* (love-in-a-mist), and *Papaver rhoeas* (Shirley poppy).

Planting ornamental salad varieties

Young plants of decorative fall salad varieties, such as endives and the colorful ornamental kale, can be planted among the other border plants wherever space becomes available.

Cutting back biennials

Some biennials can be coaxed into flowering another year if they are cut back hard after flowering. Hollyhocks, foxgloves, Iceland poppies, and sweet Williams usually produce new growth which will last the winter to bloom a second time if you cut them back to the ground as soon as their flowers fade.

Planting biennials

Young plants of many of the hardier biennials can be planted outdoors now in the borders where they are to bloom next year, for example: hollyhocks, Canterbury bells, sweet Williams, and sweet rocket.

BULBS

Planting

Bulb planting continues to be an important task in late summer. First on your agenda should be to get any fall-flowering bulbs that are still waiting to be planted into the ground as quickly as possible.

Now is also the best time to replant any narcissus bulbs that you dug up after flowering and stored over the summer. Clean and divide them, discarding any obviously diseased bulbs. Tiger lilies may be propagated by removing the bulbils (see below).

Some spring-flowering species should be planted as soon as they can be obtained; for example, dog's tooth violets (*Erythronium*), crown imperials (*Fritillaria imperialis*), snowdrops (*Galanthus*), snowflakes (*Leucojum*), and grape hyacinths (*Muscari*) all do best if they are out of the ground for as short a time as possible.

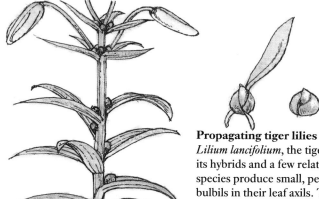

Propagating tiger lilies
Lilium lancifolium, the tiger lily, its hybrids and a few related species produce small, pea-sized bulbils in their leaf axils. These can be removed and propagated much like seeds.

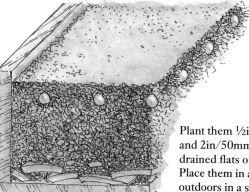

Plant them ½in/15mm deep and 2in/50mm apart in well-drained flats of sandy compost. Place them in a coldframe or outdoors in a sheltered seed bed.

Planting madonna lilies

Unlike most other lilies, madonna lilies (*Lilium candidum*) should be planted now in late summer, during their short dormant period; for most of the rest of the year, this species bears foliage and, in order to flower the following summer, must form a flat rosette of leaves in fall, which remains green throughout the winter.

Madonna lilies require a well-drained soil. The bulbs should be planted with their tips no more than 2in/50mm below the surface. Place them in informal groups of five to eleven bulbs about 8in/200mm apart.

Planting eremurus

It is best to plant eremurus, the imposing foxtail lily, in late summer. Choose a warm, sunny location with good drainage. If your soil is sandy and well-drained, then a planting hole 6–8in/150–200mm deep is sufficient. In heavy and poorly drained soil, dig the hole to a depth of 20in/500mm; fill in first with a 8in/200mm layer of gravel and cover it with 4in/100mm of good sandy soil.

The planting hole must be wide enough to spread out the fleshy, octopuslike roots. Fill in with good garden soil so that the large central bud is covered to a depth of 4–6in/100–150mm.

Fertilizing

Every two weeks apply applications of a quick-acting liquid fertilizer to dahlias, gladioli, tuberous begonias, and other tender summer-flowering "bulbs" that are still in full bloom. Dahlias especially can be kept blooming for weeks on end if they are fed regularly with a foliar fertilizer. As well as maintaining flowers of good quality, feeding now with a phosphorus-rich balanced fertilizer helps produce strong bulbs, corms, and tubers to be dug later for winter storage.

THE WATER GARDEN

A pool in biological equilibrium usually demands little attention during late summer, though in general, the regular housekeeping tasks described for early summer and midsummer should be kept up during this season.

LAWN AND FLOWER MEADOW

Lawn mowing after vacations

If your lawn was untended and has grown long while you were away for a summer vacation, do not be tempted to cut the grass short at the first mowing, as you will only succeed in giving bothersome weeds a chance to gain a hold. Bring it back into top shape gradually. Raise the lawn mower blades so that they cut no more than half the height of the tallest blades of grass; that will shorten the grass to a manageable length without weakening the grass plants. Irrigate thoroughly if the soil under the lawn is dry. A few days later – five to seven depending on weather and growth conditions – you can mow a second time, adjusting the mower to cut the grass a little shorter than before. Repeat this procedure for the next few weeks, until the grass is at the right height for your type of lawn.

Cutting the flower meadow

A flower meadow which needs a second cutting may be scythed now. The timing will depend on the species composition of your meadow, but on no account let a flower meadow go into winter with grass that is too long.

Sowing a new lawn

In areas with severe, cold winters, now is the best time to sow a new lawn, early spring is the second best. (See page 35.) Soil temperature and rainfall are both normally high enough to encourage rapid germination of grass seed. In areas with less severe winters, sowing can continue into early fall or be left until early spring.

PATIO AND BALCONY

Fertilizing container plants

Annuals and other classic container, tub, or window box plants should still be fed weekly with a balanced liquid fertilizer. Well-fertilized and cared for, they will continue flowering until frosts begin.

Permanent plantings of shrubs and herbaceous perennials in containers should not receive any further fertilizer till next spring. To survive the winter, they should be encouraged to cease active growth now and to ripen their shoots in preparation for cold weather.

Pelargonium cuttings

If you prefer to overwinter pelargoniums as young plants from cuttings, these should be taken now to ensure strong plants before winter sets in. Choose plump shoots and make cuttings about 4in/100mm long. Insert them in a mixture of sand and peat; they should take root quickly.

CHAPTER 7

EARLY FALL

"Behold congenial autumn comes,
The sabbath of the year!"

John Logan

The unmistakable, and always reliable, signal for the beginning of early fall is the appearance of the pink flowers of the autumn crocus (*Colchicum autumnale*). Almost simultaneously, the dark berries of the European elder (*Sambucus nigra*) ripen, together with the sealing wax red hips of the English dog rose (*Rosa canina*).

Autumn crocus, as in its natural habitat, flourishes and looks good growing in grass. The leafless flowers rising from the bare soil are often called "naked ladies" or "naked boys". The corms should be planted in midsummer, about 6–8in/150–200mm apart in an irregular fashion to make an informal, natural effect. They grow best in cool, moist, deep and fertile soil, but need shallow planting: 2–2½in/50–60mm is sufficient. *Colchicum speciosum*, a closely related species from the Near East, normally flowers about three weeks later than *C. autumnale*. The cultivars of *C. speciosum* have larger, showier, and more vulnerable blooms than those of the native plant.

Left Because it resembles the true crocus, meadow saffron, *Colchicum autumnale*, is also known as autumn crocus. Seen here with bramble leaves, its own will not appear until spring.

THE EARLY FALL GARDEN

The flowering year in the garden rapidly draws to a close in early fall, as longer nights and calm clear skies allow temperatures to fall. Now is the time to take advantage of what is likely to be the most stable period of good weather in the entire year, often known as "Indian Summer" or "Old wives' summer." Major garden maintenance projects that require a stretch of fine weather are best planned for early fall.

Fall gardens brim over with brilliant yellows and warm, glowing reds, mauves, and browns of the many composites now in flower – chrysanthemums, coreopsis, gaillardias, heliopsis, helianthus, heleniums and rudbeckias. This is also the season to enjoy some of the most perfectly formed roses of the year. These late-flowering roses can form the backbone of a warm and sunny garden in early fall, which is just as rich in floral scents and colors as it was in midsummer. A garden design planned around them, with pinks, blues, and white, offers a welcome relief to the more usual and sometimes strident yellows and oranges, and allows the pink-flowering colchicum into the composition.

Shrub roses

One of the older shrub roses is 'Comte de Chambord,' a delightful Portland rose, ideal for even the smallest garden, thanks to its small, compact growth habit. 'Comte de Chambord' is sturdy and robust, erect in form but not more than about 4ft/1.2m tall. The large, densely filled flowers are of rich clear pink with an intense and heady damask rose fragrance. This first-class plant with its large, attractive gray-green leaves combines a genuine old rose character with repeat flowering, making it one of the best choices for any rose garden.

Just as venerable, 'Reine des Violettes' is a hybrid perpetual shrub rose which combines the charming flower shape of the old gallica roses with a perpetual flowering habit and soft gray-green foliage. The wonderfully perfumed flowers are a deep, velvety violet. This rose makes an upright bush, about 4–5ft/1.2–1.5m tall; it requires good cultivation if it is to give the best performance.

Right Late-flowering perennials such as mauve hardy asters and white shasta daisies (chrysanthemums) give a burst of color before night-frosts end the display.

Although bred early in this century, 'Ferdinand Pichard' has the aura of an even more antique rose. Its large, cup-shaped flowers are clear pink, striped and splashed with vivid crimson; the pink soon fades to blush while the crimson darkens to purple. The blossoms are not completely double but possess a distinct fragrance; they combine well with the rich green foliage. Generally considered to be the best of the striped roses, 'Ferdinand Pichard' is particularly valuable because it continues to bear its flowers intermittently throughout the summer and fall, after its first glorious flush is over. It forms a small bushy shrub, about 5ft/1.5m tall, making it ideal for the smaller garden.

'Nevada' is a much larger shrub rose, growing easily to a height and breadth of 8ft/2.5m. It is a superb rose which combines dependably repeated flowering with the graceful growth habit of a wild rose. It makes a shapely dense shrub with long, arching, almost thornless canes which are smothered along their entire length with large semidouble blossoms. The creamy white flowers open flat to reveal a center of yellow stamens; individually they are a trifle blowsy, but together their mass effect makes a breathtaking floral show. 'Nevada' is a vigorous and thoroughly healthy rose, scarcely ever attacked by mildew. After a first glorious performance in early summer, it flowers intermittently throughout the summer and often gives a good performance in early fall.

Perhaps the most powerfully fragrant of all the roses, 'Mme Isaac Pereire' bears huge flowers, often as large as 5in/120mm across. They are rich rose-red shaded with magenta, cupped at first, opening to a flat and quartered saucer, the petals being rolled back at the edges. It can be grown effectively as a large shrub or small climber, trained to a pergola or trellis; it will easily reach 6½ft/2m. The foliage is large, bold, and deep green in color. The sumptuous flowers appear in several bursts, but those in early fall are the finest of the year. When well grown, in rich fertile soil, 'Mme Isaac Pereire' is unequaled for beauty of form, richness of color, and intensity of scent.

The legendary Bourbon rose, 'Zéphirine Drouhin,' is deservedly one of the most popular for performance and length of flowering season. The fragrant semidouble flowers are of a bright cerise-pink. The young shoots and leaves are bronze-red at first, changing to gray-green as they mature. As a climber 'Zéphirine Drouhin' will easily cover a wall to a height of 10–15ft/3–4.5m, but beware – red brick does not become her. Unfortunately this rose is susceptible to mildew – its only defect – but this can be overcome by planting against a northfacing wall, where it thrives better than any other rose. It can also be grown in the open, as a shrub.

Any perpetually flowering climber is to be cherished, particularly if it has such lovely, exquisitely shaped, and deliciously fragrant blossoms as 'New Dawn.' This legendary American rose bears small pink blossoms, produced freely in clusters for many weeks from midsummer through early fall. 'New Dawn' may be pruned to form a lax shrub or grown as a hedge; on a pillar or pergola, it will frequently remain short, but given the benefit of a wall, it will achieve 13–19ft/4–6m. This rose is noted for its plentiful, glossy foliage which remains virtually free of disease throughout its growing season.

Blue-flowering shrubs

True blue-flowering shrubs, which complement so well the pinks and reds of the rose blossoms, are scarce in the garden at all seasons, so we are doubly lucky to have caryopteris and perovskia, two attractive shrubs with flowers in shades of blue that may be at their prime during early fall and blossom at the same time as the last roses.

Caryopteris × *clandonensis* is a hybrid shrub with grayish green aromatic foliage, which is covered during late summer and early fall with abundant feathery clusters of blue flowers. The most valuable named hybrids are 'Heavenly Blue,' with bright lavender blue flowers, and 'Kew Blue,' with flowers of a darker, richer blue. Caryopteris forms a knee-high mounded shrub which fits perfectly into a mixed border. It prefers a sunny location but is not at all particular about soil, so long as it is well drained. Its shoots freeze back in severe winters, but, even so, nothing is lost: caryopteris flowers on the current season's new growths and needs to be pruned back hard each spring in order to maintain its best form and flower production. Cutting back each shoot of the previous year's growth to about two pairs of buds forms a compact bush and produces stronger new shoots with larger trusses of flowers.

Perovskia atriplicifolia, known as Russian sage, also freezes back to the ground regularly in harsh winters, but responds well to the same pruning treatment as caryopteris. This beautiful Himalayan shrub has finely cut, aromatic gray foliage and white stems; it bears long spikes of lavender blue flowers in late summer and early fall, which blend perfectly with the powdery gray foliage. Russian sage grows 3–5ft/0.9–1.5m tall; its long, stiff branches make a loose, open upright shrub. Since it does not spread widely, several can be grouped together with good effect. It thrives in any good, well-drained soil on a sunny site. The distinctive overall tone of blue-gray makes perovskia a wonderful partner for pink roses. The hybrid 'Blue Spire' has larger flowers of a warm lavender-blue and deeply cut leaves.

Much smaller than Russian sage, two relatively uncommon *Nepeta* species, late-flowering relatives of the popular catmint, are every bit as valuable for their attractive blue flowers. *N. nervosa* is a lovely species with brilliant gray-green leaves marked with conspicuous veins and pretty, pale lavender-blue flowers borne in 'dense cylindrical spikes. It grows 12–20in/ 300–500mm tall as a loosely upright, bushy herbaceous perennial. *N. sibirica* grows about twice as tall and bears its radiant lavender-blue flowers in distinctly separated tiers on erect leafy stems throughout late summer and early fall. Each flower is about 1in/25mm long or slightly larger. Like the other members of the *Nepeta* genus, this charming herbaceous perennial requires a well-drained soil. If it likes your garden, it will spread freely.

For a rich indigo blue, a thoroughly uncommon color this late in the year, there is no plant better than the perennial leadwort (*Ceratostigma plumbaginoides*). The foliage takes on scarlet and maroon tones in late fall, while the plant is still in flower. This native of China has slender, much-branched spreading stems that produce erect leafy shoots up to 12in/300mm high, each terminating in a dense cluster of flowers. Ceratostigma flowers continuously from late summer until the first frost, each blossom being about ½in/15mm in diameter. Any well-drained soil in full sun suits it perfectly well. Although it is not always easy to establish, once it gets going it develops rapidly and extensively, spreading freely by slender underground rhizomes, making it a first-class ground-cover plant and excellent for planting in dry walls, where the blue flowers make a pleasant contrast against the stone.

Other fall-flowering shrubs

Two delightful Chinese subshrubs are too seldom planted, although they are easy to grow and produce masses of lovely pink blossoms in early fall: mint bush (*Elsholtzia stauntonii*) and bush clover (*Lespedeza thunbergii*). Although not closely

The venerable Bourbon rose 'Mme Isaac Pereire,' raised in 1881, flowers from summer onward but saves the finest splendid, heavily perfumed blossoms for early fall. The beauty of this vigorous, arching rose knows few rivals.

related, they require the same treatment and growth conditions: fertile, well-drained soil in full sun. Both freeze back regularly to the ground in winter just like caryopteris, but, with a bit of protection around the roots and hard pruning in the spring, they sprout again willingly to flower on the current year's new shoots.

Elsholtzia stauntonii makes an erect bush, up to 3¼–4ft/1–1.2m tall, with leaves that smell of mint when crushed. Throughout early fall, the plant is covered with terminal cylindrical spikes composed of masses of tiny lilac-pink flowers. Its leaves are dark green with a fine powdery bloom. *Lespedeza thunbergii* is larger, growing to about 6ft/1.8m. In early fall, often well into late fall until frost finally puts an end to its show, bush clover is covered with rich crimson-purple pea flowers, so that the overall appearance is much like that of a magnificent purple-flowering laburnum. It sprouts anew from the ground each spring to form a graceful bush with elegant, silky branches. At flowering time, the stems are often bowed to the ground by the masses of blossoms, carried in small bunches in loose, terminal panicles, each 2–2¾ft/600–800mm long. In a mixed planting, towards the back of the border or in a raised position on a bank, its graceful arching stems can be seen to good advantage.

Herbaceous perennials
Early fall is the main season for the many popular hardy aster cultivars, mostly hybrids of *Aster dumosus*, *A. novae-angliae*, and *A. novi-belgii*. Beautiful as they are, there is also another small group of less well-known North American asters which deserve to be planted in the early fall garden, largely because they have maintained much of their original charming species character.

Aster cordifolius, a native of open woodlands, is an excellent perennial to cultivate in light shade. This variable species grows up to 5ft/1.5m tall and bears small violet, blue, or white flowers with yellow centers in loose panicles. The wild form may need staking, but there is a shorter cultivar available that can do without any such assistance: 'Ideal' bears lavender-blue flowers in large trusses and grows to 3–4ft/0.9–1.2m tall.

The closely related heath aster (*A. ericoides*) is better known and has several excellent cultivars that are short enough never to require staking. Generally white, but occasionally blue or pink, the small, dainty flower heads are arranged along the wide-spreading branches of loose panicles. Unlike most other asters, this species from the open prairies loves full sun and is very tolerant of drought. The heath asters are perfect for informal, more natural mixed plantings; they possess an elegant, upright form and minute, vivid green heath-like foliage, which is attractive throughout the summer months before these plants come into blossom in early fall. What is more, the light and airy, graceful flower trusses are also suited for cutting. The best among the named cultivars are: 'Blue Star,' in pale blue, 28in/700mm tall; 'Erlkönig,' in pale violet, 3¼ft/1m tall; 'Golden Spray,' white with a touch of yellow, 32in/0.8m tall; and 'Schneetanne,' white, 4ft/1.2m tall. These cultivars are resistant to aster wilt and can grow for years on one spot without need of division.

A. × *frikartii* is a plant of exceptional beauty, perhaps the best of all the garden plants in this important genus. A robust hybrid, it flowers continuously from midsummer to late fall with lovely blue blossoms, each with a bright orange central disk. Its habit is elegant and refined, with erect stems growing to a height of about 30in/750mm, sturdy enough never to need staking. The single flowers are large, 2½–2¾in/60–70mm in diameter and are borne on long stems, making them excellent for cutting. There are two named cultivars which are readily obtainable: the excellent 'Mönch,' with warm lavender-blue blossoms, and 'Wunder von Stäfa,' with large, sky-blue blossoms. The cultivars of *A.* × *frikartii* prefer sun and deserve the best soil and a prominent position in the garden, where they blend well with pale pink and pale blue flowers and also grey foliage plants.

The calico aster (*A. lateriflorus* 'Horizontalis') is a tall erect plant, reaching 4–5ft/1.2–1.5m in height, with numerous, dense horizontal branches. The minute dark green foliage turns to coppery purple in early fall; at the same time the branches are studded with tiny white to pale pink flowers. The central disks are at first yellow but soon turn to purple, so that the general effect is a cloud of rosy lilac with a hint of coppery brown, a subtle and elegant combination of form and color. In its native habitat in eastern USA, *A. lateriflorus* inhabits open woodland and open areas along beaches. Consequently, in the garden it does best in full warm sun, but requires plenty of moisture from the ground.

The tall Japanese anemone hybrids combine particularly well with late-flowering roses and asters. The simple, refined beauty of their flowers places them among the loveliest plants of the entire garden year, as if nature had saved them up as a late surprise. These hardy herbaceous perennials tend to wander about at will, occupying any spots that suit them. Among the best cultivars are 'Honorine Jobert,' with pure white flowers, each with a conspicuous bunch of yellow

'Honorine Jobert,' a Japanese anemone of exquisite charm, flowers for weeks on end throughout fall. A vigorous branching perennial, with dark green, deeply divided leaves, it grows rapidly in any moist spot in sun or light shade.

stamens, about 4ft/1.2m tall; 'Prinz Heinrich,' a deep pink form, growing 2½–4ft/0.8–1.2m tall; and 'Queen Charlotte,' a silvery rose, about 3¼ft/1m tall. Fall-flowering anemones grow in any good garden soil, in full sun (where they need plenty of moisture) or partial shade. All are invasive, but still worthwhile for the reward of their long-lasting floral display.

Equally suited for sun or light shade, *Polygonum campanulatum* is another Asiatic perennial for a moist cool spot in the early fall border. This distinctive member of the knotweed genus is unusual as it bears its pink bell-shaped flowers in loose terminal panicles rather than in dense bottlebrush heads like most of its relatives. *P. campanulatum* grows up to three or four feet/(a meter or more) tall. It is a stout, invasive plant with attractively veined, dark green foliage. It makes an outstanding display from midsummer till frost. The tiny floral bells, carried in airy masses on the elegant branching panicles, make a stunning effect when planted in large groups toward the front of the border where the flowers can hang freely.

Ornamental grasses

Some of the ornamental grasses are at their best during early fall. *Pennisetum orientale* produces feathery bottlebrush plumes of pale pink, with long projecting purple hairs, that are just as colorful and decorative as any flowers to be seen in the garden now. This perennial grass is ideal for a solitary position in full sun. Its charming arching plumes, about 1½–2ft/450–600mm tall, are borne well above the small dense clump of attractive light green foliage. It is particularly valuable because of its unusually long flowering period. It will require some winter protection in areas with cold, snowless winters.

PLANTS FOR EARLY FALL

Blue and mauve
Buddleja davidii cultivars
Caryopteris × clandonensis
  'Heavenly Blue,' 'Kew Blue'
Hibiscus syriacus cultivars
Hydrangea involucrata
Perovskia abrotanoides
P. atriplicifolia + P.a. 'Blue
  Spire'
Aconitum × 'Arendsii'
A. carmichaelii + A.c. 'Barker's
  Variety,' 'Kelmscott'
Aster cordifolius 'Ideal,'
  'Silverspray'
A. dumosus hybrids
A. ericoides 'Blue Star'
A. × frikartii 'Mönch,' 'Wunder
  von Stäfa'
A. novae-angliae cultivars
A. novi-belgii cultivars
Ceratostigma plumbaginoides
Clematis × bonstedtii
  'Crépuscule'
C. heracleifolia + C.h. davidiana
Echinops ritro 'Veitch's Blue'
Nepeta nervosa
N. sibirica
Scabiosa caucasica
Crocus sativus
C. speciosus 'Artabir,' 'Oxonian'

White and cream
Abelia × grandiflora
Buddleja davidii cultivars
Calluna vulgaris 'Gold Haze'
Clethra alnifolia
C. barbinervis
Hibiscus syriacus cultivars
Potentilla fruticosa 'Abbotswood,'
  'Manchu'
Clematis 'Huldine'
C. ternifolia
Anaphalis margaritacea
Anemone × hybrida 'Honorine
  Jobert'
Aster dumosus hybrids
A. ericoides 'Golden Spray,'

'White Heather'
A. novi-belgii cultivars
Chelone obliqua 'Alba'
Chrysanthemum arcticum
  (*Arctanthemum*)
C. indicum (*Dendranthema*)
  hybrids
C. serotinum (syn.
  Leucanthemella)
Cimicifuga japonica
C. ramosa
C. simplex 'White Pearl'
Polygonum weyrichii
Saxifraga cortusifolia fortunei
Scabiosa caucasica cultivars
Acidanthera bicolor (*Gladiolus
  callianthus*)
Colchicum autumnale 'Album'
C. speciosum 'Album'
Crocus speciosus albus
Cyclamen hederifolium album
Galtonia candicans

Yellow and orange
Hypericum calycinum
H. 'Hidcote'
H. × moserianum
Potentilla fruticosa 'Arbuscula,'
  Goldteppich,' 'Kobold'
Campsis radicans 'Flava'
Clematis tibetana vernayi (*C.
  orientalis*)
Chrysanthemum arcticum
  'Schwefelglanz'
C. indicum hybrids
Coreopsis grandiflora cultivars
Gaillardia hybrids
Helenium 'Septembergold,'
  'Goldrausch'
Helianthus atrorubens 'Gullick's
  Variety,' 'Monarch'
H. decapetalus 'Capenoch Star,'
  'Maximus Flore Pleno'
H. microcephalus
H. salicifolius
Heliopsis helianthoides scabra
  cultivars

Kirengeshoma palmata
Kniphofia 'Bressingham Comet,'
  'Bressingham Gleam,' 'Green
  Lemon,' 'Limelight'
Ligularia dentata 'Desdemona'
Oenothera missouriensis
Rudbeckia fulgida deamii
R. laciniata 'Golden Glow'
Sternbergia lutea

Red and pink
Abelia × grandiflora
Buddleja davidii cultivars
Calluna vulgaris 'Carmen,'
  'County Wicklow,' 'H. E.
  Beale,' 'J. H. Hamilton,'
  'Mullion,' 'Peter Sparkes,'
  'Schurig's Sensation'
Elsholtzia stauntonii
Fuchsia magellanica 'Gracilis'
F. 'Riccartonii,' 'Mme
  Cornelissen'
Hibiscus syriacus cultivars
Lespedeza thunbergii
Campsis radicans
C. × tagliabuana 'Mme Galen'
Clematis 'Ernest Markham,'
  'Gipsy Queen,' 'Kathleen
  Wheeler,' 'Lady Betty
  Balfour,' 'Ville de Lyon'
Anemone hupehensis 'Praecox,'
  'Prinz Heinrich,' 'September
  Charm,' 'Splendens'
A. × hybrida 'Queen Charlotte,'
  'Rosenschale'
A. tomentosa 'Robustissima'
Aster dumosus hybrids
A. lateriflorus 'Horizontalis'
Aster novae-angliae cultivars
A. novi-belgii cultivars
Chelone obliqua
Chrysanthemum arcticum
  'Roseum'
C. indicum hybrids
Gaillardia hybrids
Helenium 'Baudirektor Linne'
Kniphofia 'Bressingham Flame,'

'Fyrverkeri'
Lavatera thuringiaca
Physostegia virginiana 'Vivid'
Polygonum amplexicaule
  'Atropurpureum,' 'Firetail'
P. campanulatum
Sedum cauticola + S.c. 'Ruby
  Glow,' 'Vera Jameson'
S. spectabile 'Carmen,' 'Brilliant,'
  'Meteor,' 'September Glow'
S. telephium 'Munstead Red,'
  'Autumn Joy'
Colchicum autumnale + C.a.
  'Atropurpureum'
C. speciosum hybrids
C. bornmuelleri
Cyclamen hederifolium

**Plants for bees and
butterflies**
Buddleja davidii cultivars
Calluna vulgaris cultivars
Caryopteris × clandonensis
  cultivars
Clethra alnifolia
C. barbinervis
Elsholtzia stauntonii
Hypericum species
Lespedeza thunbergii
Perovskia abrotanoides
P. atriplicifolia
Potentilla fruticosa cultivars
Aster species + hybrids
Chrysanthemum (*Dendranthema*)
  single-flowered species +
  hybrids
Coreopsis species + cultivars
Echinops ritro
Gaillardia hybrids
Helenium hybrids
Helianthus atrorubens
H. decapetalus
Nepeta nervosa
N. sibirica
Rudbeckia species

EARLY FALL TASKS

TREES AND SHRUBS

Planting and transplanting evergreens

Conifers and the hardier broadleaved evergreen trees and shrubs are best planted now in early fall. Plant them as soon as possible, however, so that they have time to make sufficient new roots to supply their leaves with water to replace transpiration losses throughout the winter months. Evergreen hedges as well as solitary shrubs can be planted now, but less hardy species are better planted in early spring.

Early fall is the best time of year to move conifers and other evergreen shrubs. Transplanting any tree or shrub is a major operation which needs to be thoroughly considered and well prepared.

Removing evergreens for transplanting
Mark out a circle 2-4ft/600-1200 mm diameter round the tree or shrub (depending on its size).

A few weeks before removing the shrub, dig a trench beyond the circle 1ft/300mm deep, severing any side root. This promotes the growth of fresh feeder roots closer to the main stem.

Use the spade to cut away roots and soil, leaving a root ball light enough to carry but with the minimum of roots severed. Light soil will mean a smaller root ball than a heavy clay soil.

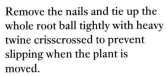

Cut away much of the soil under one side and then finish cutting away the soil completely from under the other side of the root ball. Ease a large, half-rolled-up piece of burlap sacking underneath. Undercut the rest of the root ball, roll the sacking underneath and through to the other side and wrap it tightly round the root ball, securing it with long nails. Use the spade to ease the whole of the ball out of the hole and tip the ball to remove the spade.

Remove the nails and tie up the whole root ball tightly with heavy twine crisscrossed to prevent slipping when the plant is moved.

Propagating evergreens

Broad leaved evergreen shrubs are most easily propagated from cuttings, taken in early fall from this year's new shoots. These can be semiripe stem cuttings, cut just below a node, or cuttings taken with a heel. To make a heel cutting, pull the shoot away from the parent plant leaving a thin sliver of bark and wood from the old stem. Many evergreen cutting roots more easily if taken this way. See page 156 for cutting techniques.

Preparing the soil for planting

Planting time for deciduous trees and shrubs begins in late fall after they have naturally shed their leaves. But, if you are planting a new garden or a large mixed group of trees and shrubs, prepare the planting site now, so that the soil has several weeks in which to settle. Dig the planting area two spade heights deep (double dig), removing rubble, roots, perennial weeds, and rocks. Loosen the soil and work in plenty of well-rotted garden compost. When the time comes you will be able to plant quickly, as individual preparation of each hole will no longer be necessary.

Preparing for winter

Recently planted trees and shrubs should be prepared now for the coming winter. New plantings require the most care, particularly during the first two or three years. Remove perennial weeds, keep the soil surface loose, and water and mulch if necessary. When weeding and digging between the plants, keep well clear of the roots to avoid damaging them and do not dig deep in the ground close to the stem, particularly when working around plants such as rhododendrons which have shallow root systems.

Complete your hoeing, digging, and mulching before leaf drop; when the leaves fall, they can remain undisturbed where they lie, to give extra protection to the root zone during winter.

ROSES

Dead heading

Stop deadheading all recurrent or perpetual flowering shrub roses and climbing roses, so that the plants' growth can harden off before the arrival of winter frosts. Cut off any obviously diseased leaves; this helps to prevent the spread of mildew and other fungal diseases that often strike at this time of year.

Pruning ramblers

Climbing and rambling roses that flower only once each summer can be pruned now, if you have not already done so in late summer (see page 104 for pruning technique).

Weeding and mulching

If your rose bushes are growing in an open bed, without an underplanting of annuals, herbaceous perennials, or a ground cover of some kind, then do be sure to keep the bed free of weeds. If necessary, loosen the soil surface lightly and apply an organic mulch.

Suckers and new shoots

If the rootstock of a grafted rose is sending up suckers, remove them from the point of origin as soon as they are detected (see page 85).

Some roses appear never to want to stop growing and in early autumn continue to produce soft new shoots that cannot possibly ripen sufficiently to withstand the winter frosts. This is a particular problem if the soil is extremely fertile or if nitrogen-rich fertilizer was applied too late in the summer. However, you can promote the ripening of the rose canes by applying a potassium-rich fertilizer now, if you have not already done so in late summer.

CLIMBING PLANTS

Planting and watering

New climbing plants can be planted during early fall if they are available in containers. The soil is still warm enough during this season to promote rapid new root growth.

Do remember, however, to water newly planted climbers regularly, especially those growing on walls, until they have become established. The soil in a bed at the foot of a wall is often the driest in the garden and climbers planted there must be encouraged to root deeply so water deeply and thoroughly.

HERBACEOUS PERENNIALS

Dividing summer-flowering perennials

Summer-flowering perennials that have become crowded or are showing signs of aging can be lifted and divided (see page 159) after they have finished flowering. Renew the soil and work in plenty of ripe compost or other humus before replanting small, robust pieces of the divided plants. Perennials that flower in fall should not be divided until spring.

Planting peonies

Early fall is still a good time to plant peonies (see page 105).

Preparing to plant perennials

If a new perennial border is to be planted later in the fall, dig the soil now, to allow time for it to settle before planting begins. Before digging, take a soil sample for analysis, to determine the nutrient content of the soil in each bed. This will enable you to make any necessary amendments and avoid overfertilizing.

Most herbaceous perennials can remain in position for at least three to five years, so prepare the soil well to a depth of 18–20in/450mm–500mm working in plenty of ripe compost. In areas with extreme winters or heavy soil, delay planting perennials until early spring.

ANNUALS AND BIENNIALS

Planting biennials
There is still time to plant hardy biennials in the beds where they are to flower next spring, for example: hollyhocks (*Alcea*), daisies (*Bellis*), wallflowers (*Cheiranthus*), foxgloves (*Digitalis*), alpine wallflower (*Erysimum*), honesty (*Lunaria*), forget-me-not (*Myosotis*), Scotch thistle (*Onopordum*), Iceland poppies (*Papaver nudicaule*), and pansies (*Viola* × *wittrockiana*).

In areas with very cold winters, the more tender biennials, such as *Cheiranthus*, should spend the winter in the shelter of a cold frame, until they can be safely planted in pre-spring.

Sowing hardy annuals
If you live in a region where winters are mild, you can sow some of the hardier annuals now for early flowers next year, for example: *Calendula, Centaurea, Delphinium, Eschscholzia, Iberis*, and *Nigella*.

BULBS

Planting spring- and summer-flowering bulbs
Bulbs for the spring and summer garden must be planted in early fall if they are to have enough time to grow a strong root system before frost sets in. Bulbs usually reach garden stores by early fall plant them as soon as you are able to buy them. Before planting, prepare the soil well. Work in some ripe compost and add bone meal.

Lay out every bulb on the surface where it is to be planted. You can then judge the distribution and, if necessary, make minor adjustments in the planting plan. Plant the bulbs, one at a time, using a bulb planter or trowel. When in doubt about the planting depth, a good rule of thumb to follow is to set them three times as deep as the bulbs' greatest dimension.

Bulb planting depths
Planting depths are given for a variety of bulbs. Planting depths depend on the size of the bulb and its flowering height. Because depth is important, each bulb is drawn to a larger scale than its flowering height in spring and summer.

Potting up bulbs for forcing indoors

Now is the time to pot up spring bulbs for flowering in the house during the winter. Not all bulbs are suitable for indoor use, but hyacinths, tulips and daffodils adapt well to the forcing process. Other possible species are crocus, dwarf iris and chionodoxa. When buying bulbs for forcing indoors, select the largest you can find and pot them as soon as possible. You will get a well-balanced mass of flowers and foliage by planting as many bulbs as the pot will hold, placing them so that they almost touch. For a spectacular show of tulips or daffodils, plant the bulbs in two layers in a deep container.

Plant the bulbs in an ordinary potting soil or a soil mix of equal parts of garden soil, sand and peatmoss. Fill up the pot with soil so that when the bulbs are placed on the soil, the tips of smaller bulbs will be ¾–1¼in/20–30mm below the rim of the pot while the tips of large hyacinth and narcissus bulbs should just show above the rim. Position the bulbs and fill in enough soil to leave a half-inch/centimeter of space below the rim of the container. Water the pots well and label each one.

Planting bulbs in pots

For a massed effect plant in two layers in a deep container. Set the upper bulbs (if you are planting different-sized bulbs these will also be the smaller) in between the spaces left by the lower layer. If you are planting tulips, place them so that the flat sides face the rim; the first broad leaves that emerge will then form an attractive border.

Forcing

The preliminary stage is crucial. Once the bulbs have been potted, they must be stored in a cold, dark place and the pots must not be allowed to dry out. You need to provide a temperature between 40–50°F/4° and 10°C until sufficient roots have grown to permit forcing. The time may take as little as twelve or as long as sixteen weeks depending on the species.

Once the pots are filled with roots, which can usually be seen emerging from the drainage hole at the bottom, it is time to begin forcing. Do not expose the plants to room temperature all at once but place the pots at first in a room with around 59°F/15°C and indirect light. After a few days move them into brighter light with temperatures between 64° and 71°F/18° and 22°C. Crocuses and daffodils, in particular, prefer the cooler temperature whereas hyacinths and tulips flourish at 68°F/20°C.

Removing tender bulbs

The bulbs and corms of tender summer-flowering species, such as gladiolus *Acidanthera* (now *Gladiolus callianthus*), *Tigridia*, tuberous begonias, *Crocosmia*, *Canna* and *Caladium*, must be dug up before frost for storage indoors over winter. As soon as the foliage starts to turn yellow, usually about six weeks after the blossoms have faded, it is time to remove them. The many, pea-sized bulblets and cormlets that have formed at the top (or, in the case of gladioli, at the base of the parent

2 Right Cut the stalk to leave about 2in/50mm. Spread the bulbs out to dry in a warm, airy, preferably sunny place. Once dry, lay the bulbs in flats or open paper bags and store until spring.

Gladiolus corms

Right Gladioli are treated in the same way except that, after drying, discard the old corm with its roots attached, and store the plump new daughter corms for planting and flowering next spring. Treat the tiny cormlets like the bulblets (*above*).

Care of tender bulbs

1 Left Many bulbs and corms do best if they are dug up and stored over winter. This should be done well after blooming, when the leaves have yellowed. Loosen the soil with a fork, so as not to damage the bulb and bulblets, dig them up and remove any soil.

3 Left Free the new bulblets and store them separately. Planted and lifted annually, they will flower in about three years.

corm) can be used to build up your stock.

Store in a dry, well-ventilated place where the temperature stays between 41°F/5°C and 50°F/10°C. At higher temperatures the corms and bulbs tend to shrivel.

Planting lilies

Bulbs of most lilies should be planted now as soon as they can be obtained. Early fall is the best time to plant most lily species and hybrids, except the Madonna lilies, which must be planted earlier, in late summer (see page 106). Prepare the soil thoroughly to a depth of at least 12in/300mm. Most lilies prefer a loose, fertile soil with plenty of humus, so dig in liberal amounts of good ripe compost, leaf mold, well-rotted manure, or composted tree bark before planting. Good drainage is essential – waterlogged soil is fatal to all lilies.

Planting depth depends largely on the size of the bulb and the manner in which roots are formed. Lilies which develop roots from the base of the bulb only should be planted with the tips of the bulbs not more than 2in/50mm below the surface. This group includes most species of European origin and many native American lilies. Stem-rooting lilies, such as *Lilium regale* and the popular hybrid 'Enchantment,' need to be set much deeper, so that their tips are covered to a depth two or three times the height of the bulb. In loose, friable soil, choose the greater depth; if your soil is heavy, plant at the shallower depth. Whatever depth you select, be sure that there is an inch or two of good soil beneath the bulb. It is important to make the planting holes large enough so that the roots can spread outward and downward without crowding.

WATER GARDEN

Tidying the pond

In the water garden, aquatic plants and those in the low and water-edge areas will die back as the season progresses and the nights become colder. It is especially important now to continue removing all dead leaves, faded flowers, and stalks which would foul the water. Use a fish net to strain out as much duckweed as you can. Leave the underwater shoots of oxygenating plants untouched: they will continue to give off oxygen throughout the winter, even under ice, and will help maintain a healthy pool.

Planting bog plants

The planting season for aquatic plants is long past, as the water is already much too cold to allow them to become established before winter. However, now is a good time to plant many of the hardy bog plants: marsh marigold (*Caltha*), cotton grass (*Eriophorum*), soft rush (*Juncus*), water forget-me-not (*Myosotis*), and knotweed (*Polygonum*).

LAWN AND FLOWER MEADOW

Lawn mowing

If the lawn has been allowed to grow longer during the heat of summer, it can now be cut again at the normal height, so long as the weather is mild and the grass is growing rapidly. How often and by how much depends on the growth rate of the grass; this depends on the weather, how well fertilized the grass is, and on the quality of the grass. You must, therefore, consider the length of the grass and adjust mowing height and frequency accordingly.

As a rule of thumb, a utility lawn should be cut back to a length of 1½in/40mm as soon as it reaches 3in/80mm. A fine luxury lawn should be cut back to 1¼in/30mm whenever it grows to a height of 2½in/60mm.

Toward the end of this season, as soon as the weather begins to turn so cool that lawn grasses cease to grow so rapidly, reduce mowing frequency and raise the mower blades once again by about ¼–½in/5–10mm, so that the grass is neither too long nor too short as the season comes to a close.

Sowing a new lawn

In many regions early fall is a good time to sow a new lawn or to reseed bare patches in an existing lawn. The ground is still warm enough for the grass seed to germinate quickly and the new lawn will have enough time to become established before winter (for sowing procedure, see page 35). Your choice of seed mixture should be governed by the soil conditions and climate in your garden as well as your requirements and expectations.

For a fine luxury lawn choose a mixture of about 80 percent Chewings fescue (*Festuca rubra commutata*) and about 20 percent browntop bentgrass (*Agrostis tenuis*); these two grasses form the basis of most seed mixtures for fine lawns, and make a fine, dense, compact lawn that tolerates close mowing. Occasionally creeping red fescue (*Festuca rubra rubra*), a grass tolerant of both wet and dry soils, is also included in mixtures for luxury turf.

In addition to these grasses, general purpose mixtures for utility lawns usually include a strain of perennial rye grass (*Lolium perenne*), a somewhat coarser, heavy-duty grass, together with meadow grass (*Poa pratensis*). Neither of these species will tolerate close mowing and should not be present in a mixture if you expect a fine luxury lawn. However, for a higher-quality utility lawn, look for a mixture that specifically contains a low-growing, fine-bladed variety of perennial rye grass. (Read the labels carefully.)

There are also mixtures for shady sites, but cutting higher and less frequently than usual are more important here than buying a special mixture.

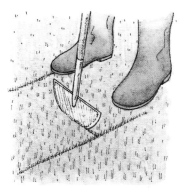

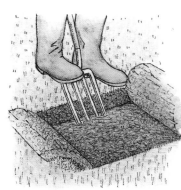

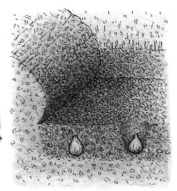

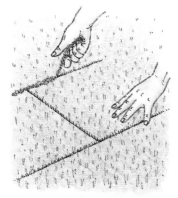

Planting bulbs in the lawn
Use a sharp spade or edging tool to mark out strips of lawn and to divide them into manageable lengths.

Slice under the surface to a depth of 1½-2in/40-50mm, leaving most of the grass roots intact. Roll the sod back and loosen the soil with a fork.

Plant the bulbs and firm the soil. Make sure it is level before gently treading the sod back into place. The sods will soon settle.

Infill by sprinkling soil along the edges. The method shown here is an alternative to using a bulb planting tool, which cuts out sod cylinders.

Naturalizing bulbs

Many spring-flowering bulbs are especially suitable for naturalizing in the rough grass of a flower meadow; once they are established they will continue to flower and increase year after year with little attention. This method of growing bulbs mimics the natural conditions in which many species (*Narcissus, Crocus, Colchicum, Fritillaria, Leucojum,* and *Galanthus,* for example) are found in the wild. However, consider carefully before planting bulbs in your lawn: the bulbs' foliage must always be allowed to mature before the grass is cut and that means no mowing until early summer. Up to that time, the dying foliage of the bulbs and the tall grass will appear untidy. It is also obvious that bulbs have no place in a first-class lawn, as any prolonged period without mowing necessarily leads to deterioration of the lawn.

Should you decide to grow bulbs in this way, aim for a natural, informal effect. Start by cutting the grass, which makes planting much easier. Then, taking one species at a time, tip the bulbs out of a bag, allowing them to roll gently over the grass. Planting them where they come to rest will ensure a pleasingly random pattern of flowers. Do not mix colors and species within one group, but make bold clumps and sweeps of a single species and allow the groups to mingle and merge only at their boundaries.

PATIO AND BALCONY

Preparing for cold weather

This season normally brings an end to gardening activities on the patio and balcony; the time has come to make preparations for the coming winter and for next spring's first flowers as well. Plants growing in containers should no longer be fertilized and should receive less water so that new growth is not encouraged. The plants should be induced to ripen and harden their shoots sufficiently before winter sets in.

Any shrub roses and permanent hardy container plants that are to remain outdoors during the winter may, however, profit from feeding with a potassium-rich fertilizer, which accelerates the ripening of their new growth. Move all of your tender container plants to their winter quarters before the first serious frosts.

The miniature water garden

Hardier aquatic plants may remain in place in the miniature water garden if you can ensure that the water does not freeze. Pack the entire container in an insulating material and install a small aquarium heater, strong enough to maintain a temperature above 38°F/4°C. Tropical water lilies and other tender aquatics must be brought indoors, to be overwintered in a room cool enough to maintain near-dormancy.

Planting up for spring

Now is the time to plant boxes and other containers with spring-flowering bulbs. Apply the same rules of planting as described on page 118. The first to appear in spring, when the weather is often still inclement, will be especially welcome when you can see them from indoors.

CHAPTER 8

FALL

"Now Autumn's fire burns slowly along the woods,
And day by day the dead leaves fall and melt . . .
. . . and now the power is felt
Of melancholy, tenderer in its moods,
Than any joy indulgent summer dealt."

William Collingham

The full season of fall is marked by the ripening of beechnuts, horse chestnuts and acorns. About the same time the leaves of several European native trees assume their fall colors. In Central Europe and Great Britain, the European whitebark, *Betula pendula*, and horse chestnut, *Aesculus hippocastanum*, are usually the first to color, followed by the small-leaved linden, *Tilia cordata*, English oak, *Quercus robur*, and European beech, *Fagus sylvatica*.

Now is the time of richly colored leaves, bright nuts, and ripe red berries, with the fall sun accentuating their fiery brilliance. Although this fall spectacle is brief, a garden planted with well-chosen trees and shrubs can offer the most breathtaking display of the year as the foliage takes on its vivid fall color – reds, oranges, yellows, and golds. Berries in white, blue, and black are common too, and can take their place in the decorative design.

On sunny days bees are still gleaning the last nectar from heathers, sedums, and the autumn-flowering crocus. We can still enjoy the late lingering scents of a few shrubs that flower now, such as *Hamamelis virginiana* and *Osmanthus heterophyllus*.

At this time of year a period of fine and peaceful, sunny weather eventually yields to a cooler, more unsettled period which coincides with leaf fall of most native deciduous trees. The first trees to lose their leaves in late fall are the European whitebark, the small-leaved linden, the horse chestnut, and the English oak, followed a few days later by European beech.

Leaf fall is usually accompanied by the first heavy night frosts. The last native trees to drop their leaves are the larch and the broadleaved linden. Work in the garden can be continued until the ground begins to freeze, when most jobs, certainly all planting operations, must cease.

THE FALL GARDEN

Even though there are so few plants flowering at this time of year, there is no need for a lack of lively color in the garden in fall. At the lowest level of planting, the many species and cultivars of fall-flowering crocus (*Crocus speciosus, C. banaticus, C. goulimyi,* and *C. longiflorus*) provide a long-lasting spectacle of blue and mauve tones which fit so well with the more fiery colors of the changing leaves and glistening berries.

The lasting quality of the berries varies greatly. Birds tend to eat the softest, darkest blue, and black berries first. Though frost may have little visible effect on hard berries such as rose hips, haws, cotoneaster, or holly, it softens their pulp and makes them more palatable to the hungry flocks. Some holly berries color in autumn and remain attractive till spring. Certain cotoneaster and barberries hold their fruits in fine condition throughout the winter; snowberries usually hang until they turn brown and rot, some time after New Year. Fruits of the *Viburnum opulus* last longer even though they are appetizingly red. But most red or orange ornamental fruits, such as pyracanthas and mountain ash, last for much shorter periods: the birds seem to have their own menu plan which they follow as they strip one lot of berries after another through the fall and winter.

Most European trees and shrubs depend for good fall leaf color on a good night frost followed by warm sunshine a week or so before they start to die. However, the leaves of a great many deciduous trees from the temperate regions of eastern North America and East Asia change color naturally due to their aging process that begins long before the leaves die, well in advance of any severe frost. They, too, are enhanced by periods of sunny warm days and cold nights. If your garden has an acidic soil then you are in luck, because many of the woodland trees and shrubs that produce spectacular foliage do best in acidic soils; however, there are plenty of shrubs that are very happy in alkaline conditions.

Large trees for fall color
Some of the finest trees in fall are also some of the largest ornamental deciduous trees and may be too large for planting in a small modern garden. However, should your garden be spacious by all means include them; you will be rewarded with an annual color display long before they reach maturity.

The scarlet oak, *Quercus coccinea*, is a large North American tree and one of the finest and most reliable for fall color. It will grow to a height of 65ft/20m or more and requires only a limefree soil to grow happily – and for an oak, rapidly. The clone 'Splendens' has been selected for its reliably rich scarlet coloring. It is worth seeking out.

Most of the color in the garden at this time of year, will be the warm, intense shades of fall foliage and bright berries. All the fall hues enhance one another and blend perfectly with the muted tones of late-flowering shrubs and perennials.

Euonymus europaeus, the European spindle tree, is unrivaled for dramatic effect in fall when its foliage turns to brilliant shades of scarlet, crimson, and orange. It makes a long-lasting contribution to the fall garden since it also has highly colored pendulous fruits that remain long after the leaves have dropped. They are especially showy when the shocking pink capsules open to reveal the shining orange seeds.

The red maple, *Acer rubrum*, can grow to a giant 130ft/40m tall in its native soil in Canada; in Europe, however, it seldom exceeds 33ft/10m. The attractive palmate dark green leaves turn to a mixture of rich red and scarlet in fall. Three clones are well worth tracking down: 'Scanlon,' a medium-sized tree, has two-toned leaves that consistently turn a rich, tawny crimson; 'October Glory' and 'Schlesingeri' are specially selected for the brilliance of their fall leaves, which turn a rich deep scarlet before dropping. The leaves of red maple do not color nearly so well on alkaline soils.

Another large tree from eastern North America, the sweet gum, *Liquidambar styraciflua*, has palmate leaves somewhat similar in shape and size to those of many maples. This tree is valuable for its stately form and handsome foliage. In summer the lobed leaves are glossy and lively bright green; in fall, especially if the tree is growing in good deep soil that is moderately moist, the foliage exhibits a gorgeous mixture of shades of purple, crimson, and orange. Like many other trees, liquidambar raised from seed colours rather unreliably and may have an unpredictable habit. Two well-shaped clones which always color well are 'Lane Roberts' and 'Burgundy'.

Nyssa sylvatica, the tupelo from eastern North America, is a slow-growing, but fairly large tree which naturally inhabits swampy, poorly drained land. Outside its native territory, the tupelo grows best in a damp, loamy, limefree soil. With time it forms a dense crown, easily approaching 100ft/30m in height, although in Europe it remains considerably shorter, like so many North American trees. The glossy dark green leaves are handsome in summer but their chief value lies in their glorious array of scarlet, orange, and yellow in fall.

Smaller fall trees
For the small garden, there is also an excellent selection of smaller trees and shrubs for fall color. Among the many valuable oriental maples are a number of particularly lovely cultivars. *Acer davidii* 'George Forrest,' for example, is a vigorous cultivar of Pere David's maple from China. 'George Forrest' makes a loose, open crown with elegant spreading branches and is without a doubt one of the best of the hardy Asiatic maples for the small garden. In summer the large dark green leaves with their rhubarb red stalks are attractive, but this small tree makes its main show in fall when the

The tupelo tree, *Nyssa sylvatica*, is one of the most reliable trees for showy fall foliage. It needs a moist limefree soil and, if well-situated, will give a spectacular annual array of gold, orange, and red. It dislikes root disturbance, so it must be planted as a young, well-growing container plant; it will fail to thrive if the roots receive the slightest damage.

red-tinged winged seeds hang in clusters among the vivid red and orange leaves.

Among the several cultivars of the full-moon maple, *Acer japonicum*, are two which are distinguished for their fiery fall foliage: *A.j aconitifolium* makes a large rounded bush or small tree, about 8ft/2.5m high, with soft green, very finely divided leaves which turn to rich ruby crimson in fall. The cultivar 'Vitifolium' is very different in appearance and has broad, conspicuously lobed leaves like those of a fig tree. They are remarkable for their large size, being up to 6in/150mm long and wide, and are soft green in spring and summer but color gloriously in fall: the inner mass of foliage may remain a vivid green while the outer branches ignite into shades of orange, scarlet, crimson, and purple.

Acer palmatum, a species of Japanese maple represented by countless desirable cultivars, includes many which color well in fall. 'Lutescens,' for example, has glossy, handsomely divided leaves, tinted a dark, coppery green during the summer, but changing to a clear butter yellow in fall. 'Shishigashira' is a large, slow-growing form with distinctive upright habit. The bold palmate leaves are dark green in summer but turn to a deep shade of old gold.

Closely related to the witch hazels, *Fothergilla major* is a compact, slow-growing but ultimately fairly large shrub from the southern USA. It is charming in the spring with its profusion of fragrant white bottle-brush flowers which appear before the leaves. Fothergilla is very decorative in fall when the leaves turn yellow, orange, or crimson before falling; it colors best if grown in a sunny position.

Gray beard is the picturesque name for the oak-leaf hydrangea, *Hydrangea quercifolia*, a small shrub from the southern USA. It bears white flowers in the summer, but is of value chiefly for its magnificent fall colors. In favorable seasons, the large oaklike leaves turn crimson, orange, or purple. This hydrangea should be given a sunny, sheltered spot with a moist, fairly rich, acidic soil.

It is perhaps not widely appreciated that deciduous azaleas are often colorful in fall before their leaves drop. The foliage of *Rhododendron luteum*, a beautiful and hardy shrub, growing to about 10ft/3m, turns to rich shades of crimson, purple, and orange. A second exquisite azalea species, the Korean *R. schlippenbachii*, has large, pale pink, saucer-

The flaming foliage of *Enkianthus campanulatus* makes it one of the most spectacular shrubs in fall. It is valuable both as a solitary specimen or planted in combination.

In the shade, the leaves of the iron tree, *Parrotia persica*, turn to shades of golden yellow. In spring it bears small red flowers on leafless branches. It does best in rich, moist well-drained soil.

shaped flowers in early spring. The attractive leaves are the largest and most striking among azaleas; suffused with reddish-purple when young, they turn to yellow, orange, and crimson in fall.

Enkianthus campanulatus is a fairly large Japanese shrub of erect habit, hardy to zone 5 and easily grown in any moist, limefree soil, in sun or partial shade. It is attractive in the spring when hung with myriads of long-lasting, bronze-yellow, cup-shaped blossoms, but its great beauty comes in fall when the leaves change to various glowing shades of red and yellow.

Parrotia persica, the iron tree, is another member of the witch hazel family, but from the Middle East. It is a very large shrub or medium-sized tree with widely spreading branches which are marbled and flaked in green, gray, and brown. Parrotia is one of the finest small trees for fall color; the large leaves turn to a glorious mixture of crimson and orange tinged with bronze and pink, and, in the shadiest parts of the tree, golden yellow.

One of the last shrubs to change color and also one of the brightest is *Photinia villosa*, a small elegant Asian tree closely related to the hawthorns. It carries hawthornlike flowers in spring, which are reliably followed by bright red berries. Photinia turns to a vivid orange mixed with scarlet and gold tints that last well into winter.

Fall color where soil is neutral or alkaline
Should your garden soil be neutral or alkaline, there are still many first class trees and shrubs which can give you plenty of good foliage color. The two largest trees for fall color on alkaline soils are of ancient origin. The leaves of both *Ginkgo biloba* and the North American tulip tree *Liriodendron tulipifera* change to a pure butter yellow before falling.

Of the smaller trees for neutral or alkaline soil, the Norway maple, *Acer platanoides*, is a dense but attractive tree in its wild form; it grows vigorously and turns in a good season to a clear, bright yellow. There are several cultivars available that are even more dependable and richly colored. 'Cucullatum' and 'Schwedleri' both grow to large upright trees; they turn to a wonderful bright yellow. 'Reitenbachii' makes a medium-sized tree. Its large, five-lobed leaves unfurl with a strong red tinge, are bright green throughout the summer, and finally change to a rich dark red before falling.

Cotinus coggygria, the smoke tree from southern Europe, grows only to 10–13ft/3–4m. Its rounded, gray-green leaves color dependably each year; they turn to yellow or red and remain long on the tree. The smoke tree gets its name from the clouds of fawn-colored flower heads that envelop the shrub in summer. Both flower color and fall color are brightest in the hybrid cultivar 'Flame,' with leaves that turn a glorious orange and scarlet before falling.

Chittam wood is the common name for *Cotinus obovatus*, the rare and beautiful North American cousin of the smoke tree. It grows to 30ft/9m in the southern USA but scarcely exceeds half that height in Europe. The spring foliage is pinkish bronze; in fall the leaves turn to various shades of scarlet, orange, yellow, and violet. Given a favorable site, it can easily be the most brilliantly colored of fall shrubs.

The golden rain tree, *Koelreuteria paniculata*, is a small spreading tree that grows in any good loamy soil but which needs a long, hot summer in order to give a good crop of flowers. When happy, it is a mass of deep yellow flowers in late summer. The large, handsome, ferny leaves open a vivid lobster red in the spring, changing to a soft bronze-green during the summer; in fall they turn a rich golden amber.

There are at least three sorbus species that are especially suited for planting in the small garden for attractive fall fruits as well as foliage color: *Sorbus americana* is a small tree with stiffly upright branches. The small bright red berries borne in large dense clusters are much loved by birds – while they last they are very showy. As a bonus, the leaves turn to apricot or red before falling. *S. esserteauiana*, a small open-crowned tree, produces tightly clustered small scarlet berries which are especially valuable because they ripen and color later than most other sorbus: If this lovely mountain ash has sufficient moisture, its leaves will turn to rich red before falling. *S. sargentiana* is considered by many to be the finest of the rowans, a relatively large tree, up to 30ft/9m tall and as wide. The large handsome leaves unfurl mahogany brown; in fall they color brilliantly to a rich orange-red. The display of scarlet fruits is spectacular; they are late to ripen and individually small but are borne in such large drooping clusters that, together, the rounded berries make a magnificent show.

Fall fruits and berries

Leaf color may be the main garden feature in mid-fall but many shrubs and small trees, both deciduous and evergreen, are now heavily laden with attractive fruits and shining berries. The majority of the berried shrubs associate splendidly with the brightly colored foliage. But in late fall, after the last dead leaves have been stripped from the trees, the berries still have much to offer. Although their season is often brief, they prevent the garden from seeming empty and barren during the last few weeks before winter. They include the milky white of the snowberry, the pinks, reds, oranges, and yellows of the hollies, mountain ash, cotoneasters, barberries, and viburnums, and the bright purple of the beauty berry.

The beauty berry, *Callicarpa bodinieri giraldii*, up to 6ft/1.8m tall, is a Chinese shrub, hardy to zone 6 and highly valued for its unique lilac-colored berries which are carried profusely among the rose-tinted fall foliage. It is ideal for a sunny, sheltered, woodland spot with good rich acidic soil and makes an arresting fall picture planted among yellow- or purple-leaved shrubs or in front of a gray stone wall. Cross-pollination is necessary for berries so plant severl shrubs together.

For acidic soil, there is a first-class North American holly that deserves cultivation in the garden: the deciduous species *Ilex verticillata*. Reaching 10ft/3m in height, its small oval leaves are purple-tinged, especially in the spring: in the fall they turn to yellow before dropping. The glossy scarlet berries ripen before the leaves fall but are relatively long-lasting and are borne in such numbers that the shrub makes a blazing visual impact.

There are countless barberry species and cultivars, evergreen and deciduous, dwarf or almost tree size, with red, orange, yellow, blue, or black berries; they all prefer a warm loamy soil. Among the best for berries in late fall are four deciduous species: *Berberis aggregata*, *B. koreana*, *B.* × *carminea* 'Buccaneer,' and *B. wilsoniae*.

Deciduous members of the genus euonymus, which includes the European spindle tree, are shrubs which scarcely draw any attention in spring or summer, for their flowers and green foliage are without distinction. In fall, however, when the foliage turns to brilliant scarlet, crimson, or orange and the fruits ripen, they are dramatic and decorative. All euonymus

The hardy Mongolian climber, *Clematis tangutica*, flowers well into fall, when its nodding lemony yellow blossoms appear together with the ripening silky silvery white seed heads.

The attractive holly, *Ilex aquifolium* 'Bacciflava', dependably bears heavy crops of bright yellow fruits, which make an eye-catching display among the glossy, dark green foliage.

grow best in a good loamy soil in a sunny, well-drained site, although many are fairly shade tolerant.

A dwarf creeping shrub, effective at close range or massed as a ground-cover plant in the rhododendron garden, the North American wintergreen, *Gaultheria procumbens*, seldom exceeds 6in/150mm in height. It has lustrous dark green foliage which hides little pinkish white, drooping flowers; they must be seen close up to be appreciated. In late fall, the evergreen foliage takes on a red tinge and the plants are dotted with large bright red edible berries. They have a pleasant tart taste.

Skimmia japonica is a small rounded evergreen shrub with showy red berries and clusters of sweetly fragrant white flowers in spring. Be sure to plant at least one male clone such as 'Rubella' to ensure that females such as 'Veitchii' or 'Nymans' produce berries. The smaller *Skimmia reevesiana* bears scented hermaphroditic flowers, so that a single plant is able to produce its dark crimson berries.

Photinia davidiana is a vigorous evergreen shrub noted for its vivid changes of color during fall. Although an evergreen, some of its tough leathery leaves turn scarlet and yellow. Its clusters of brilliant red berries cover the bush and last well into winter. The matt fruits are apparently too dry to be of much interest to the birds.

The evergreen hollies are single-sex plants and it is essential to select a female clone if berries are desired and to plant a male holly in close proximity to ensure adequate pollination. Where winter temperatures fall low, plant one of the North American hybrid hollies, *I.* × *meserveae*. These so-called blue hollies can easily endure temperatures below −14°F/−25°C without any damage and they are similar in leaf form, habit, and overall appearance to *I. aquifolium*. The female clones 'Blue Princess' and 'Blue Angel' are especially prolific. The male clone 'Blue Prince' bears countless white blossoms in early summer and is an excellent pollen donor for the other blue hollies as well as for many *I. aquifolium* cultivars, which all bear more heavily when 'Blue Prince' is near.

PLANTS FOR FALL

Very few garden plants flower at this time; some important exceptions are:

Blue and mauve
Caryopteris × *clandonensis*
  hybrids
Ceratostigma plumbaginoides
Gentiana sinoornata
Hosta tardiflora
Crocus banaticus
C. goulimyi
C. longiflorus
C. sativus
C. serotinus
C. speciosus 'Conqueror'

White and cream
Calluna vulgaris 'Alba Plena,'
  'Christina,' 'Long White'
Elaeagnus × *ebbingei*
Osmanthus heterophyllus
Prunus × *subhirtella*
  'Autumnalis'
Clematis terniflora (*C.*
  maximowicziana)
Fallopia aubertii (*Polygonum*
  aubertii)
Anaphalis triplinervis
  'Silberregen'
Crocus ochroleucus
Galanthus reginae-olgae

Yellow and orange
Potentilla fruticosa cultivars
Sternbergia lutea

Red and pink
Calluna vulgaris 'Annemarie,'
  'Battle of Arnhem,'
  'Cramond,' 'Finale,' 'H.E.
  Beale,' 'J.H. Hamilton,'
  'Marleen,' 'Peter Sparkes,'
  'Schurig's Sensation,'
  'Underwoodii'
Elsholtzia stauntonii
Erica carnea 'Eileen Porter,'
  'Praecox Rubra'

Lespedeza thunbergii
Viburnum × *bodnantense*
Sedum 'Herbstfreude' ('Autumn
  Joy,')
Cyclamen hederifolium

Scented flowers
Elaeagnus × *ebbingei*
Hamamelis virginiana
Osmanthus heterophyllus
Viburnum × *bodnantense*
Crocus longiflorus

**Trees, shrubs, and climbing
plants with fall leaf color**
Acer – many sp., especially:
A. capillipes
A. cappadocicum
A. circinatum
A. davidii
A. tataricum ginnala
A. griseum
A. japonicum cultivars
A. palmatum cultivars
A. pensylvanicum
A. platanoides
A. rubrum
A. saccharum
A. saccharinum
Amelanchier laevis
A. lamarckii
Berberis – many deciduous
  species, especially:
B. aggregata
B. dictyophylla
B. koreana
B. × *carminea* 'Fireflame'
B. thunbergii cultivars
B. wilsoniae
Betula species
Cercidiphyllum japonicum
Chionanthus virginicus
Clethra alnifolia
C. barbinervis

Cornus 'Eddie's White Wonder'
C. florida
Cotinus coggygria
C. 'Flame'
C. obovatus
Cotoneaster bullatus
C. divaricatus
Crataegus pedicellata
C. persimilis 'Prunifolia'
Enkianthus campanulatus
Euonymus alatus
E. latifolius
E. oxyphyllus
E. planipes
Fothergilla gardenii
F. major
Fraxinus excelsior
F. ornus
Ginkgo biloba
Hamamelis × *intermedia* 'Jelena'
H. japonica
H. mollis
Hydrangea petiolaris
H. quercifolia
Koelreuteria paniculata
Larix decidua
Liquidambar styraciflua
Liriodendron tulipifera
Malus coronaria 'Charlottae'
M. tschonoskii
Metasequoia glyptostroboides
Nyssa sylvatica
Oxydendrum arboreum
Parrotia persica
Parthenocissus quinquefolia
P. tricuspidata
Prunus sargentii
Pyrus calleryana
P. ussuriensis
Quercus alba
Q. coccinea
Q. dentata
Q. palustris
Q. rubra
Rhododendron luteum
R. schlippenbachii
R. vaseyi

Rhus typhina
Ribes aureum
Sassafras albidum
Sorbus alnifolia
S. commixta + *S.c.* 'Serotina'
S. 'Embley'
S. sargentiana
Viburnum dentatum
V. furcatum
V. prunifolium

**Trees, shrubs, and climbing
plants with decorative fruits**
Berberis species + cultivars
Callicarpa bodinieri giraldii
Celastrus orbiculatus
Chaenomeles cultivars
Clematis tangutica
C. tibetana vernayi
C. vitalba
Cornus species
Cotoneaster species + cultivars
Crataegus species
Elaeagnus umbellata
Euonymus species
Gaultheria species
Idesia polycarpa
Ilex species + (female) cultivars
Malus species + cultivars
Mespilus germanica
Photinia davidiana (*Stranvaesia*
  davidiana)
P. villosa
Pyracantha cultivars
Rhodotypos scandens
Rosa species, especially:
R. moyesii
R. rugosa hybrids + cultivars
R. glauca
R. pendulina
R. sweginzowii
R. villosa
Skimmia japonica – female
  cultivars
Sorbus species
Viburnum species

FALL TASKS

GARDEN WILDLIFE

Birdhouses

Many native bird species naturally nest in cavities and crevices in old trees, rather than constructing nests. However, lately, the preference for "clean" gardens (and farms, parks, and even woods), has severely reduced available nesting sites, such as old decaying trees, in many areas. Fortunately, a number of bird species will accept man-made birdhouses and you can do much to encourage the bird population in your garden by supplying these "cavities." A wide variety of commercially made birdhouses are available or you can make your own. Late fall is the best time for erecting birdhouses because new houses which have been allowed to weather outdoors during the winter are more acceptable to the birds in the spring and they can also serve as welcome roosting shelters for birds that remain in the garden during the cold winter months.

Clean out all birdhouses in your garden during late fall. This prevents parasites from overwintering in the old nest debris.

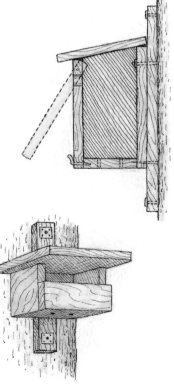

Birdhouses for small birds

The house *above* is designed for birds such as titmice, with a hole 1¼in/30mm across to keep out larger birds and an openable side for cleaning. The one shown *right* is for birds such as wrens that prefer a view when incubating. Use well-seasoned durable wood and rustproof nails, and drill two or three small holes in the floor for drainage.

THE SOIL

Soil sampling

A good gardener should know as much about his soil as possible; he should know of what general type it is, its pH value, and levels of the most important nutrients. He will then know what plants will grow best in it and how to fertilize it economically and intelligently. Soil deficiencies can often be corrected in one way or another, whether these have been caused by years of mismanagement or by a season of garden production.

Fall is the ideal time to take soil samples from the garden for analysis. Should the results of the analysis show the need to add lime to raise the pH or nutrients or other soil improvers, these can then be carried out during the winter months, so that the soil is in optimal condition for the next growth season.

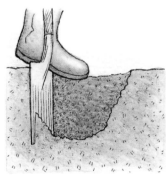

Taking soil samples

Dig a series of holes about 10in/250mm or more deep, all over the area to be tested. One side of the hole should be smooth and vertical. Scrape soil from the wall of the hole, taking care to obtain a uniform amount from each layer. Repeat the process for each hole. Mix the samples thoroughly to obtain a representative sample. Then place about 1lb/50g in a clean plastic bag, ready for analysis.

If you plan to submit your soil sample to a professional laboratory for analysis, an instruction booklet will normally be provided describing their preferred method for taking a soil sample; follow their instructions as closely as possible. But whether you plan to analyze the soil yourself with one of the commercially available testing kits or to submit the sample to a professional testing laboratory, collecting the soil sample is the first and perhaps most critically important part of the testing procedure.

There are often large variations in soil nutrients in various parts of a garden, so it is important to collect a number of samples from different locations in the test area. Also, always be sure that your collecting tools and containers are clean and not contaminated with fertilizer, manure, or lime.

For most flower and vegetable plots, it is sufficient to sample the top layer of soil to a depth of 10in/250mm; wherever a lawn is to be installed, a sample of the top 4in/100mm is sufficient. However, where deep-rooting plants such as trees and shrubs are to be planted, it is advisable to take two separate samples for analysis: one of the topsoil to a depth of 8in/200mm and a second from the subsoil layer between 8 and 16in/200mm and 400mm depth.

Preparation for spring planting

If you intend to plant new herbaceous or mixed beds next spring, you may want to dig over the area to be planted and prepare the soil now. The benefits of fall digging are most evident with heavy clay soils, of course, which will be much easier to work after the freezing and thawing actions of winter have broken up any large clumps and loosened the structure of the soil.

While digging, incorporate lime, sand, garden compost, peat, manure, composted shredded tree bark, or whatever your soil needs to improve its fertility. By planting time next spring, any measures you take now to improve the soil will already have had a chance to take effect.

TREES AND SHRUBS

Planting deciduous woody plants

Late fall is normally the best season of the year for planting deciduous trees and shrubs, especially those dug up from the open ground. Selling and planting usually begin as soon as the plants have lost their leaves and planting can continue as long as the soil is neither frozen nor too wet to work. Planting in this season is in most cases advantageous because the soil is still warm enough to allow the plants to make new roots before winter sets in, roots which will then be better able to support new growth when the leaf buds open in spring (for planting procedure, see pages 152–153).

Planting a deciduous hedge

Throughout fall, many nurseries offer a good selection of small, bare root or balled deciduous shrubs especially suited for planting in a hedge. These plants are almost always much less expensive than comparable specimens for solitary planting.

About a week to ten days before planting, you should start preparing the soil where the hedge is to grow. First dig a trench 20–40in/0.5–1m wide and two spade depths, loosen the subsoil and incorporate into the topsoil whatever material is needed to improve its structure and fertility (compost, peat, sand, manure, etc.) before refilling the

Planting a hedge

1 Mark out the line of the hedge with string. Dig a trench broad enough to take the roots of the hedge plants without crowding. (If you are planting a double row for a really thick hedge, make the trench twice as wide.) Dig a trench deep enough to mix in a good layer of compost and manure for the new roots to grow into. Soak the roots before planting.

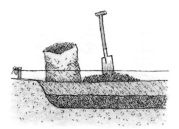

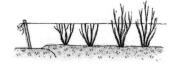

2 Place the plants according to the recommended spacing along the trench. Fill in and firm the soil, leaving no air pockets.

Water in well. If the roots have burlap wrapping, leave it in place, after freeing it from around the stem.

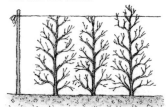

3 If there is any danger that winter winds might rock and loosen the shrubs, cut them back now. Otherwise, leave the first pruning until pre-spring. Place

string strung between two canes for an even cutting height.

trench. Once the improved and loosened soil has settled again planting can begin as detailed above.

Tree stakes and ties

Check that stakes and ties on all newly planted trees are intact and secure enough to hold up to winter storms. Remember that the aim of staking a tree after planting is to keep the stem perfectly steady *at the base* until the roots have grown strong enough to anchor the plant on their own. Some freedom of motion of the crown and upper trunk serves to strengthen the wood and is desirable, as long as no damage due to rubbing against the supports can occur. Check to see that no ties are so loose that the tree can rub against its stake or against the string or rope itself, causing abrasion of the bark. Ties should not be so tight that they might cause strangulation when growth resumes in spring; any tie which threatens to bite into the cambium layer of the bark should be loosened and retied.

Any form of support should be removed as soon as it is no longer needed. Staking should normally stay in place for two years, seldom longer. When removing a stake, saw it off at ground level rather than risk injury to the tree's roots, which might result from rocking the stake back and forth.

Watering evergreens
If the fall has been dry, and rainfall insufficient to build up a moisture reserve in the soil, then you may need to give evergreen trees and shrubs a last thorough watering before frost sets in. Pay special attention to rhododendrons and other evergreens with shallow root systems and to all freshly planted shrubs which have not yet been able to establish enough deep-reaching roots to fill their water requirements. Remember: all evergreens continue to transpire water from their leaves and needles on sunny winter days, even when the ground is frozen.

Preparing for winter protection
Material for winter protection of tender shrubs should be organized now, well before protection is actually needed. See that you have everything you will need on hand, in case the weather suddenly takes a turn for the worse. However, do not be stampeded into putting up screens or laying evergreen branches too early. In most cases it is wisest to wait as long as reasonably possible; if you cover too early, you only invite mice and other rodents to make their homes beneath the covering. It is usually best to wait until the ground is frozen to a depth of 2in/50mm or more before taking action. The materials used must be loose enough to admit air freely and not pack under the weight of snow; among those commonly used are dry leaves, straw, bracken fern, and evergreen branches. Whatever material you choose, do not spread it too thickly; in most cases one layer just dense enough to shade the ground completely is sufficient. Its purpose, to mitigate the effects of alternate freezing and thawing and to give protection from sun and wind, is the same as the effect of deep snow cover. It is not intended to keep plants warm!

Be prepared to protect the more tender evergreens with burlap screens or conifer branches stuck in the ground. Install them to afford shade from the sun and to break the force of winter's cold blasts.

Fallen leaves
In woodland and semiwoodland areas, in shrub plantings, and under hedges, shrubs and trees not standing in grass, it is often better to let fallen leaves remain as a natural mulch. Check once in a while that they have not piled up in layers too thick for the well-being of any herbaceous perennials or other small plants that may be underneath. If they threaten to smother rather than protect, level them out with a fork or rake. Never allow leaves to lie for long on lawns, where they weaken the grass by cutting off light and air and encourage growth of harmful fungi.

On no account should fallen leaves simply be carted away as rubbish. They are a "crop" to be harvested, and can be used as directly as a surface mulch or composted, either alone, to give leaf mold, or in combination with other waste vegetable material.

Trimming deciduous hedges
Formal deciduous hedges can still be trimmed in late fall; in fact there are definite advantages to leaving pruning till so late in the year. Once the leaves have fallen, it is possible to see clearly just where to prune. Also, leafless pruning eliminates the sight of ragged, brown-edged leaves which shearing in summer so often produces. Because hedge plants are now in a dormant state, you can prune back, except in cold areas; the wounds will heal without problem.

Hardwood cuttings
Probably the easiest method for the propagation of many hardy, mostly deciduous trees and shrubs is by means of hardwood cuttings taken during this season. Of course, hardwood cuttings may be taken at any time during dormancy, but the best time for them to take root is just after the leaves have fallen. Cuttings taken from leafless shoots are almost always more successful than soft, leafy cuttings because water loss due to transpiration is reduced to a minimum. Hardwood cuttings taken now may be planted at once or buried in moist sand or peat outdoors, or put in a coldframe and planted the following spring. See page 156 for cutting techniques.

ROSES

Planting roses in fall
If you live in an area with hard winters, planting roses in spring is generally safer. However, there are good reasons for planting roses in fall – with one exception: standard or tree roses should always be planted in spring, as the winter protection of freshly planted tree roses is problematical. If you plan to buy either very new or very old cultivars, which may not be available in large numbers, you will want to order early for fall planting, unless you decide to wait for the mail order catalogs in spring. Also, nurseries may charge more for roses held in cold storage over winter, so if you buy in fall you can save money, but you run the risk of losing a plant or two during the first winter.

If your garden is sheltered and the winter usually stays mild in your region, then planting in mid-fall is favorable. But, wherever you live, don't be rushed into planting too soon; wait until most plants have lost their leaves. However, in many areas the period with optimal planting conditions is short and so you should not delay. To guarantee success the soil must still be warm enough to allow the roses to grow new roots before winter. If by spring the plants have made plenty of new roots, these will then be able to supply the fresh leaves and shoots with sufficient water and nutrients from the soil to ensure a rapid start.

Try to choose a mild, dry day with an overcast sky. The soil should not be so wet that it is easily compacted; neither should the roots dry out during planting. Cut back only the ends of damaged roots, leaving all healthy roots unpruned; leave the canes unshortened until spring, when they receive their first pruning.

After planting (see page 15) and watering in well, mound up the bushes with soil; later, after the ground has frozen, they should receive the same winter protection as tender plants (see page 148–149).

Protection from wind: cutting back and tying in

While the pruning of garden roses is better left until spring, it is often wise to cut back any long canes that may be whipped around by winter wind. If any of your roses are growing on a windy, exposed spot, then you should cut back long stems as much as necessary to prevent their being damaged by winter storms. If unhindered, buffeting by the wind can loosen the bush, sever its root hold, and even kill the plant.

Inspect your climbing and rambler roses to ensure that they are tied in securely against wind and that none of the long new canes is in danger of being torn or broken.

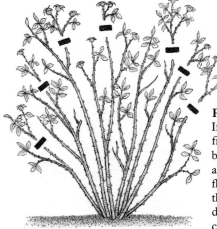

Protecting roses from wind
If your roses are likely to suffer from exposure to wind, cut back some of the longest stems after the shrub has finished flowering. Removing up to a third of the stem will reduce the danger of wind rock which causes broken roots and weakened stems.

Fallen rose leaves

Gather up fallen rose leaves as long as they continue to drop. Healthy leaves may be composted, but if you had any incidence of black spot or rust on your roses during the past summer, all the leaves should be disposed of, to prevent the spores of these two enemies of the rose from overwintering. It pays to be assiduous about raking up and removing dead rose leaves as they fall and a bit of effort now can do much to ensure the health of your roses next year. Of all the diseases which attack roses, black spot and mildew are the most pernicious. Both infect primarily the leaves, eventually killing them and causing them to drop. Both diseases can spread rapidly from midsummer onward and strip the leaves from the bushes. Each infected leaf that falls carries with it millions of spores which overwinter on the dead leaves or in the soil, ready for an attack the following year. In this case, good hygiene is the best remedy.

CLIMBING PLANTS

Planting climbers

Reliably hardy deciduous climbing plants can still be planted as long as weather permits. In general, climbing plants are subject to the same rules and restrictions for planting as other shrubs or roses: try to plant your climbers as early in this season as possible, and avoid planting when the ground is frozen or wet. Water well and be prepared to protect plants against sun and wind. Evergreen climbers are better planted in early spring, when the danger of desiccation due to winter sun and wind is past.

Watering climbers growing on walls

If the soil at the base of the wall is in rain shadow or if the climbers have not had time to establish a root system deep enough to guarantee an adequate supply of water, you may need to give them a thorough soaking, before freezing weather sets in. If necessary, follow up with a thick organic mulch to help protect the roots and the soil from extremes of winter weather.

Secure climbers before winter

Inspect your climbing plants to be sure that they are secure for the coming winter and can withstand winds, and damage from heavy rain, or snow and ice, just as for roses (see page 148).

HERBACEOUS PERENNIALS

Planting

Mid-fall is an important planting season for many herbaceous perennials. As long as the soil is still warm and not too wet, they will make new roots quickly. If they can get a good start now, they will grow faster and flower better next year than perennials planted in the spring. However, if your soil is heavy and inclined to remain cold and wet for long periods in winter, then it is much safer to delay planting. Some perennials, such as ferns, ornamental grasses, and any especially tender species, are always better left until spring.

As soon as leaves are falling, you should complete any remaining planting as quickly as possible. Soon it will be too late for safe planting in all but the lightest, warmest, best-drained soils and you may have to postpone further planting till the spring.

Tidying up borders
Some time after the first severe frosts, when the foliage of your herbaceous perennials has withered and the last flowers have faded, the time has come for the annual cleanup in the herbaceous beds and mixed borders. Avoid being in too great a rush, however; as long as the leaves are green and capable of photosynthesis it is better to allow them to stand a while longer. They can still transport energy to the roots to be stored for new growth next spring. Most truly herbaceous plants may be cut back almost to ground level as soon as their leaves have died back, but there are some important exceptions: ornamental grasses and any perennials with decorative seed heads or stems which look good covered with frost or snow should be left standing, as well as any stalks bearing seed for birds.

Most of the debris can safely be put on the compost pile, except, of course, any obviously diseased plants, which should be removed from the garden. Woody stalks should be chopped into pieces about 4–6in/100–150mm long in order to accelerate composting. Remove stakes, brush sticks, and other supports at the same time. Brush sticks can be chopped up and added to the compost pile along with the other dead stalks and leaves. Intact stakes and canes should be cleaned and stored in a dry place for next year.

Winter protection
Tender perennials, as well as many alpine plants, which come from mountainous regions where they normally enjoy the excellent winter protection provided by a thick layer of dry snow, will need artificial protection against the damp cold and harmful winter sun which are common in snowless gardens. Cover plants that are at risk with dry leaves and enough weightier material such as conifer branches or bracken to hold them in place. Take care not to smother small evergreen plants under too thick a layer nor to cover the centers of rosette-forming plants. For best results, spread an organic mulch around the base of each plant to protect the soil from repeated thawing and freezing and top with a loose covering of conifer branches or bracken as protection against the drying effects of wind and sun. It is best to wait until the ground is frozen before installing winter protection.

ANNUALS AND BIENNIALS

Thinning and planting out biennials
Biennials (as well as annuals) sown in late summer or early fall should be thinned out somewhat to prevent their becoming over-crowded and spindly and to reduce the danger of disease. Do not thin as drastically as you might in spring, but leave a space of about 2–2½in/50–60mm between the plants; the final thinning will be done in early spring after the rigors of winter are over.

In warm areas, now is still a good time to plant hardy biennials wherever garden plots are vacant, for example after summer bedding annuals have been removed. Biennials are always grown to almost full size before they are transferred to where they are to bloom and, as long as the soil is open and warm, good strong young plants of forget-me-not, pansies, daisies, primulas, Canterbury bells, and sweet Williams can be successfully transplanted to their final positions. However, do try to finish planting before fall leaves have dropped, or the weather may turn cold too soon for the biennials to become well enough established to withstand the winter unscathed. Freshly planted biennials should be watered thoroughly whenever the soil shows signs of drying. As soon as the ground has frozen once or twice, check the young plants to be sure that all are sitting firmly in the ground, then bring out a loose protective covering (such as conifer branches) if you cannot expect a lasting snow cover in your area.

BULBS

Planting spring bulbs
If you have not yet finished planting all your spring-flowering bulbs, you still have some time. But do try to get them into the ground as soon as possible, so long as the soil is still relatively warm and not so wet that it is unpleasant to dig. The bulbs must have enough time to sprout roots before the ground freezes if they are to flower satisfactorily next spring.

Potting bulbs for forcing indoors
There is also still time to pot hyacinths, daffodils, and tulips for forcing indoors in late winter. The sooner you pot the bulbs, the sooner you can enjoy their flowers since most bulbs require a minimum of twelve weeks' cold storage after potting before forcing can begin (see page 118).

Planting lilies
Fall is frequently a good season in which to plant bulbs. Many shipments of new lily bulbs are not sent out from the nurseries until late fall, so you may find yourself with a collection of prize lilies waiting to be planted. Newly purchased bulbs can still be planted in

the garden as long as the weather is good and the soil neither too cold nor too wet to be easily workable. If the bulbs arrive too late to permit planting outdoors you should pot them up in a good potting soil and place the pots in a very cool, but frostfree greenhouse, shed, or garage for the winter. In the spring, the lily plants (for they will begin to sprout before you can get them into the ground) can be planted in the beds where they are to grow as soon as weather permits.

Removing tender bulbous plants

Be prepared to dig all tender bulbs, corms, and tubers for winter storage but do not remove them too soon. While the leaves are green

Removing dahlias
1 Once the leaves have blackened, cut off the stalks about 2in/50mm above the ground. Stalk and leaves can be added to the compost pile. This is a good time to renew any labels that have faded or torn.

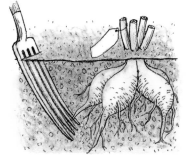

2 Using a fork, ease the tubers carefully out of the ground, taking great care not to spear or break them. Wounds would allow the entry of organisms that can rot the tubers during their winter storage. Leave the tubers to dry off for a few days.

3 Gently remove the soil still sticking to the tubers before packing them in flats and boxes filled with peatmoss. The best place for winter storage is a cool, but frostfree, dry, and airy basement or shed.

and capable of photosynthesis they are still working to fatten their underground storage organs with energy for next year's growth. Wait until the first strong frosts have blackened the foliage of your dahlias, caladiums, cannas, tuberous begonias, and montbretias before you start digging.

WATER GARDEN

Preparations for winter – dead leaves
During the course of fall, your water garden will once again require your attention and you will need to make the first preparations for coming winter. Do all you can to prevent dead leaves and other vegetation from landing in the pond, where it would decay and foul the water. Clear away untidy foliage from poolside plants after frost has turned them brown.

Cut back all dying water plants, with the exception of reeds and rushes. Some of these should be left standing to poke through the ice in winter; their protruding stalks help keep the water supplied with oxygen, even when the surface is frozen. If you do cut back rushes and other plants with hollow stems, be sure not to cut below the expected maximum water level; these plants can "drown" if their hollow stems fill with water.

Winter protection for aquatic plants
Tropical aquatic plants such as water hyacinth, *Eichhornia crassipes*, fairy moss, *Azolla caroliniana*, and water lettuce, *Pistia stratiotes*, which are sometimes grown as exotic summer guests in the water garden, need to be brought indoors well before the first night frosts. These plants can be overwintered in an aquarium or even in a bucket of water in the greenhouse. However, to survive they need plenty of light and water temperatures which do not drop below 48°–54°F/8°–12°C. If you cannot provide sufficient light to maintain good leaf color, then keep the plants cool, closer to the 46°F/8°C minimum.

Certain other plants are only borderline hardy, as they originate from the warmer temperate regions of the globe. Some of these aquatics and bog plants are especially attractive and are well worth the efforts required to bring them securely through our less-hospitable winters, for example, gold club, *Orontium aquaticum*, water hawthorn, *Aponogeton distachyos*, pickerel weed, *Pontederia cordata*, and false skunk cabbage, *Lysichiton americanus*. These plants should not be allowed to freeze solid for any length of time. If the plants are growing in containers, these can be moved to a deeper part of the pool which will not freeze. Where this is not possible, for example, if the plants are growing in a low area which can be expected to freeze over, a layer of conifer branches over the plant will give some protection. Be sure, of course, to remove the branches in spring, before new growth begins.

Water lilies can be allowed to die back naturally. Except for tropical water lilies, which must be brought indoors for overwintering in an aquarium or basin, all water lilies are perfectly safe in the pond where they are growing as long as water depth is at least 12in/300mm above their crowns.

Water lilies can also be left in a drained pool over the winter. Cover the crowns with a generous layer of straw and the entire pool with a layer of plastic sheeting (to prevent its refilling with winter rain or snow).

Checklist of other protective measures:
- Concrete pools with vertical sides may need the protection of styrofoam blocks along the edges to absorb the expansion of the ice as the surface freezes.
- If there are fish in a pool that is likely to freeze solid, they must be netted and brought indoors. It is better to ensure that the pool does not freeze completely.
- To protect the pool from freezing, thick styrofoam sheets may be floated over part of the surface. These alone or in combination with a simple aeration pump, which must be kept running as long as temperatures are below freezing, will usually be all that you need to bring your pool, aquatic plants, and fish safely through the winter. Expensive heaters are seldom necessary.
- All water pipes and hoses which might freeze should be drained and secured.
- Any air or water pumps which are not to remain in operation should be drained, cleaned, and brought indoors.

LAWN AND FLOWER MEADOW

Fall feeding
If your lawn is to maintain its bright green color throughout the winter months, you may want to fertilize it in mid-fall. Avoid a fertilizer containing nitrogen which encourages growth (harmful in cold regions) and fungal disease (in milder, wet areas). However, to encourage root growth and not leaf production you can use a fertilizer with a relatively low nitrogen content but good levels of phosphorus and potassium.

Mowing before winter
Some grasses may now be growing more slowly, so mow them much less frequently. Raise the blades of your mower to the proper winter height for your type of lawn and continue to mow whenever needed. As much as possible avoid mowing when the grass is wet with dew or rain and never attempt to cut grass during frosty weather. Plan to mow a final time in late fall so that the grass is not too long when winter sets in; a lawn that is too long as it goes into winter is more susceptible to diseases.

If your flower meadow has grown too high since the last cutting, it should be scythed once again; the grasses should never be so tall that they will be lodged by winter's rain and snow. It is especially important to mow now if your flower meadow is planted with bulbs; you want the grass to be so short that it does not obstruct the beauty of the spring flowers.

Raking up leaves
The lawn is one of the few areas of the garden where fallen leaves cannot be tolerated. Rake up the leaves from your lawn regularly, at least once a week, and remove them to the compost pile.

Moss and thatch – spiking and dethatching
Moss in the lawn is often a sign of compacted soil. Now is a good time to combat moss by spiking (aeration), but be sure to finish the job before the ground becomes too wet from fall rains or hardened by frost. It is also good practice to remove dead grass (thatch) using a rake or dethatching tool (see pages 160–161).

PATIO AND BALCONY

Planting for winter
Window boxes, tubs, and other containers should be planted up for color in winter and early spring on the patio and balcony. There is a wide selection of small broad leaved evergreens and conifers, heaths, and other dwarf winter-flowering shrubs as well as diminutive winter-flowering perennials and small spring-flowering bulbs which are all perfectly suited for restricted space and close-up viewing, so you can allow your fantasy to roam free. (You might even consider acquiring a second set of containers for your balcony: one for summer planting, the other for a permanent planting comprising mainly plants with winter interest if you live in a warm area.)

Overwintering container plants
All tender container plants that need to be overwintered indoors should be brought inside as soon as frost threatens. However, many plants, particularly those of Mediterranean origin, are surprisingly hardy and those which withstand a few degrees of frost are better left outside on the patio or balcony as long as possible.

When moving plants into their winter quarters, it is good practice to break all flowers and unopened flower buds, and cut back any soft, unripe shoots. At the same time, prune off any obviously diseased leaves or shoots.

The winter quarters need to be as bright as possible and cool but frostfree. For most container plants, the optimal winter temperature lies between 40° and 54°F/5° and 12°C; seldom do they require more warmth.

CHAPTER 9

WINTER

"At Christmas I no more desire a rose
Than wish a snow in May's new-fangled mirth;
But like of each thing that in a season grows."

William Shakespeare

According to the biological calendar, winter is the longest season of the year in most regions. It is also the season that shows the widest variations according to geographical location – altitude, latitude, and distance from the ocean. These play a decisive role in determining the weather and winter's duration, which can vary by as much as six weeks.

There are no phenological indicator, or signal, plants for winter – all of our native plants remain securely dormant from late fall till just before spring (see *Pre-spring*). Not until the snowdrops start to flower can we expect the first signs of nature's reawakening, signaling the end of winter, as the natural cycle of the seasons once again moves on to begin a new year of growth and hope.

In the initial phase of winter, the days are frequently dark, overcast, and dreary due to low clouds which can block out the sun for days on end. Precipitation, which falls mostly as rain, can be heavy and long-lasting. The second phase of winter is generally marked by a sudden, massive temperature drop, accompanied at first by clear weather but often followed by snow. In late winter, temperatures start to rise as the days become longer. Occasionally there may be a short spell of unseasonably mild weather, but it is wise to ignore such a false spring, for it rarely lasts and cold weather is almost certain to return.

THE WINTER GARDEN

Winter is the moment of truth for any garden. As soon as the flowers have faded and the deciduous trees and shrubs have been stripped to their bones, the framework, the supportive skeleton of your garden plan and planting design, becomes dominant. Paths, walks, hedges, and walls, all elements that provide background and form for your plantings, must stand on their own merits now, for the eye is no longer engaged – or distracted – by the bounty of floral color. If the logic and design of you garden "works," and is pleasing, then you can be satisfied thay you have gone far toward achieving the most important goal in designing any garden. For it is possible to make a garden that is beautiful and pleasing to all the senses at all seasons, whether sleeping under a blanket of snow in deepest winter or exploding with extravagant masses of fragrant blossoms in summer.

Practice looking at you garden in winter with the critical eye of a visitor. Judge the shapes and outlines of your trees and shrubs, the backgrounds provided by evergreens and hedges and then look for color interest, which is so rare and therefore so valuable during the winter season.

There are very few plants which actually flower during the winter. In all but the mildest areas, most plants which are normally described as winter-flowering usually blossom during pre-spring. (There are a few exceptions: see page 144.) Most of the color interest in the winter garden will be created by evergreen foliage plants, particularly those with variegated leaves, and by trees and shrubs with decorative fruits or attractive, beautifully colored bark and stems.

Because the palette of bark and stem colors is restricted, color combinations in winter are not a problem in garden designs. The glowing young stems of the scarlet willow, *Salix alba* 'Britzensis,' with their open texture, make an admirable show in winter whether next to yellow-stemmed willows, crimson dogwoods, cinnamon-barked maple, or the purest white birches. Yellow- and orange-colored barks are especially beautiful with birch bark against a dark background. A small group of European whitebark birch planted with one or two golden willows, *S. a. vitellina*, for example, assume a warm glow in the reflected light of the cheery willow branches. Colorful young shoots of willows and dogwoods and the trunks and branches of birches, snakebark maples, and some of the original cherries take on a warm radiance in the light of the low-lying winter sun. Remember, though, that these trees and shrubs with their thin bare stems inevitably have a certain frailty; conifers and broad-leaved evergreens are needed to give substance and form to the winter garden scene.

Evergreens in the winter garden
Nothing is more capable of lending texture, volume, and visual depth to a planting design than evergreen shrubs. Bold sweeps of evergreen ground-cover plants such as ivy, pachysandra, or vinca threading through beds and borders are important in unifying the winter garden. Use a combination of evergreen trees, shrubs, and ground-cover plants to build up a framework.

As frost outlines the last leaves and seed heads in the winter garden, bold shapes and textures come into their own. Here the elegant trellis and mellow brick wall provide for a background to clumps of euphorbia and evergreen foliage.

Evergreen hedges and tall conifers provide a solid permanent backdrop, with sharp accents, furnishing the interesting shapes needed to enliven the winter scene.

The green of your evergreens will most likely be the primary background color in your garden in winter. The evergreens give a range of moods to choose from when planning the composition of hedges or plantings which are to serve as background to trees and shrubs with colorful bark and shoots Conifers vary widely in size and shape, and their ever-"green" foliage can assume an almost limitless spectrum of hues of green and displays a surprising variety of textures as well. Indeed, because evergreens are so important during the long winter months, you should take care to pick conifers that have the silhouette, density, texture, color, and, most important, the scale which best suits your garden. There are a multitude of shades of green, between the pale, frosty grey-green of certain junipers and the darkest greenish-black of the sombre yew.

Bright bark color
There is nothing that characterizes a frozen winter landscape better than the dazzling white trunks of European whitebark birches. This association of white trunks with winter cold and snow is so strong that any trees with white, or even very pale gray, bark conjure up this image. Trees with warm brown trunks or with shaggy, dark cinnamon bark relieve the icy cold, while the smooth green and white snakeskin stripes on the trunks of some maples are crisp and clear on overcast days.

The graceful birches are valuable in the winter garden because of the delicate tracery of their slender branches as well as for their lovely milky white, pink, or orange-brown bark. In most species, the main trunk is just as attractive in summer beneath the open canopy of leaves as it is in winter when bare of foliage, which earns these fast-growing, very hardy trees a place in even the smallest garden.

White is the color most often associated with birch bark, at least by gardeners acquainted primarily with the European whitebark birch, but there is an exotic species which excels even this birch for pure dazzling whiteness of bark, the Himalayan birch, *Betula utilis jacquemontii*. With its paper-thin bark peeling in strips to leave behind a smooth surface of purest white, this tree is one of the most conspicuous in winter because even the branches high up in the crown, of no greater thickness than a finger, are milky white. It grows fairly quickly to a medium-sized, wide-spreading well-shaped tree, but perhaps is not so graceful of habit as the European whitebark birch. It is, however, one of the best trees for brightening up a shady corner or the edge of a wood, where it joins the lawn. Planted with shrubs that have highly colored stems where the slanting winter sun can catch them, this birch will delight you all winter long.

The North American paper birch, *Betula papyrifera*, is also a handsome tree in winter with its creamy white, paperlike bark, which peels in large patches to reveal a tinge of orange and buff beneath. It has the cleanest, smoothest trunk of any birch and remains white clear to the ground, even when large, not becoming black and rough like the European whitebark birch. *B. papyrifera* grows to 65ft/20m high; it makes a large, open crown of branches and eventually requires more space than the European whitebark birch. Although it lacks some of the delicate grace of the European species, this is an attractive tree for any garden large enough to accommodate it.

Several species of birch have warm-colored bark in shades of pink and orange. *Betula albosinensis*, for example, is a Chinese birch with exceptionally beautiful, silky-textured bark of a shining orange-brown color covered with a pink and gray bloom. The Russian rock birch, *Betula ermanii*, a wide-spreading birch from Asia, hardy to zone 5, has bark of a creamy shade of apricot pink, peeling away in thin strips to reveal patches of dull white shaded with orange-brown. The youngest branches are brighter in color, almost white. *Betula maximowicziana*, the monarch birch, is clearly the king of the birches; this Japanese tree has the largest leaves of any birch, a good 6in/150mm long and almost as wide. They are shaped much like those of the linden, are glossy rich green in summer turning in fall to dark shades of old gold. Beautiful at all times of the year, but especially decorative in winter, the bark is dark orange-brown, maturing to gray, and striped horizontally with gray-brown, in parts orange and pink.

As a genus, the maples seem to reserve many of their loveliest traits till the end of the year; not only are there numerous maples with breathtaking fall leaf colors, several of them are just as beautiful bare of all foliage, when their unique bark colors and textures enchant throughout the winter months. But even in summer, the bark of many species contributes to the trees' special appeal, since the foliage is seldom so dense as to hide the bark completely. The trunks of many have handsomely striped, "snakeskin" bark, others have bark which peels off in layers to reveal paler colors beneath.

The coral bark maple, *Acer palmatum* 'Sangokaku,' is one of the most shapely of the Japanese maples. A small, neat, erect, dome-shaped tree, its finely-drawn twigs take on a glowing coral red color in winter, particularly when the winter sun strikes its branches. The coral bark maple is hardy to zone 5 and will reach 30ft/9m; like all Japanese maples, it prefers a rich, moist soil. 'Sangokaku' also has good bronze-green foliage during summer, turning to a soft yellowish orange in fall. *A. capillipes*, the red snakebark maple, is another small Japanese species, one of the group of handsome trees with striated, "snakeskin" branches, which also includes the closely related species *A. grosseri*, *A. pensylvanicum*, and *A. rufinerve*. *A. capillipes* is the only one of this group to have shiny leaves. Its bark is clearly and brightly striped with white on gray-green but the youngest shoots are dark red. It grows rapidly when young, but, as the branches tend to arch over, it seldom reaches a height of 33ft/10m. It is hardy to zone 6 and tolerant of a wide range of soils, although most suited to a woodland situation. Indeed, it thrives best if the trunk is lightly shaded

Betula utilis jacquemontii, the brightest of the white-barked birches, is a handsome open-branched tree, whose leaves turn a clear yellow. It grows quickly to a height of 30ft/9m.

from the sun. The young leaves and shoots are rich pink in the spring; the fall coloration is variable, as a single tree may have leaves of yellow, orange, or crimson.

One of the most beautiful of the snakeskin maples, the Chinese species *Acer grosseri* has striking green bark, striped with white. It is a small tree, seldom exceeding 19ft/6m even in its native habitat. *A. grosseri* is particularly distinctive because it maintains the bright markings on its trunks until the bole is large, after which it gradually becomes brown and gray and corky in texture. It grows quickly and develops a handsome crown with long arching branches, which sweep to the ground like a fountain of green. The leaves color magnificently in early fall, turning to bright shades of tawny orange.

Acer pensylvanicum, known as moosewood, is a small North American tree with prettily striped bark and extraordinarily large leaves. During the winter, moosewood is one of the most attractive maples, renowned for its fascinating jade green bark striped with silver and white. The leaves, which may be almost 8in/200mm across, have a pink tinge on opening and turn bright yellow in fall. Moosewood grows to 30ft/9m in its home in eastern USA, but in Europe seldom reaches more than 19ft/6m. It carries erect branches, which are at first green, becoming reddish brown before finally asuming the beautiful green and white snakeskin pattern. There is a clone

A warm and welcome sight in the midst of winter: the bark of *Prunus serrula*, the Tibetan cherry, is a beautiful, polished mahogany brown with strikingly regular horizontal striations.

A tree of an entirely different appearance, the paper bark maple, *Acer griseum*, is a fascinating feature in the winter garden; the old and tattered, rust colored bark on the trunk and largest branches flakes and curls back to reveal the cinnamon-colored underbark. The paper bark maple grows to about 26ft/8m in cultivation, is hardy to zone 6 and not at all fussy about soil. It forms a shapely little tree, often with many limbs, which originate low on the main trunk and rise steeply to make an upright fan silhouette. In summer, it has a pleasantly cool appearance which changes completely in fall when the whole tree ignites in a memorable blaze of red and purple. But it is mainly for the warm brown tones of the bark of the bare branches in winter that *A. griseum* is so treasured. If you choose to plant the paper bark maple in your garden, try to obtain a young tree that branches from low down, so that you receive full benefit of the rich raggy brown bark. It associates well with the winter-flowering heath, *Erica* 'Springwood White,' planted as a carpet at its base.

For smooth, glistening bark on thick, sturdy boles, it is hard to beat the ornamental cherries and scarcely anyone can resist the temptation to touch the glossy, mahogany red trunk of a tree like the Tibetan cherry, *Prunus serrula*. In fact, you should plant the Tibetan cherry beside a well-used path where its shining branches can be felt by passersby since this will help keep the bark highly polished. During late summer and fall, the old bark gradually peels away in strips, revealing the polished young bark. Virtually no other tree, except perhaps *Acer griseum*, produces such a striking effect. *P. serrula* will normally reach 13ft/4m after five years and eventually a maximum height of about 33ft/10m; it grows rapidly as a young tree, but slows down as it ages. It is well suited for planting in a prominent spot in a yard or in a front garden near the entrance way. It is charming in summer with its dainty, willowlike, dark green foliage, that turns to a clear tawny orange in fall. The small white flowers which hang in clusters among the branches in early spring are not so glistening honey color, it darkens with age to pale orange-

The bark of the Manchurian cherry, *Prunus maackii*, is less highly polished but nevertheless attractive; from a unique, glistening honey color, it darkens with age to pale orange-brown and dark orange before flaking much like a birch. The Manchurian cherry is a small wide-spreading tree, eventually reaching 40ft/12m in the wild state. It is related to the bird

called 'Erythrocladum,' the pink moosewood, in which the young shoots are a bright coral pink with paler stripes. Its mature branches and trunk are a pale salmon pink with overtones of beige and gray. The young shoots turn bright crimson as the leaves drop in fall. 'Erythrocladum' has what may be the most brilliantly colored bark of any hardy tree, brighter still than the willows and dogwoods. It is, however, a plant of weak constitution. Neither moosewood nor pink moosewood is very tolerant of alkaline soils.

Obviously closely related to moosewood, the Japanese *Acer rufinerve*, known as the gray-budded snakebark maple, is a small tree growing to about 30ft/9m. It resembles moosewood in leaf shape and markings on the branches. The predominant stem color is a cool silvery gray-green; the bright green bark is conspicuously striped with white and the youngest twigs are a contrasting reddish pink. This attractive maple is quite simple to grow and it looks its best in winter if you can position it in front of a dark background.

In the slanting light of the winter sun, the young shoots of crimson *Cornus alba* 'Sibirica' stand out well against the dark background of an evergreen hedge. In the foreground the variegated form of the evergreen shrub *Euonymus fortunei* provides a solid base, anchoring the dogwood firmly in the overall design.

cherries and flowers late in the cherry season with little erect spikes of fragrant white blossoms. The bright yellowish green young leaves make a striking contrast with the peeling bark on the mature branches. In fall when the leaves turn to amber and gold and in winter after the leaves have fallen, the little tree is a source of glowing golden warmth. You might continue this effect by planting a thick carpet of eranthis underneath to bring a sunny highlight when they flower at winter's end.

Shining stems

The dogwoods and willows are fast-growing vigorous trees and shrubs, which need regular hard pruning to restrain their expansive tendencies and to produce brilliantly colored young shoots (the older branches eventually become dull to a drab brown). So to take advantage of the intense coloration of the young growths, make sure that the stems are cut back every year or every other year (see page 29).

The violet willow, *Salix daphnoides*, has deep plum purple colored bark. Because winter is such a dark season in most regions, it is always the bright colors that receive preferred treatment, but even so, this lovely willow is very attractive on its own and can be effective against a light background. Its young shoots, which are purple overlaid with a fine bloom, are main attraction in the garden; they are at their best if the plant is pruned back to the main trunk every other year.

The dogwoods always seem to be most effective in large, isolated masses, such as a thicket near a large lawn or alongside a quiet body of water, where their brilliant colors can be reflected in the still black surface of the pond or stream. With its bright red shoots, the wild form of *Cornus alba*, the red bark dogwood, is attractive enough to plant in the garden; however, many gardeners prefer to plant the less rampant clone *C. a.* 'Sibirica' which has much more intense crimson stems. Though its color is definitely superior to the wild form, it is not so tenacious and should therefore not be pruned back completely each year. There is also a *C. alba* clone with deep purple, almost black young shoots called 'Kesselringii.'

The yellow dogwood, *Cornus stolonifera* 'Flaviramea,' is a dense, medium-sized shrub from North America, which spreads and suckers with abandon on any moist soil, so be prepared to restrain it – unchecked, it will make dense thickets up to 6½ft/2m tall. But cut back hard faithfully each year in early spring, it can be tamed and encouraged to make plenty of pretty young shoots which are yellow to greenish yellow. It is then of a similar height and habit to *C. alba* 'Sibirica,' with which it creates a most effective and vivid contrast. Because crimson 'Sibirica' does not grow as vigorously as its yellow-stemmed cousin, it should outnumber the yellow if a balanced effect is to be maintained. A combination of yellow and red dogwoods can be effective, especially when planted as long parallel bands of color among a path or steam.

The real path to success with these dogwoods is to keep them eternally young by regular pruning in early spring. Other than this, they require no upkeep.

Salix alba 'Britzensis,' the scarlet willow, is doubtless the best willow to plant for a spectacular display of scarlet stems in winter. It responds well to pruning annually or every second year. To make a large bush, the scarlet willow may also be cut back to the ground every second year in early spring, just before the buds break. The young shoots are a brilliant orange-scarlet, which is set off well by the old wood which is yellow in color. Planted together with a group of pruned dogwoods, the scarlet willow makes a wonderful background for a bank of winter-flowering heaths.

The golden willow, *Salix alba* 'Vitellina,' is a related clone and a truly ancient plant, known in Europe since Roman times. It looks bright and cheerful in winter with its long wands of brilliant egg-yolk yellow. Left unpruned, 'Vitellina,' although less vivid in color, is nevertheless an attractive wide-spreading tree, growing to a height of about 30ft/9m. Its ideal site is near water, where the reflection can double the effect; it also grows in a poor, dry soil.

PLANTS FOR WINTER

Yellow and orange
Chimonanthus praecox
Hamamelis species + cultivars
Jasminum nudiflorum

White and cream
Erica carnea cultivars 'Snow
    Queen,' 'Springwood White'
Prunus subhirtella 'Autumnalis'
Viburnum farreri
Helleborus niger 'Praecox'

Red and pink
Erica carnea 'White Beauty,'
    'Vivellii,' 'December Red,'
    'Pink Spangles,' 'Praecox
    Rubra,' 'King George'
Hamamelis species + cultivars
Viburnum × bodnantense 'Dawn,'
    'Charles Lamont'
Helleborus atrorubens

Scented plants
Chimonanthus praecox
Hamamelis species + cultivars

Viburnum farreri
V. × bodnantense 'Dawn'

**Trees and shrubs with
decorative fruits and berries**
These fruits or berries usually
remain till Christmas.
Berberis species + cultivars
Cotoneaster, some sp., especially:
    C. conspicuus
    C. dammeri
    C. franchetii
    C. horizontalis
    C. microphyllus cochleatus
    C. sternianus
Euonymus europaeus 'Red
    Cascade'
Ilex species + cultivars
Malus 'Crittenden,' 'Golden
    Hornet,' 'Prof. Sprenger,'
    'Red Jade,' 'Wintergold'
M. × zumi 'Calocarpa'
Photinia davidiana
P. villosa
Pyracantha cultivars

Rosa, many species + cultivars,
especially:
    R. acicularis
    R. canina
    R. davidii
    R. glauca
    R. moyesii
    R. pendulina
    R. eglanteria (*R. rubiginosa*)
    R. rugosa
    R. sweginzowii
    R. villosa
    R. willmottiae
Skimmia japonica 'Nymans,'
    'Veitchii'
S. reevesiana
Sorbus esserteauiana
S. sargentiana
S. 'Joseph Rock'
Viburnum opulus

**Trees and shrubs with
colorful bark**
Acer capillipes
A. davidii

A. griseum
A. grosseri
A. laxiflorum
A. palmatum 'Sangokaku'
A. pensylvanicum + *A. p.*
    'Erythrocladum'
A. rufinerve
Betula albosinensis
B. ermanii
B. utilis jacquemontii
B. × koehnei
B. maximowicziana
B. papyrifera
Cornus alba 'Sibirica,'
    'Kesselringii'
C. stolonifera + *C. s.* 'Flaviramea'
Prunus maackii
P. sargentii
P. serrula
Rubus cockburnianus
Salix alba 'Britzensis' + *S. a.*
    vitellina
S. daphnoides

WINTER TASKS

WILDLIFE

Winter feeding of birds

Whenever the garden lies under a blanket of snow, you may want to set up feeders to attract songbirds into the garden. It is then that their need is greatest; the natural food supply is at a minimum and they require extra food for energy and warmth or, in prolonged periods of ice and snow, to prevent starvation.

Remember, however, that winter feeding reaches only a small percentage of the native bird species and, of these, probably none is an endangered species. Winter feeding will not affect the population of any species in any significant way, but it will concentrate some birds locally where you want them – that is, around your house. As long as you follow certain guidelines there is no reason not to feed songbirds during winter. There are five general principles to bear in mind:

(1) Begin feeding as soon as freezing temperatures set in or a blanket of snow covers the ground and continue feeding only so long as snow and frost persist.

(2) Never feed so that food lies on the ground where it can become wet or contaminated by bird droppings. Moldy, spoiled food is dangerous for birds. Do everything you can to maintain a clean feeding area in order to avoid disease transmission; for the same reason, several small feeders are better than one large feeder.

(3) Choose a feeder construction that keeps the food dry and is cat-proof (and, if possible, pigeon-proof – for example, one with a low enough roof). For seed, a hopper-type feeder is best although a mesh basket will do.

(4) It is not necessary to buy expensive bird food for winter feeding. Beef suet is a favorite winter food of most insect-eating birds, just as sunflower seeds, millet, and hemp seeds are eagerly eaten by all seed-eaters.

(5) Cease feeding before the birds start nesting.

THE SOIL

Soil care

As long as the weather allows working outside in the garden, winter is an excellent time to take steps toward improving your garden soil. If analysis (see page 130) has shown, for instance, that your soil is too acidic and needs liming to raise the pH or that it requires some other additive to eliminate a basic deficiency or to improve its structure, you should take advantage of any period of quiet, dry weather to spread lime or whatever material is indicated over the surface of the beds. During winter these materials will continue to work slowly in the soil so that, by the time spring arrives, the treatment will have taken effect and the soil will be in prime condition to promote rapid growth.

Liming can be of immense benefit if properly done, but harmful if carried to excess and there are three things you need to know before you even consider spreading lime: first, what is the present pH of your soil, is it acid or alkaline? If already alkaline, then there is, of course, no reason whatever to spread lime. Second, what is the optimal pH level for your type of soil? A sandy or peaty soil, for instance, has a more acidic optimum than a heavy clay soil. Third, what is the preferred pH value for the plants you wish to grow?

If you have a "normal" garden soil, neither too sandy nor too heavy and are not planning to plant such "specialist" species as rhododendrons, heaths or other acid-loving plants, then the best policy is to adjust your soil to a pH around 6.5. The pH value for sandy or peaty soils should be closer to 5.8, while that for heavy clay should be somewhat higher, close to 7.

The amount of lime to apply also depends on the soil type: to raise the pH one unit, say from pH 5.5 to 6.5, a sandy soil requires about 11½oz/sq.yd (270g/sq.m) of ground limestone; a loam, 22½oz/sq.yd (540g/sq.m) and a heavy clay, 33¾/sq.yd (800g/sq.m). Should it be necessary to raise pH more than one unit, use several annual dressings of smaller quantities rather than a large amount all at once.

In most situations, the natural trend is for soil to become more acidic with time, so liming is often required. There are, however, situations where it may be desirable to make the soil more acidic, which is somewhat more difficult than raising the pH. Sulfur can be used with success, applied at a rate of about 5¾oz/sq.yd (135g/sq.m); the incorporation of acidic peat can also assist the process.

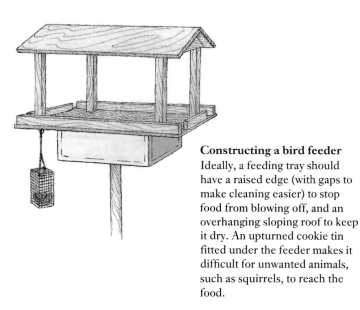

Constructing a bird feeder
Ideally, a feeding tray should have a raised edge (with gaps to make cleaning easier) to stop food from blowing off, and an overhanging sloping roof to keep it dry. An upturned cookie tin fitted under the feeder makes it difficult for unwanted animals, such as squirrels, to reach the food.

Heeling in plants
Dig a trench big enough to accommodate the roots laid closely together as possible. Quickly shovel soil and damp peatmoss over the roots to prevent them from drying out, and firm in lightly with your foot. Water the soil if dry.

TREES AND SHRUBS

Planting and heeling in

Planting of deciduous trees and shrubs can continue as long as the soil is neither frozen nor too wet to work. However, if they cannot all be planted in their allotted spots before bad weather sets in, they must be heeled in until weather and soil conditions allow planting again.

Heeling in keeps bare root plants alive and in the best possible condition if they cannot be planted immediately because of frosty or wet weather or if the ground has not yet been prepared for them. They can remain heeled in for a week or more, or even over the winter, until conditions are favorable for planting.

Choose a sheltered, lightly shaded location to heel in your plants. Position trees in the trench with their tops slanting toward the winter sun at an angle of about 45° to minimize exposure to the sun.

Protecting evergreen shrubs
Protect young or small evergreen shrubs from wind and sun by surrounding them closely with cut conifer branches stuck into the ground and angled to cover the plant.

Where the shrubs are in beds, heap up fallen leaves or pack straw around the plants to protect them from freezing and thawing. Use cut branches to keep the material in place.

Checking lifting by frost

Alternating periods of freezing and thawing weather may heave newly planted shrubs, particularly smaller plants with shallow roots like young heaths. Frost heaving can tear tender young roots and disrupt contact between the root ball and the soil around it, causing the plant to dry out and die. So, whenever the soil thaws, check new plantings and firm up the soil around any plants that have been loosened and, if heaving has been extreme, dig out and replant, taking care to firm the soil well.

Winter protection

Evergreen shrubs and trees, broad-leaved as well as certain conifers, may need protection against the drying effects of winter sun and wind. Winter protection is especially important for broad-leaved evergreens in areas where they are on the borderline of hardiness or if the garden is on an exposed site. The chief concern is to make certain that water is not lost from the foliage more rapidly than it can be replaced by the roots.

Fallen leaves may generally be left where they lie as a mulch under trees and shrubs. Wait until the ground is frozen to a depth of an inch or two before spreading any protective mulches – the most important function of winter covering is to keep the ground uniformly frozen and so to prevent roots from being torn and young plants heaved out of the soil by alternate freezing and thawing.

Rejuvenating deciduous hedges and shrubs

Rejuvenate neglected or overaged hedges and shrubs, which have become bare at the base or too large for their space, by radical pruning in winter. Choose from among several pruning methods which differ

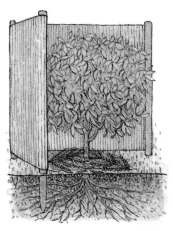

Protect larger shrubs and hedges by constructing a screen, using burlap or old straw matting attached to a framework of strong stakes driven firmly into the ground. The screen should be placed around two sides of the plant so that it gives protection both from the prevailing winds and from the winter sun.

mainly in degree of severity.

The simplest – and most radical – method, useful for shrubs which produce a thicket of stems from ground level, entails cutting away all shoots to a height of about 12in/300mm. During the coming year many new shoots will grow, about two-thirds of which should be cut out in the following winter, leaving the strongest, best-situated shoots.

A second, less radical method entails cutting out one-third to one-half of the shoots, usually the oldest, each winter for two or three years in succession. This will probably be the method of choice when rejuvenating hedge shrubs, since the hedge remains largely intact.

Formal hedges that have grown too large or have been neglected are generally best rejuvenated by cutting back one face at a time, allowing the hedge plants a year to recuperate between operations. If possible, fertilize several months before a heavy rejuvenation pruning.

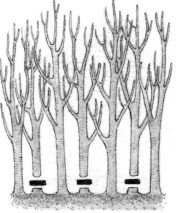
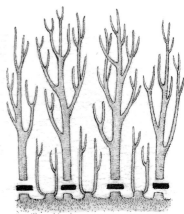

Partial pruning

The methods shown here (*right* and *below*) are suitable where hedges or shrubs are over-aged or need radical reshaping but for practical or aesthetic reasons you do not want to lose all the growth at once.

Above This method is useful for a shrubby, informal hedge where you want to retain some height and privacy or in a mixed hedge planting where one species has outgrown the others. In the first winter (*left*) cut out alternate stems (or the overvigorous ones). In the second (*above*) new shoots will have sprouted, so cut back the remaining stems.

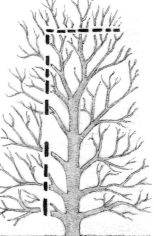
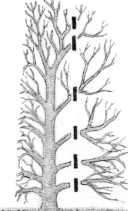

Above For shrubs that need radical rejuvenation without losing growth or flowers completely for one season, cut out approximately one-third to one-half of the stems (*left*) now, and remove the rest in the second or third years (*above*).

Above For formal hedges, particularly where the hedging plant is slow-growing or would suffer if cut back completely, cut back severely the sunnier side and top in the first year (*left*), and prune the other side a year or two later.

Watering evergreens

Water broad-leaved evergreens and conifers during periods of unusually dry, sunny, or windy weather if the ground is not yet frozen. Evergreens continue to transpire water from their leaves throughout the winter; if the lost water cannot be replaced from the roots, the shoots may suffer and die back – most "frozen" shoots are actually caused by a lack of water.

Freeing evergreens of heavy snow

Serious breakage can result from the accumulation of snow on branches, especially those of certain evergreens. Wet, heavy snow is obviously much more damaging than the light, fluffy kind. Free branches of accumulated snow as soon as possible after any snowfall, before it has a chance to become wet and heavy or freezes solid. Shake the branches gently or push them upward with a broom or rake. Avoid pulling branches downward, however, as that adds to the strain and may break them.

Pruning summer-flowering shrubs

If your summer-flowering shrubs have been less willing to flower and have made less new growth than usual, pruning now can coax them to make new shoots and flower buds. Cut away the oldest wood, as well as any weak, diseased, damaged, or poorly situated branches to leave an open, pleasingly shaped shrub with plenty of strong, well-placed young growths. For light pruning operations you can safely wait till the end of winter; but, if radical pruning (rejuvenation) is necessary, try to complete it as early in winter as possible.

Fertilizing in winter

Deciduous trees and shrubs, particularly those standing in grass, may be fertilized during the course of winter, whenever the ground is not frozen. Feeding at this time of year ensures that the nutrient salts will be washed past the grass roots into the tree root zone (see page 64).

Conifers, particularly the Serbian spruce, *Picea omorica*, may show symptoms of magnesium chlorosis: the needles turn yellow, with no transition between the green and yellow parts of the needles; young needles may be wholly affected while older needles become yellow only toward the tips. Magnesium deficiency occurs in light, acidic, sandy soils, and these should receive a dressing with epsom salts during winter. Apply the salts, which contain about 10 percent magnesium, according to the results of a soil analysis (see page 130).

Hardwood cuttings

Hardwood cuttings for propagation of many deciduous shrubs can still be taken in winter; however, the cuttings taken as early as possible in the dormant period have the best chances of success (see page 156).

Protecting roses in winter

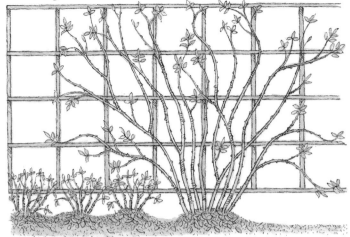

Above Though protection is important, it should not be brought into place too early. Wait until there have been two hard frosts before you mound up soil around the bases of bushes and of climbers to protect the graft union.

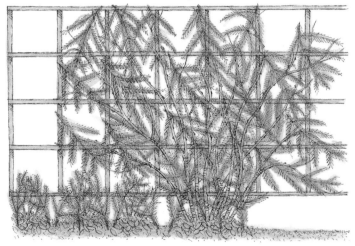

Above When the ground freezes to a depth of 2¾in/70mm, cover climbers with a curtain of conifer branches or burlap sacking. Cover bushes with leaves, straw or other loose material. It is important that air is able to circulate around the canes; stagnant moist air under winter protection is more harmful than no protection at all.

ROSES

Protection from extreme winter cold

Most serious winter injury to roses results not from low temperature but from sudden or frequent temperature fluctuations. A rapid rise or extreme drop in temperature can rupture cell walls in the rose canes and kill them. The second primary cause of winter damage is from drying winds. Especially when the ground is frozen, winter winds can dry out exposed canes and, if the canes have been injured by the cold, the weakened cells are unable to resist water loss; when that happens you find shriveled and blackened canes in the spring instead of plump green wood.

Contrary to what you might expect, one purpose of winter protection is to keep roses cold, not warm. What you want to promote are thoroughly dormant canes at as constant a temperature as possible – ideally in the range 23° to 14°F/−5° to −10°C. Much more important than most gardeners realize is the need to protect the roses from wind and winter sun. In really cold temperatures (below 14°F/−25°C), climbers and ramblers will need to be unbound, laid upon the ground and covered with soil and a layer of conifer branches. The same method can also be applied to tree roses after they have been untied from their supports.

HERBACEOUS PERENNIALS

Winter protection

If you haven't completed covering tender perennials, there is still time to do so. Once the soil is frozen, take advantage of any snowless period to cover where it is necessary. Also, check the winter protection in your mixed and herbaceous beds periodically to be sure that it is still in place. After windy storms you may have to adjust or renew coverings of straw, or conifer branches.

Cleaning up beds and borders

Whether you choose to clean up your beds and borders of herbaceous perennials at the end of the year or to leave such housecleaning tasks until pre-spring is largely a matter of personal choice and experience. However, if the dead and tattered vegetation disturbs the appearance of the garden or if there is danger that winter winds might loosen the plants or tear them from the ground, it is better to cut their withered tops back to a height of 12in/300mm or less. Otherwise, as long as they are not diseased, leave dried stalks and leaves – they protect the crowns of the perennials and provide cover for countless small insects and other invertebrates, the majority of them useful.

Sowing for cold germination

The seeds of many perennials will not germinate unless they are exposed to a period of cold temperatures to break their dormancy. For optimal germination, such species as monkshood, many primulas and gentians, meconopsis, alliums, members of the lily family, and most alpine plants require a cold period for six to twelve weeks after sowing, with temperatures around the freezing point. Sow the seed early in winter in flats or pots, and place them outside in a shady spot. A covering of conifer branches helps to reduce the danger of drying out.

ANNUALS AND BIENNIALS

Protecting biennials

Wallflowers, cheiranthus, and other more tender biennials need the protection of a light covering of conifer branches or salt hay in colder regions, particularly during snowless periods of the winter. Protect them from the vagaries of winter weather, but be sure that their foliage does not become smothered under wet, packed leaves or debris.

BULBS

Storing summer-flowering bulbs

Use the relatively quiet weeks of early winter to finish cleaning and sorting the bulbs, corms, and tubers of acidanthera, gladioli, tuberous begonias, dahlias, and cannas for winter storage. Pack them in open boxes of peatmoss in a cool, dark place.

Forcing bulbs

As soon as growth starts to show, the first of your potted bulbs (see page 118) can be brought indoors for forcing; wait until the leaves are 1½–2in/40–50mm long and, especially important with hyacinths, until the flower buds are visible above the necks of the bulbs. The bulbs now need bright, cool conditions to produce sturdy, well-formed flowers, so place the pots in a sunny position indoors with a temperature around 50°F/10°C and water when necessary. Once the leaves develop and the flower buds just begin to show color, you can move them to a cool, bright living room. The flowers will last longer if temperatures stay between 59° and 68°F/15° and 20°C.

WATER GARDEN

Winter protection

If you have not done so already, remove, clean, and service any pumps that are not needed over winter before the pool freezes over.

If there are fish in your garden pool, it is important that the surface does not remain frozen for more than a few days at a time and you must ensure that the pool never freezes solid to the bottom. Keep at least a part of the pool surface free of ice to allow the escape of toxic gases resulting from decay of plant remains.

Protecting the pond in freezing weather
If the pond freezes over, melt a hole in the ice. A bundle of hollow reeds placed in the hole and staked to the pond bottom will provide aeration – especially important if there are fish in the pond.

Where winters are not too severe, part of the pond surface may be kept free of ice by floating a ball or placing some polystyrene blocks around the edges.

Never make holes in the surface ice by hammering as this may stun or even kill the fish. Instead place a bucket, plastic bottle, or tea kettle filled with boiling water on the ice to melt through the surface layer. Be sure first to secure the vessel with a string tied to the handle so that it does not disappear into the depths when it does thaw the ice!

In regions with extremely cold winters, or during severe cold snaps, provide further insulation by pumping enough water out of the pool through the hole in the surface ice to reduce the water level by 2–2¾in/50–70mm and create an air space between the water and the ice. Inserting a bundle of reeds in the hole may also help prevent it from freezing over.

LAWN AND FLOWER MEADOW

Winter care
In most regions, lawns enjoy a period of rest and recuperation in winter. Avoid walking on the lawn as much as possible during the winter months, especially when the ground is frozen hard or if there is frost on the grass. However, during periods of dry, mild weather, rake up fallen leaves and other debris and remove them.

A moderately thick blanket of snow is the best protection against winter damage, so do not remove it. But don't pile up snow on the lawn when shoveling it from your walks, paths, or patio.

During periods of thawing weather, take note of any patches on the lawn where water stands and fails to drain off. Mark such spots now, while they are apparent, so that you can dig French drains or another sort of drainage in spring, when the ground is dry enough to work.

Take advantage of the quiet period of winter to clean, oil, and overhaul your lawn mower. Empty and dry gasoline tanks to avoid corrosion. Spring is bound to come much sooner than you think, so get your lawn tools in tiptop shape now, before the time for the first mowing catches you unprepared.

PATIO AND BALCONY

Watering
Evergreen shrubs and other plants in containers that remain outside as part of a permanent planting need water during the winter! Even when the soil is frozen the plants continue to lose water from their leaves or needles; because the water reserves in containers are much more limited than in the open ground, these plants are especially vulnerable to damage due to lack of water. So-called frost damage is most often damage due to desiccation. So don't forget to water your containers on the patio or balcony whenever the soil is dry and not so frozen that it cannot absorb any water.

Fuchsias and geraniums
Fuchsias, geraniums (pelargoniums), and other tender balcony plants that have been brought indoors for the winter should be checked periodically. Cut away blossoms and flower buds, dead or diseased leaves, and any parts showing fungus attack. Aim to maintain a constant, moderately cool temperature, water sparingly, just often enough to keep the plants from wilting, and ventilate as much as possible.

CHAPTER 10

GARDEN TECHNIQUES

THE SOIL

Preparing for planting

In a garden where the plants are growing well and the soil is generally in good condition, all you need do to prepare for planting is dig a hole large enough to accommodate the roots without crowding and to mix the excavated soil with compost or other suitable organic matter to improve its fertility and structure.

In a new garden, however, or one in which the soil has been neglected, you will need to make extensive preparations for planting. Dig over the entire area, to a depth of 1½ft/450mm, removing stones, tree roots, builders' debris, and the roots of perennial weeds. This will loosen compacted topsoil and, most important, subsoil. Work in abundant quantities of garden compost, well-rotted manure, composted tree bark, or other suitable organic material. Use composted tree bark rather than peatmoss as much as possible when amending soils, since limiting the use of peatmoss in gardens will help to conserve world peat moors and other wet areas, the natural habitats of many endangered species of animals and plants. Composted tree bark has a higher nutrient content than peat and is also better able to absorb mineral salts from applied fertilizers. In other respect it is just as effective as peat; however, it usually has neutral pH value, whereas peatmoss is decidedly acidic. If soil analysis (see page 130) indicates deficiencies, mix in the required amounts of the appropriate mineral fertilizers.

When you are planting isolated trees or shrubs in grass or on any spot where the whole area is not cultivated, dig the site at least 2ft/600mm deep and 4ft/1.2m wide for every tree or large shrub and 1⅔ft/500mm deep and 3¼ft/1m wide for smaller plants. Be sure to break through any compacted subsoil at the bottom of the hole.

Mulching

After planting, spread a layer of organic material over the soil. Mulching can halve the amount of water lost through surface evaporation and it also insulates the soil, damping excessive temperature fluctuation, and reduces the likelihood of compaction and erosion. Good mulch materials include shredded tree bark, half-rotted leaves, garden compost, well-rotted farmyard manure, or a mixture of these. A thick layer of mulch – between 2–4in/50–100mm deep – also prevents the growth of annual weeds but is unsuitable if you want to underplant with creeping ground cover.

TREES AND SHRUBS

Planting bare root trees and shrubs

Most hardy deciduous trees and shrubs can be planted with bare roots at any time during their dormant period from late fall until early spring. Although not in active growth, their roots may have been damaged when dug from the open ground and must be protected from frost, drying wind, and sun until they have been planted.

Dig the planting hole about 1ft/300mm wider than the spread of the roots and just a bit deeper than they reach. Enrich the soil you have excavated. Roughen and loosen up the soil around the sides and especially at the bottom of the hole, so that there is a gradual transition between the existing topsoil and the enriched mixture with which you backfill. Supporting stakes for bare root trees should always be driven in *before* the tree is planted (see page 154). Almost every tree has a natural front and back, so choose a position which allows you to fit the stem snugly against its stake.

Just before planting the tree or shrub, examine its roots and cut back to sound tissue any that are broken or damaged. Spread the roots out evenly and take care that the base of the stem is level with the soil surface. Usually the old soil mark will guide you.

With the plant in position start filling in the soil around the roots. Shake the tree gently up and down in its hole so that the soil finds its way in among the roots and no air pockets remain. You may find it helpful to bind the tree loosely to its stake while you shovel in the soil. Firm up the soil as you go by treading it carefully. Once the hole is half filled and the soil well firmed, flood it with water to eliminate air pockets around the roots; when the water has seeped away, finish refilling the hole, firm up, and bind the tree to its stake.

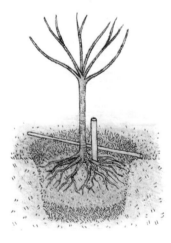 

Bare root planting
Position the tree in the hole using a straight piece of wood to ensure that the new soil level will correspond with the old soil mark on the stem.

When you have finished planting, make a saucer shape in the soil around the plant. Water again so that the entire soil volume around the roots is completely saturated.

Planting balled-root trees and shrubs

Conifers, broadleaved evergreens as well as many deciduous trees and shrubs are often sold with their roots in a ball of soil, tied around with burlap. They, too, will have been dug from the ground, losing part of their roots in the process. They are just as vulnerable to damage as bare root plants and are not to be treated like container-grown plants, which are much less susceptible to injury.

Burlap is all that holds the root ball intact, so handle with care. Do not move the plant by the stem or trunk because this may loosen the root ball: instead cradle it in your arms, with one hand supporting the bottom. If the fabric wrapping is not man-made or treated with preservative, it will be biodegradable and need not be removed from the root ball; to avoid strangling the stem, loosen the knots or cut open the top of the wrapping, but not until the root ball has been placed firmly in the planting hole.

If the root ball is dry, soak it with water for two or three hours before starting to plant, so that it is moist throughout. This is safer than watering after planting, as a dried-out ball can be impervious to water once it is underground.

Dig and prepare the planting hole as usual and enrich the excavated soil with compost or other suitable organic material. Fork over the bottom of the hole to break through any compacted layer, but tread it in lightly again to prevent it from settling later when the plant is moved into place.

Balled-root planting
Carefully lower the plant into the hole. Half fill and firm the soil. Water thoroughly. Undo the burlap and spread it out.

Fill and firm the soil so that it just covers the top of the ball. Make a rim around the hole to form a reservoir for water and irrigate thoroughly.

Planting container-grown trees and shrubs

Container-grown trees and shrubs can be planted at virtually any time of the year, even during the growth period, whenever the soil is loose and not frozen solid. Even so, spring and fall remain the ideal seasons for planting and it is best to avoid periods of drought and extreme heat or cold.

Digging the planting hole and other preparations for planting are essentially the same as for balled-root plants. It is equally important to ensure that the plant is moist before it goes into the ground; if a container appears to be dry – a plant which seems to be too light for its size is always suspect – submerge it in a tub of water until air bubbles stop rising from the soil.

If you plant trees and shrubs while they are in active growth, water them throughout the first year until they have established an adequate root system.

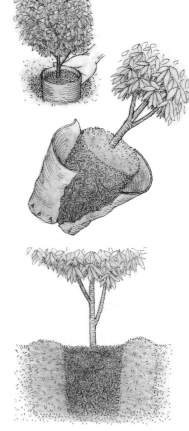

Planting from containers

1 Place the container in the hole to check the depth. The surface of the container soil should be level with the surrounding soil.

2 Remove or cut away the container and check the roots. If they are pot bound (wound tightly around the root ball) tease them out carefully so that they can be spread in the hole.

3 Holding the plant by its stem, place it in the hole, and fill, firming and watering as you go. Make a rim around the root ball to form a reservoir and soak thoroughly.

Staking trees

If you plant large trees, they will need some support because the roots, some of which will have been severed when the tree was removed from the ground, will not be able to withstand the force of wind in the crown. Depending on the vigor of the tree and the windiness of the site, after one or, at the most, two growing seasons enough new roots will have grown into the surrounding soil to provide stability, and the stake and tie should be removed so they do not damage the trunk.

The length of the stake above ground should be no more than one-third of the height of the tree, allowing the upper stem and crown some freedom of movement. Well-grown trees have strong enough stems to hold the crown erect, so the primary purpose of the support is to hold the root collar steady until the roots have established anchorage. Trees that are allowed to sway in the wind develop a larger stem diameter and stronger wood than trees staked so that all

movement has been eliminated; firmly staked trees also tend to grow taller and once the staking is removed, tend to be more vulnerable to wind damage.

In general only taller conifers will need the help of a stake; wherever staking is unnecessary, omit it; as long as the root ball cannot rock, the plant will do better without a stake.

Pruning hedges

All formal hedges require regular shearing – basically a special kind of indiscriminate pruning – to maintain their shape. Hedging plants normally have buds and branches so close together on their stems that you can cut practically anywhere and still be close to a growing point.

The basic tools you need are a sturdy pair of pruning shears and a hand or electric hedge trimmer. An electric hedge trimmer is quicker and, unless you are experienced with hand trimmers, it makes it easier to achieve a uniform clean cut. For broadleaved evergreens with large leaves, such as holly or *Prunus laurocerasus*, it is best to use pruning shears. Hedge trimmers tend to mutilate too many of the leaves which then remain an eyesore for many months.

Choosing a hedge shape is basically a matter of personal taste, so long as you remember to maintain a slight inward taper so that the base is wider than the top. This taper allows sunlight to reach the foliage at the base of the hedge and keeps the hedge dense and green all the way to the ground. In regions with heavy winter snows, a flat-top hedge may be more subject to breakage than one with a ridged or rounded top that can shed snow more readily.

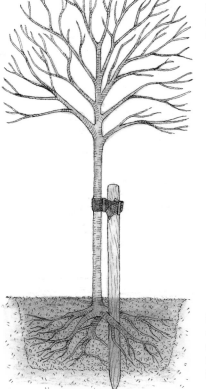

Staking bare root trees
Left Choose a round stake, larger in diameter than the tree. Insert it into the hole before planting. Attach it with a tree tie, or in such a way that the stem cannot rub against the stake.

Staking balled-root trees
Above After planting, drive the stake in at an angle pointing into the prevailing wind. Take care to avoid the root ball.

Pruning formal hedges
Left A simple wooden frame can be used as a cutting guide for a low hedge.

Right For a large or growing hedge it may be easier to use a wooden framework that can be adjusted to the height and angle of the hedge. Hang a lead weight from the frame and use it to check the vertical.

To maintain sharp clean hedge lines, you can stretch strings to act as guidelines for the pruning shears or you may use wooden templates. Informal hedges normally need no regular pruning, but are treated just like flowering shrubs. Do not shear them, but cut individual branches back as necessary to maintain a dense, attractive appearance. Rejuvenate a mature hedge just like any shrub by cutting out, at ground level, a part of the oldest stems each year over a period of several years.

Pruning flowering deciduous shrubs

Pruning seems to be one aspect of gardening practice that causes many gardeners serious difficulties. However, by observing a few simple rules, you can easily avoid making mistakes.

Some shrubs require virtually no regular pruning at all. With flowering shrubs such as the magnolias and hamamelis, for example, all that is necessary is to remove dead, diseased, or damaged shoots whenever you see them. Only occasionally will you need to cut out, during the dormant period, any badly located branches that spoil the natural, attractive outline of the shrub.

Other flowering shrubs that benefit from regular, even annual, pruning can be classified in two main groups according to their pruning requirements, which in turn are largely dictated by their flowering season. In the first group are the deciduous shrubs that flower in spring or early summer, producing their blossoms on growths made during the previous year. Prune these shrubs as soon as their flowers have faded.

The second group comprises the deciduous shrubs that flower from midsummer to fall on growth made during the current year. Prune shrubs in this group in pre-spring and early spring, just before new growth begins, in order to allow the maximum time for new flowering wood to be produced.

In principle any pruning cut should be just above a bud. The cut should be at a slightly oblique angle across the stem; the bottom of the cut should be just level with the bud, on the opposite side of the stem, which ensures that the cut is close to the bud but not so close that the bud is damaged or is in danger of drying out. Use only the sturdiest, sharpest pruners to ensure that every pruning cut it clean, with neither ragged edges nor torn or loosened bark.

Pruning cuts

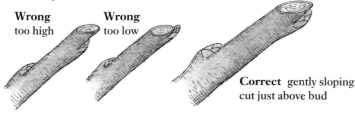

Wrong too high   **Wrong** too low

Correct gently sloping cut just above bud

All pruning is simple if you anticipate the results of any particular cut. Remember that pruning stimulates new growth and the more severe the cut, the stronger the new growth will be. First, remove all dead, damaged, or diseased wood, weak or exhausted branches and any that rub; always cut back to living, healthy tissue. Then cut out any thin, weak growths from the center of the shrub to create free circulation of air and access for light. This encourages the development of sound, well-ripened wood and reduces the incidence of disease.

Once you are left with only sound, healthy growths, pause to consider how you should proceed, keeping in mind just what the objectives of pruning are: to maintain vigorous, youthful, healthy

Pruning for spring flowers
Below After flowering (*left*) cut back to two strong buds (*middle*). Fresh new growth appears in late summer (*right*) and will produce flowers next spring.

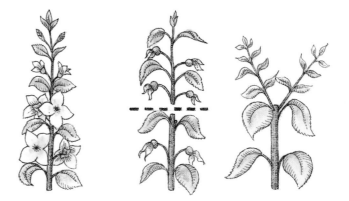

Pruning for summer flowers
Below Cut back last year's growth to two strong buds (*left*) in pre- and early spring. New shoots grow (*middle*) producing flowers in summer (*right*).

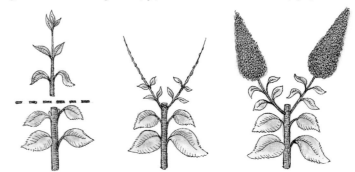

growth and the natural shape and balance of the plant. Except for topiary or hedges, regular pruning should never be necessary to maintain a smaller size; if you find that you need to prune to keep a shrub within bounds, you have planted the wrong shrub!

To correct the form of a lopsided shrub, try to envisage how the plant will respond to pruning. If it has grown unevenly, with strong branches on one side and weak growth on the other, your first impulse may be to cut the strong growth back hard to bring it down to the same height as the weaker side. Don't do it! This will have the opposite effect and accentuate the unbalanced shape. Instead, prune back the *weak* growths severely, to a point where strong buds can be seen, and prune the strong growths only slightly. After about two years, vigorous branches from the weak side should have balanced the shape of the shrub.

Taking cuttings from soft and semiripe wood

In principle, cuttings taken from softwood and those taken from semiripe wood require much the same treatment and the methods for rooting either type differ only slightly.

After you have taken and planted the cuttings water them well and cover with glass or plastic, to prevent loss of water, until growth of new leaves indicates that rooting has been successful.

Soft and semiripe wood cuttings
1 Left Cut a shoot about 4in/100mm long, just below a leaf node.

2 Right Remove the lower leaves and dip in rooting hormone (semiripe) or fungicide (softwood).

3 Left Make a hole with a dibble and insert the cutting 1½in/40mm deep in a suitable potting mix.

Taking hardwood cuttings

Hardwood cuttings are the easiest method of propagating many woody plants. Take them during the dormant period, soon after leaf drop in fall. Because the shoots are leafless, they are unlikely to fail due to loss of water.

Straight young growths that are only one year old generally root most easily.

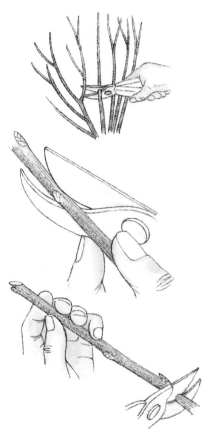

Hardwood cuttings
1 Right Choose a young, straight shoot and cut fairly low down on the stem.

2 Right Pick a good strong bud for the top bud and make a normal slanting pruning cut just above it.

3 Right Exactly 6in/150mm below the top bud make the bottom cut straight across the stem.

4 Right Where winters are severe, store cuttings over winter in a box of moist sand in a cool place until pre-spring.

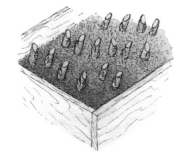

5 Left After overwintering or, where winters are not too severe, immediately after taking the cuttings, make a narrow trench in any sandy fertile soil and insert the cuttings vertically in the ground.

6 Left Firm back the soil over the cuttings leaving about 1in/ 20-30mm projecting above the surface. When the cuttings have made new growth (usually by the following fall) they may be transplanted.

1 Bend a young, vigorous stem to the ground and mark a position on the soil about 10in/250mm from its tip. At this point, dig a hole with one straight side away from and one sloping side toward the plant.

2 Trim the leaves from around the part of the stem that will come to rest under the soil. Cut a small slit in the underside of the shoot at the point where the roots are to grow.

Layering

Layering is a useful method of propagating many woody plants, especially when only one or a few new plants are desired. Because the stems are rooted before they are severed from the parent plant, there is no danger of loss due to dehydration, which makes the method extremely valuable for rooting many choice, rare plants which are difficult to root by other means.

3 Bend the stem to the ground without strain, peg it down in the hole, and bend the tip upward against the straight side.

Propagating by layering
This method can be used with most plants that have stems pliable enough to be brought easily to the ground and pegged.

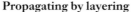

4 Fill in the hole and water well. If necessary, insert a small stake to support the upright shoot. Keep the spot moist, weedfree, and well mulched until active new growth indicates that rooting has been successful and the new plant can be severed and transplanted.

ROSE CARE

Roses are no more difficult to grow than any other garden plant, provided you pay attention to a few simple rules and let yourself be guided by common sense. True, roses are susceptible to several diseases and pests, but, by and large, a robust rose is able to live and cope with most of them. Indeed, the first line of defense against pests and diseases is in the health of the plant itself. Constant spraying will never make a healthy rose out of one that is sickly because of unfavorable climate, wrong exposure, impoversiehd soil, faulty watering, or inadequate feeding.

Choosing and positioning

To begin with, choose robust varieties suitable for your location and be sure you buy strong, healthy plants. Any variety that is permanently weak and diseased in your garden should be replaced, without remorse, with another, more resistant species or cultivar.

Always plant in a spot which is sunny and warm, but at the same time open and airy, with free access for plenty of fresh air around and through the plants. Nothing is worse for roses than stagnant, excessively humid air or baking hot, desert dry conditions.

Roses can easily remain in one place for 25 or more years so, before planting, prepare the ground thoroughly and plant well as described on page 15. Avoid overcrowding and, wherever possible, plant your roses as solitary specimens in mixed plantings.

Fertilizing

Feed your roses so that they are neither starved nor overfed. Be especially careful with nitrogen: use a balanced fertilizer with no more than 7 to 9 percent nitrogen and spread no more than the equivalent of $1/10$-$1/7$oz/3 to 4g pure nitrogen per square yard/meter at any one time. Do not feed with a nitrogen-rich fertilizer after the end of early summer. Potassium is vital because it encourages disease resistance and accelerates the ripening of new wood. Fungus diseases, such as black spot and rose rust, are much less serious if the soil is well supplied with potassium. At the same time, maintain a nearly neutral soil pH of around 6.5 to 7 (see page 145) and avoid overliming, which can cause chlorosis.

Pests

Inspect the roses regularly, so that you can detect problems early, before they have a chance to get out of hand. Individual chafer beetles, moth caterpillars, leaf roller grubs, Japanese beetles, and other large pests can easily be picked off by hand and destroyed: isolated infected shoots or leaves can be cut away before the disease can spread.

An imperfect or nibbled leaf here and there should never be cause for alarm nor should an occasional aphid ruin your enjoyment. Instead of trying to maintain an antiseptic garden, aim for a balance between plants, their pests, and the natural predators that feed on them in turn. Learn to know the pests on your roses and reach for poisonous chemicals only as a last resort. Sudden explosions of pest populations are likely to disappear as quickly as they appeared and remember, useful predators are much more susceptible to poisonous sprays than the pests themselves. Learn to tolerate a minimal presence of pests; without them, the beneficial predators cannot exist.

Aphids, for example, are found nearly everywhere, making their debut in early spring on the tender new growths. Fortunately, aphids are also the easiest pest to control. Simply washing them off with a fine spray from the garden hose during the morning hours is often just as effective as a poisonous spray. Tiny red spider mites are warm weather pests and may develop rapidly when the weather is hot and dry. The simplest way to combat them, again, is with your garden hose: use a fine, strong spray of water to wash the undersides of the leaves thoroughly. If you repeat this for several days in succession, it will disrupt their breeding cycle and eliminate the pest better than any of the available chemical sprays.

Diseases

The ugly fungus diseases – black spot, powdery mildew, and rose rust – are often more serious than insect pests, but they can also be held at a tolerable level without poisonous sprays. Black spot is probably the most devastating of foliage diseases and may be the most difficult to control. It is encouraged by potassium shortage and warm, wet weather in summer, and is spread by splashing water, which carries the spores from diseased leaves to new foliage. Cut off and destroy any diseased leaves you discover. Black spot spores live through the winter on old leaves on the ground, so clear the area of fallen leaves. Poor drainage, poor air circulation and shading by overhead trees also encourage black spot.

More widespread, powdery mildew is a fungus found wherever roses are grown. It is encouraged by closed-in conditions, dryness at the roots, and excessive feeding with nitrogen. It flourishes during periods of high humidity, but not during rainy weather. In contrast to black spot, it needs dry leaves to become established. Roses in overcrowded, shady gardens are more prone to mildew than those in sunny beds where they have free air circulation through and between the plants. Careful mulching also helps reduce mildew attacks.

Rose rust is relatively uncommon and occurs primarily in hot dry soils which are deficient in potassium. Hygiene and sufficient feeding with potassium go far toward preventing rose rust.

Hygiene and watering

Hygiene is the best way to prevent fungus diseases: never allow fallen leaves to accumulate under the bushes. Rake up and destroy all fallen, diseased leaves and any diseased prunings. Keep the soil under the roses well cultivated, loose, and either mulched or planted with ground-cover plants. Both mulch and ground-cover plants help to reduce fungus diseases: they prevent splash from the soil during rain and watering and also lower the humidity of the air around the bush.

During dry spells, water the soil only and avoid wetting the foliage as much as possible (unless you are deliberately dislodging pests). Try not to splash the leaves with muddy water. Water seldom, but thoroughly: never give less than 4½–6½ gals/20–30 litres per square yard/meter at one time, but, whatever you do, avoid compacted or waterlogged soil, which encourages black spot.

HERBACEOUS PERENNIALS

Planting
Plant herbaceous perennials according to the same general principles you follow when planting shrubs. Perennials will usually be bought as young container-grown plants, but, when you are replanting perennials which you have dug up and divided, you have bare root plants which require essentially the same treatment as bare root shrubs.

Because your herbaceous perennials will remain in one spot for several years before they need to be dug up, divided, and replanted, it pays to spare no efforts to prepare the soil thoroughly before planting, since no amount of work later can equal the value of initial digging and improvement. If you are planting an entire border or a large section of a plot, dig and prepare the whole area at the same time. Incorporate plenty of good garden compost or other organic matieral as well as a long-acting fertilizer.

Aim to prepare the soil so thoroughly that, once planting begins, you can proceed without interruption; getting the plants into the ground quickly helps minimize losses. Humid weather and overcast skies are the best conditions for planting. Just before planting, immerse container plants in water for a couple of hours to ensure that the root balls are thoroughly moist. Protect the roots of bare root plants with wet burlap or wet newspaper until they are safely in the ground. Before planting it helps to lay out the plants in their assigned places so that you can make any last minute adjustments to the plan. However, leave the pots and wrappers on the plants until you are ready to start planting.

With a hand trowel, dig each hole large enough to accommodate the root ball or spread-out roots without cramping – about twice the width of the root ball is ideal. Fortify the soil that is to be used to refill the hole with ripe garden compost. Rest the plant on a cushion of this improved soil and fill in the hole so that no air spaces remain. As you fill, firm the soil with your fingers, water each plant individually, using a watering can or hose, and make sure that it is positioned firmly. If there is no promise of immediate rain, thoroughly soak the entire planted area to the full depth of the roots. A few days later, when the soil surface has dried somewhat, loosen the soil between the plants with a hoe or cultivator.

Division
Division consists of splitting one plant into two or more fragments, each of which has roots and either viable shoots or buds capable of developing into shoots. It will succeed if you follow a few simple guidelines (see below and over page).

Dividing perennials
For perennials with fibrous roots, dig up the whole clump and, if the clump is small or tractable enough, simply pull apart gently by hand.

For larger more intractable clumps of fibrous-rooted plants, insert a fork downward through the center of the clump, then drive in a second fork, back to back with the first (*left above*). Pry the forks apart by pressing down and outward (*left below*). Repeat this process as often as necessary to produce small clumps of a suitable size for replanting.

For perennials with stout, fleshy or woody crowns, dig up the whole crown and use a sharp sturdy knife to cut it into pieces. Each section should have at least one strong bud and plenty of intact roots.

Regular division is necessary to keep many herbaceous perennials young, vigorous, and willing to flower; it is also a useful method of propagation, indeed the only practical way to increase the stocks of many favorite cultivars and hybrids. The best time to divide most perennials is directly after flowering, for this is when new roots and shoots are developing most actively. For those that flower in fall, the best time is the following spring.

Lift the plants carefully with a fork and shake off as much soil as possible so that you can see where strong buds and shoots originate from the crown. Many perennials have spreading fibrous roots and several stems arising from a loose crown (such as asters, chrysanthemums, heleniums, phlox, and shasta daisies). Most of these can simply be pulled apart by hand. Some – older clumps of daylilies, for example – may be pried apart by two forks back to back. Divide smaller clumps by slicing them carefully with a knife or pruning shears.

If the central part of the crown is aged and woody, without any actively growing shoots, discard it and take strong, healthy, young pieces from the periphery. Each division should have plenty of healthy undamaged roots and at least one stem or strong bud. Do not make the divisions too large: in most cases there should be no more than three stems or growth buds on each fragment; small, vigorous divisions are nearly always preferable to larger ones. After dividing, cut back the tops to compensate for the loss of roots.

Herbaceous perennials that develop a dense fleshy or woody crown (such as lupines, delphiniums, and hostas) are not easy to divide by pulling apart and need to be cut. They are best divided toward the end of their dormant period, just as their buds are beginning to swell. Before cutting them apart, wash the crown well so that you can clearly see these growth buds.

Replant the divisions as quickly as possible and water them well to settle the soil about their roots.

FERTILIZING

Once your garden plants are well established they may need an occasional dressing with fertilizer to replenish the nutrients which have been taken up by the plants as well as those which have been washed away by rain and watering. If your plants show signs of reduced vigor or indeed symptoms of a mineral deficiency, you should analyze the soil (see page 130) to determine the nature and degree of the deficiency.

Only after you have analyzed the soil should you dress with measured amounts of a suitable mineral fertilizer calculated to correct the particular needs of your soil. Widespread analyses of many garden soils during the past few years have shown that almost all gardeners tend to overfertilize, so that a great many garden soils show excesses of certain nutrients, particularly phosphorus.

Dry, surface feeding is without a doubt the simplest and most common way of spreading mineral fertilizers in all parts of the garden. It is most effective in areas with heavy rainfall, where the rain quickly washes the nutrients into the root zone. Everywhere else – or during dry periods – you need to scratch the scattered fertilizer lightly into the soil and then irrigate well. If the soil is very dry, always water well first, a day or two before you spread the dry mineral fertilizer.

Liquid feeding is especially appropriate in dry soil regions because the nutrients are in a form immediately available to your plants. Herbaceous perennials, bulbs, annuals, roses, and smaller shrubs can easily be fed using a watering can to sprinkle the nutrient solution over the soil around the plants. Trees and large shrubs can easily be fed using a proportioner attached to your garden hose, which makes use of water pressure to force the dissolved plant food out to the roots (see page 65).

Foliar feeding, which delivers dissolved nutrients directly to the leaves, is the quickest method to treat a specific deficiency. Applied with a pressure spray, foliar fertilizer works best in regions of high humidity; it is also useful as a supplementary source of food where root systems have been damaged. Time the application of foliar feeding so that you can take advantage of high humidity as the fertilizer will penetrate the leaves only as long as they are damp. Feed at such a time that the sun will not dry the leaves before the nutrients have been absorbed.

LAWN CARE

Aeration
If your lawn has been trampled on and the grass is looking the worse for wear, you need to break through the areas where the surface layer is compacted before you can hope to get a good lawn established again. Compacted soil can be opened up by using an aerating tool that removes narrow cores of earth leaving holes to a depth of about 2¾in/70mm that enable air and water to reach the grass roots. For smaller areas you can use a hand spiking tool, but you may find that this is too laborious. Certainly for very large areas of lawn it is easier to use a power-driven aerator.

If your soil is heavy and full of clay, rake up and remove the cores to the compost pile. Then, either leave the holes open so that the grass roots can grow in to fill them or, especially if your soil is poor and inclined to compact, improve the quality of the soil by spreading and raking in a top-dressing of a mixture of sand, peat or compost and good garden soil.

If the soil under the lawn is of good quality, let the plugs lie on the ground until they are dry enough to crumble by dragging a rubber doormat over them. Mix sand and peat with the crumbled cores and brush or rake the mixture into the holes.

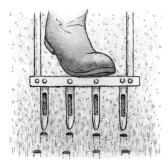

Aerating a lawn
For heavy or waterlogged areas, use a hollow-tine fork, pressed into the ground with your foot.

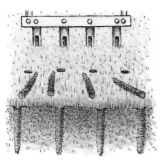

This removes plugs of soil from the compacted ground which are pushed out of the fork at the next penetration.

Dethatching a lawn
To remove thatch, press the rake down hard onto the surface of the lawn as you pull it along.

The knife-like tines of the dethatching rake will pull up the dead material while leaving the grass plants rooted.

Dethatching

A second common lawn problem is the accumulation of thatch – a layer of dead grass and debris on the top of the soil, lodged among the grass blades. A thin layer of thatch – less than 1/3in/13mm is generally desirable because it works as a mulch, cutting down loss of water, and adds springiness to the grass. A layer of thatch thicker than 3/4in/20mm can hinder the penetration of water into the soil and increase the likelihood of fungal diseases.

You can usually scratch out a moderately matted thatch with a metal lawn rake, but to open up a thicker thatch of interwoven stolons (runners) and dead grass you need to dethatch the lawn with a specially designed rake with sharp, knifelike tines. This breaks up the thatch and brings it to the surface. Like aeration, dethatching is hard work and for large areas it is worth hiring a power-driven machine. This has revolving vertical knives that slice down through the thatch to the soil surface, combing out quantities of dead material and opening up the soil. Water, air, and light can once again penetrate into the lawn, but enough rooted grass plants are left so that the lawn can recuperate quickly.

Renovation

If neglect has left your lawn in less than top shape, but it is not so poor that you need to start from scratch, you can renovate it, provided the top-soil is of good quality to a depth of at least 6in/150mm.

First mow the lawn to a height of about 1¼in/30mm and rake up all the clippings with an ordinary rake. If thatch is present, dethatch using an iron rake or special dethatching tool. Cut through the thatch layers and remove as much dead grass and other debris as possible. You will pull up loose runners in the process. Rake off any thatch and debris you brought to the surface before mowing again, with the blades set low enough to cut off any loose runners you may have exposed. Rake up and remove all the grass clippings.

If the soil is compacted, aerify it as described above, preferably using a powered machine to work over the entire lawn. If the soil is too acidic, apply the required amount of lime at this stage. Spread it when the grass is dry and work it lightly into the surface with a rake. Then spread a topdressing of a sifted mixture of good garden soil, sand, and ripe, weedfree compost or peatmoss. Work in, smooth, and level this top-dressing well with a broad rake and sow a good quality grass-seed mixture at the recommended rate. Work the seed into the soil lightly with a rake and roll the surface. As a last step, water well using a fine spray to avoid washing away the seed.

ECOLOGY

Encouraging useful predators

Natural predators in the garden can do much to reduce the necessity of using time-consuming, expensive, and potentially harmful pesticides. However, for the army of potential little garden helpers, such as songbirds, weasels, solitary bees and wasps, lacewings, syrphus flies, butterflies, lizards, and spiders, a perfectly ordered garden, brimming with showy blooms, may be no more hospitable than Death Valley. Somewhat less rigid order, a bit of calculated untidiness, and an indulgence for an occasional weed or two can make your garden a healthier, more stable setting for your plants, where they will not be so bothered by aphids, slugs, and other pests.

A garden is an artificial creation that will always require the input of work to maintain its existence; but, with a few ecological insights, you can create a garden full of beautiful flowers *and* interesting, colorful animal life. Once you have brought "nature" back into your garden, you will find that pests that earlier had to be fought with pesticides will no longer exceed tolerable numbers; you will, of course, still have aphids, for example, but they will be held in check by the larvae of lacewings, ladybugs, beetles, and syrphus flies; no longer will huge population explosions of aphids disfigure your roses.

As a start, plant plenty of ornamental plants with single flowers, instead of only varieties with fully double flowers, for these are better sources of pollen and nectar for useful insects which depend on floral nectar and pollen for food and have larvae with voracious appetites for aphids or red spider mites.

Many solitary bees and wasps nest in holes and each species has its own preferences as to where its home should be; some nest in the ground, others in narrow burrows in wood, some in hollow grass stalks, and still others in crevices in walls or rock faces. Most of them are so tiny that they often escape your attention, but they are fascinating to observe and exceedingly useful, the bees as pollinators for important crops such as fruit trees and the wasps as natural predators, which feed their larvae with still tinier animals – aphids or mites.

Many of these species prefer to excavate their own nests, but others will use abandoned beetle burrows in old wood. You can simulate this

tiny habitat by erecting short stumps or blocks of wood bored with holes of a variety of different sizes. Place the piece of wood in a dry and warm, but not hot, location, at the back of a sunny border, under a hedge, at the edge of a group of trees, or against the side of a potting shed or hang it from a tree or under the eaves of your garage.

An old stone wall is the habitat of a countless number of small plants and animals and is a wonderful feature in a garden. You can create a similarly valuable habitat by erecting a dry stone wall as a bridge between different levels or to create areas with different levels. Natural predators will soon settle in and will feed day and night on harmful insects (as well as on each other) to make up a stable, self-regulatory system of prey and predator. Lizards and toads, for example, will be some of your best allies against the voracious slugs that never seem to leave your hostas and ligularias with intact leaves.

If your garden plan does not call for a stone wall or a rock garden, a loose pile of rocks, hidden away in a sunny spot, is just as welcome for many a lizard or toad. In much the same way, a woodpile can be home and shelter for these creatures, or even a glass lizard, mole, or weasel, if you live close to the open country; all are your allies in the unending battle against slugs.

Ways to encourage predators

Nests for solitary wasps and bees
A log or block of wood about 12in/300mm long can provide nests for tiny bees and wasps. Drill a number of holes, varying from about ¹⁄₁₀in/3mm up to about ⅓in/10mm, to the full depth of your drill bit. Some species will take up residence in small hollow tubes.

Tie up bundles of bamboo, reeds, or elder stems to hang horizontally in a sheltered spot, such as under the eaves of a potting shed.

A stone wall or rockpile
Stones layered up without any mortar – from a carefully crafted dry stone wall to a loose pile of rocks – will provide a habitat for helpful predators, and can make an attractive feature in their own right. Nooks and crannies will soon be populated by myriads of creatures, such as spiders, millipedes, centipedes, beetles,

lizards, and toads – as well as solitary bees and wasps – each playing some valuable role in the garden ecosystem.

INDEX

INDEX 163

(Figures in *italics* refer to illustrations and captions to photographs)

A

Abeliophyllum 10; *A. distichum* 10, 12
Acanthus hungaricus 80–1
Acer capillipes (red snakebark maple) 141; *A. davidii* 'George Forrest' 124–5; *A. griseum* (paper bark maple) 142; *A. grosseri* 141; *A. japonicum* (full-moon maple) 125; *A.j. aconitifolium* 125; *A.j.* 'Vitifolium' 125; *A. palmatum* 'Lutescens' 125; *A.p.* 'Sangokaku' (coral bark maple) 141; *A.p.* 'Shishigashira' 125; *A. pensylvanicum* (moosewood) 141; *A.p.* 'Erythrocladum' 141–2; *A. platanoides* (Norway maple) 25, 126; *A.p.* 'Cucullatum' 126–7; *A.p.* 'Reitenbachii' 127; *A.p.* 'Schwedleri' 127; *A. rubrum* (red maple) 124; *A. rufinerve* (gray-budded snakebark maple) 142
Achillea (yarrow) 74, 96; *A.* 'Moonshine' 77, 80
Acidanthera 50, 149
Adiantum pedatum (maidenhair fern) 59
Aesculus hippocastanum (horse chestnut) 38, 122
Alcea (hollyhock) 48, 69, 89, 105, 117; *A. rosea* 101
Allium spp. 77, 149; *A. carinatum pulchellum* 77; *A. giganteum* 117; *A. sphaerocephalon* 101; *A. tuberosum* (garlic chives) 94, 94
alpine plants 134, 149
alyssum, sweet (*Lobularia maritima*) 105
Amelanchier lamarckii (snowy mespilus) 25–6
Anchusa capensis (summer forget-me-not) 68
Anemone: *A.* apennina 27; *A. blanda* 12, 26, 117; *A. nemorosa* (wood anemone) 25, 26, 27; *A.n.* 'Allenii' 27; *A.n.* 'Robinsoniana' 27; *A.n.* 'Royal Blue'; Japanese anemones 19, 112: 'Honorine Jobert' 112–13, 113; 'Prinz Heinrich' 113; 'Queen Charlotte' 113
annuals, hardy and half-hardy:

buying from nursery 68; hardening off 48–9; late-summer flowering 95–7; planting in containers 53; planting out 49, 105; pricking out seedlings 32, 32–3; sowing indoors 20, 20, 32; sowing outdoors 32, 48, 48–9, 68, 105, 117; summer care 89
Antennaria 88
anthemis 19
aphids 74, 158, 162
apple trees 7, 38, 92
aquatic plants: deadheading 90; depth of water required 34; dividing 35, 52; for miniature gardens 54; planting 51, 51–2, 69; removing shoots 90; submerged oxygenators 52; winter protection 135–6
Arabis 88
Armeria 88
Artemisia abrotanum (southernwood) 82; *A. absinthium* 'Lambrook Silver' 82; *A.* 'Powis Castle' 82
artichokes 94
Arum italicum 'Pictum' 12
asparagus 94
Asplenium trichomanes (maidenhair spleenwort) 32
Aster spp. 32, 68, 109, 112, 160; *A. amellus* 19; *A. cordifolius* 112; *A.c.* 'Ideal' 112; *A. dumosus* 19; *A. ericoides* (heath aster) and cultivars 112; *A.* × *frikartii* and cultivars 112; *A. lateriflorus* 'Horizontalis' (calico aster) 112
Athyrium filix-femina (lady fern) 59; *A. goeringianum* 'Pictum' (Japanese painted fern) 59
Aubrieta 88
autumn crocus (*Colchicum autumnale*) 108, 108
azalea *see Rhododendron*
Aztec lily (*Sprekelia*) 50

B

baby's breath (*Gypsophila paniculata*) 68, 80, 81
balcony plants *see* containers, plants in
barberry *see Berberis*
basil 94
beauty berry (*Callicarpa bodinieri* var. *giraldii*) 127
beauty bush (*Kolkwitzia*) 42, 65

bee balm *see Monarda*
bees: nests for 162, 162; plants for 13, 28, 45, 63, 84, 101, 114
begonias, tuberous: fertilizing 106; lifting 118, 135; planting 21, 21; potting up 33, 33; storing 119, 149
bellflower *see Campanula*
Bellis (daisy) 69, 117, 134
Berberis (barberry) 64, 65, 122; *B. aggregata* 127; *B.* × *carminea* 'Buccaneer' 127; *B. koreana* 127; *B. wilsoniae* 127
bergamot (*Monarda*) 97, 98, 105
berries, colorful 122, 127–8, 129
Betula albosinensis (Chinese birch) 140–1; *B. ermanii* (Russian rock birch) 141; *B. maximowicziana* (monarch birch) 141; *B. papyrifera* (paper birch) 140; *B. pendula* (European whitebark birch) 25, 122; *B. utilis jacquemontii* (Himalayan birch) 140, 141
biennials: cutting back 68, 105; planting out 117, 134; pricking out and potting on 89; protecting in winter 149; sowing 48, 69, 89; thinning out 134
birch *see Betula*
birds, feeding 145; houses for 130, 130
Black locust (*Robinia pseudoacacia*) 56
blackthorn (*Prunus spinosa*) 25, 64
blazing star (*Liatris spicata*) 81
bleeding heart (*Dicentra spectabilis*) 68, 88
bluebell, Virginia (*Mertensia virginica*) 68
borage (*Borago officinalis*) 92, 95
box (*Buxus*) 30, 85, 102
broom, common (*Cytisus scoparius*) 38, 64
buck brush *see Ceanothus*
Buddleja spp. 85; *B. alternifolia* 102; *B. davidii* (butterfly bush) 29, 74; *B.* 'Empire Blue' 76; *B.* 'Fascination' 76; *B. globosa* 102
bugloss (*Echium plantagineum*) 105
bulbs: deadheading 49–50; fertilizing 33, 49, 89; forcing 118, 149; lifting 89, 118, 118, 135; naturalizing 25, 120, 120; planting depths for spring- and summer-flowering 117, 117; planting fall-flowering 90; planting spring-flowering 105,

134; planting summer-flowering 50–1; potting up 118, 118, 134; storing 119, 149; for underplanting shrubs 12
bush clover (*Lespedeza thunbergii*) 29, 65, 111, 112
butterflies, plants to attract 13, 28, 45, 63, 84, 101, 114
butterfly bush (*Buddleja davidii*) 29, 74
Buxus (box) 30, 85, 102

C

Caladium 118, 135
Calendula spp. 68, 117; *C. officinalis* (pot marigold) 105
California lilac *see Ceanothus*
California poppy (*Eschscholzia californica*) 68, 105, 117
Callicarpa bodinieri giraldii (beauty berry) 127
Calluna (heather) 46, 46, 102
Calonyction album (moon vine) 67
camellia 14, 85
Campanula (Canterbury bells) 48, 69, 105, 134; *C. carpatica* 88; *C. lactiflora* (bellflower) 76; *C.l. alba* 76, 80; *C.l.* 'Loddon Anna' 76; *C.l.* 'Prichard's Variety' 76
campion, rose (*Lychnis coronaria*) 101
candytuft (*Iberis umbellata*) 68, 105; rocket candytuft (*I. amara*) 105
Canna 118, 135, 149
Canterbury bells *see Campanula*
Cape tulip (*Homeria*) 50
Carpinus (hornbeam) 64, 85, 102
Caryopteris 65, 85; *C.* × *clandonensis* 29, 110
catmint (*Nepeta*) 19, 68, 96, 111
Ceanothus (California lilac) 29, 76, 85, 102; *C.* 'Gloire de Versailles' 76; *C.* 'Henri Desfossé' 76; *C.* 'Topaz' 76
cedar: Japanese (*Cryptomeria*) 29; Western red (*Thuja plicata*) 30, 85
Centaurea cyanus (cornflower) 68, 105, 117; *C. montana* (mountain knapweed) 68
Centranthus spp. 104; *C. ruber* (red valerian) 78; *C.r.* 'Coccineus' 78, 78
Ceratostigma 29; *C. plumbaginoides* (leadwort) 111

Photographic Acknowledgments
All pictures by Jacqui Hurst, © Frances Lincoln Limited except:
Jacqui Hurst/Boys Syndication: 95, 98, 109, 111, 123
Jacqui Hurst © 93, 94
Geoff Dann, © Frances Lincoln Limited: 61, 113, 124, 125, 126, 128, 140
Andrew Lawson: 107, 121, 139, 141, 142
The Harry Smith Horticultural Photographic Collection: 73

Publisher's Acknowledgments
The publisher would like to thank the following for their help in producing this book: Caroline Hillier, Jo Christian, Suzanne Luchford, Ruch Carim, Lucy Rix, Katy Foskew, Ray Rogers, Joanna Chisolm; and Vicky Robinson for the index.

Illustrators
Chapters 2, 3, 4, 7, 8, 9, 10: Andrew Macdonald
Chapters 1, 5, 6: Jim Robbins

Horticultural consultant	Tony Lord
Design	Roger Walton Studio
Project editor	Sarah Mitchell
Editor	Alison Freegard
Picture editor	Anne Fraser
Production	Maureen Hegarty and Nicky Bowden
Art director	Tim Foster
Editorial director	Erica Hunningher